Textual Permanence

Textual Permanence

Roman Elegists and the Epigraphic Tradition

Teresa R. Ramsby

Duckworth

First published in 2007 by
Gerald Duckworth & Co. Ltd.
90-93 Cowcross Street, London EC1M 6BF
Tel: 020 7490 7300
Fax: 020 7490 0080
inquiries@duckworth-publishers.co.uk
www.ducknet.co.uk

A catalogue record for this book is available from the British Library

ISBN-10: 0 7156 3632 4
ISBN-13: 978 0 7156 3632 9

Typeset by Ray Davies
Printed and bound in Great Britain by
MPG Books Limited, Bodmin, Cornwall

Contents

To my parents

For never asking me, 'studium quid inutile temptas?'

Acknowledgements

There are many people who have provided me with advice and encouragement in the production of this book. I am grateful to colleagues and friends at the University of Massachusetts Amherst whose help and support have been invaluable throughout this process, particularly the members of the UMass department of Classics, and Rex Wallace, chair of the Classics department, who granted me that most precious of resources: time. I also wish to thank my colleague Brian Breed for extremely helpful suggestions regarding the final manuscript. I am grateful for a Faculty Research Grant I received from the University of Massachusetts Amherst that made possible the hiring of several diligent and efficient research-assistants: Margaret Adamczyk, Janet Danylieko, Megan Ferrier and Kyle Frackman. I also thank those who contributed useful insights as I began to develop the ideas of this book: John Bodel, Leslie Cahoon, Kathleen Coleman, Peter Knox, Patricia Rosenmeyer, Jean MacIntosh Turfa, Stephen Wheeler, a few anonymous readers along the way and particularly Sinclair Bell for his archaeological insights and invaluable textual comments. Many thanks go also to Deborah Blake of Duckworth for her splendid editorial directions. I owe special gratitude to Eleanor Winsor Leach, my former dissertation advisor, who provided many thoughtful and pragmatic suggestions in the process of this book's production: for all the things she taught me, for the generous allotment of her time, and for her friendship, I am forever grateful.

I am also thankful to all who have provided permission for the use of copyrighted material in this book. The complete text of William Carlos Williams' poem 'This is Just to Say' is reproduced with the permission of New Directions Publishing Corporation in the United States and Canada, and Carcanet Press in the United Kingdom. Portions of my article, 'Striving for Permanence: Ovid's Funerary Inscriptions' from *Classical Journal* 100.4(2005) appear with the permission of the Copyright Clearance Center. Some chapters of this book made an appearance at two meetings of CAMWS (2005 and 2006) and at the 2006 CANE centennial, and I am grateful to those who provided me feedback at those venues.

Lastly, I wish to thank all the members of my family for their support throughout this project: my parents Dan and Barb, my step-father Brad, my late step-mother Karen, my father-in-law Ernest, my siblings Sean,

Heather and Stephanie, and all my lovely nieces and nephews. I am most especially grateful to my husband John Berneche, the best of teachers, for his love, his patience and his willingness to read and listen: *lux mea, quo vivo vivere dulce mihi est*.

Abbreviations

See bibliography for complete citations.

AP = *Anthologia Palatina*.
CIL = *Corpus Inscriptionum Latinarum*.
CLE = *Carmina Latina Epigraphica*.
ILLRP = *Inscriptiones Latinae Liberae Rei Publicae*.
ThesCRA = *Thesaurus Cultus et Rituum Antiquorum*.

The following editions provided the text for citations of ancient authors most prominently featured in this book. All translations that appear in this book are my own unless otherwise indicated.

Courtney, Edward. 1993. *The Fragmentary Latin Poets*. Oxford.
Fedeli, P. 1984. *Sexti Properti: Elegiarum Libri IV*. Stuttgart.
Kenney, E.J. 1995. *P. Ovidi Nasonis: Amores, Medicamina Faciei Femineae, Ars Amatoria, Remedia Amoris*. Oxford.
———. 1996. *Ovid: Heroides XVI-XXI*. Cambridge.
Knox, Peter E. 1995. *Ovid: Heroides: Select Epistles*. Cambridge.
Lee, Guy. 1990. *The Poems of Catullus*. Oxford.
Maltby, Robert. 2002. *Tibullus: Elegies: Text, Introduction and Commentary, ARCA Classical and Medieval Texts, Papers and Monographs* 41. Cambridge.
Owen, S.G. 1915. *P. Ovidi Nasonis: Tristium Libri Quinque Ibis Ex Ponto Libri Quattuor Haelieutica Fragmenta*. Oxford.
Tarrant, Richard. 2004. *P. Ovidi Nasonis: Metamorphoses*. Oxford.

Introduction

Elegiac Inscriptions and the 'Epigraphic Habit'

The 'epigraphic habit', or 'epigraphic consciousness', of the Romans is responsible for an important part of the literary legacy of ancient Rome.[1] As many scholars have demonstrated, in far-flung places where Romans once comprised a small percentage of the population their inscriptions make up the largest percentage of recorded data. The widespread and durable nature of Roman inscriptions makes them significant primary sources in historical research.[2] But an inscription is also an opportunity for self-representation: it is a stake in the future, an expression of hope that future generations will discover and read and ponder the words granted lasting presence in enduring material; it is proof of faith in the enduring nature of one's language, one's culture, and humanity itself.[3]

Self-representation, or at least representation of the human condition, is also one aim of poetry. If the inscription in real life is, in its most distilled form, an expression considered worthy of preservation, then perhaps the inscription inserted into a poem is meant to stand out from the surrounding verses as well. The overwhelming evidence we have regarding the importance of public writing in Rome and throughout her empire suggests that what the poets are doing with these inscriptions fills a sociological need: a need for clarity of expression, for self-monumentalization and for acknowledging the potent literary connection between the poet and the reader owing to shared literacy. Such possibilities allow modern readers a vantage point by which to regard the inscriptions and thereby the poems that contain them. This study aims to examine these inscriptional moments in Roman poetry and find meaning by exploring the type, the placement, the wording and the tone of these (typically) brief passages in order to discover what they unlock about the poems in which they are embedded. Because context will be the focus of this study, there will necessarily also be attempts to link the poetic practice of inserting inscriptions into texts with the societal practices that must have influenced these compositional choices.

The appearance of invented inscriptions in Roman poetry has received periodic attention from scholars. Often the phenomenon is quickly noted as a convention of the elegiac genre, for indeed there were elegiac inscriptions long before there was a body of elegiac literature, particularly the form elegy took at Rome in the first century BC. Yet typifying such textual devices as merely generic conventions or aesthetic affectations within the bounds of the metrical format does not serve us in better understanding the poets' elegiac craft.[4] Surely we would agree that every motif, every convention the poets place at their disposal in rendering this poetic form is worthy of examination.[5] This book will therefore point attention to the significant aspects that elegiac inscriptions reveal about their poems and the societal context in which they were created.

This book recognizes, of course, that the frequency of inscriptions within elegy is related to epigraphic conventions, for elegy was often thus utilized; but this study also asserts that the frequent association that elegists make between text and record, and between poem and monument, reveals an increasing awareness of the function of poetry as a means of establishing and preserving identity in an age of political and social upheaval. The period of interest to this study is, of course, the Augustan age, and the pioneers and chief practitioners of the elegiac movement (Catullus, Propertius, Tibullus and Ovid) provide the poetic arena to which I mostly confine myself.[6] Although the primary motivation for this work was my realization that so many imaginary inscriptions appear within Augustan poetry, those verses that strongly evoke inscriptional writing will necessarily become part of my analysis as well, since I find compelling evidence that they influence and to some extent determine the later inclusion of inscriptions 'quoted upon the stone' within the poetry.

Despite the literary aspect of this exploration, it is important to note that poetic inscriptions share formal aspects with their real-world counterparts. The inscriptions found in Roman poetry match, category for category, the types of inscriptions commonly identified in epigraphic scholarship: epitaphs, votive dedications, statuary or titular inscriptions, and graffiti. Poets often depict them appearing on objects – most commonly graves – but also writing tablets, trees and specified or unspecified votive objects. Just as real inscriptions emphatically communicate vital information, inscriptional verses, insofar as they stand out from the surrounding text, lend emphasis to what they express: more importantly, they evoke the origins of the genre, tap mimetic possibilities and serve as a site for the author to reflect on his role, his reception and his status.

It must be admitted that without the original ancient texts before us we can only conjecture that it is unlikely the Romans made any indication that certain verses were inscriptions – modern editions often do us the favour of placing inscriptions in capital letters (and I have done the same in my quotations of these verses). The use of inscriptions in text, the placement of text within a text, would surely stand out in certain respects to the attentive receiver. This 'standing out' I quantify primarily by the emphasis such passages place on the process of public writing. The monumental, real-world aspects of such public writing will have important significance for my principal aim: namely, to explore the poetic ends achieved by the insertion of inscriptions, and to demonstrate that what

Roman authors 'do' with inscriptions is similar to what the inscriptions do in society: namely, record and emphasize particular human endeavours.

One issue that must be examined is the assumption that the metrical format of elegy, and its kinship to Hellenistic epigram, may be responsible for conceiving a relationship between poems and inscriptions, and this will receive examination in my first chapter. Yet the assumption that is frequently used to explain the appearance of verse inscriptions – that they are merely functions of the elegiac genre – has traditionally disregarded the strangeness of the passages, most notably their extension to the world beyond the text, and has overlooked the hermeneutic possibilities that they provide. And what of the use of inscriptions in Horace's lyric metres, and the occurrence of inscriptions in Ovid's epic poem? These mixtures demonstrate that there is more at work than metrical affinity or generic origins.[7] Rather, it is worthwhile to perceive the 'inscribed' verses as separate from what surrounds them – to notice what the poet has taken trouble to emphasize.[8] When we pay attention to these small islands of words we find a host of interesting implications: authorial self-identifications, programmatic restatements, thematic transitions, poignant expressions of the human experience, and the mimetic borrowing of the epigraphic impulse to form a permanent record of events. The contexts in which these inscriptions appear raise many issues as well, and each particular case must be considered with its surrounding text.

My choice of relating the notion of permanence to poetry is, admittedly, a problematic one. Obviously the roots of 'permanence' (*per* + *manēre*) denote the quality of 'everlasting presence; something thoroughly remaining'. Even though the poetic world is one of fluidity, where its elements are disassembled and reconstructed, one can, I believe, speak of permanence in a poem. Take, for example, Propertius' final elegy, 4.11, the 'autobiographical' eulogy of Cornelia. When Propertius has Cornelia, daughter of Scribonia (who was briefly the wife of the young Octavian), narrate the events of her own life in epigraphic fashion, he creates a characterization that assumes the reader's ability to correlate what she says to the common understanding of the life of a *matrona*. In literary fashion, he grants to Cornelia the authority to choose what her legacy might be – the love of her children, her unblemished life and the honour of her family name that she has helped to preserve. Propertius utilizes the epigraphic motif to render Cornelia permanence, and, as I will later explain, he draws together the purpose of elegy and its graphic (even epitaphic) origins.[9] The assumptions with which one reads any culturally familiar text make for that text a reinforcing support, a demonstrating proof, that what the reader understands has basis in reality. When Propertius has Cornelia speak her life, he creates a voice that lives inside the text; her character becomes a permanent fixture in the landscape of the reader's understanding of how people live, what they value and what they should not.

One can likewise see poems that do not render anything permanent.

Propertius' elegy 4.6 neither attempts to replicate faithfully the Battle of Actium nor seeks to take responsibility for its inaccuracies. In the final portion of the poem, the narrator admits that the purpose of his poem is not Augustan eulogy: it is meant for delivery at a symposium where he and other poets share their work, and marvel at each others' ingenuity on the theme of Augustan undertakings. The vision of Apollo bestriding Augustus' ship (4.6.29-30) and the of truncated conflict that ensues (55-7) places the entire episode in the dream-world of fantasy – one projected by Augustus himself, via the poet and other artists, onto Rome's collective imagination. The poem undermines the historicity of the event entirely, and drives the history-minded reader to check the public record for better information.

The verse inscription is a clever way of utilizing the common practice of making accounts permanent, but within the fluid and flimsy fiction of the poetic world. As we shall see, Ovid's Corinna, although barely a woman-in-the-flesh throughout most of the *Amores*, achieves a presence in 2.13 when Ovid's lover composes an inscription to honour the gods for saving her from death. Her condition in 2.13 is grave because she has self-induced an abortion – an act of very real consequences with which Romans were no doubt familiar. In concert with the harsh reality to which Corinna has exposed herself, Ovid grants her an inscription: *SERVATA NASO CORINNA*. This formulaic phrase, within the context of the votive practice that so many Romans understood, emphasizes the invasion of the hard, cruel world upon the elegiac fantasy: sex does lead to pregnancy, but this obvious fact plus the abortion make unsuitable appearances in the world of erotic poetry. The votive dedication acts as a further transgression of the real upon the unreal. The inscription serves other purposes as well, but its presence in this particular poem fosters the sense that the woman is real and so is her dilemma. Other purposes that poetic inscriptions serve must be addressed on a case-by-case basis, but the permanence that the inscription provides will translate not only to characters, but to actions, events, and, most interestingly, the poets themselves.

As we know, Augustan poetry refers consistently to a poetic 'ego' operating within a narrative of erotic discovery, and eschews the traditional Roman *cursus* of military service and political ambition. The attempt to make poetry a substitute for these achievements is a significant theme of the Augustan poets.[10] An intriguing, recurring practice, which this study will closely examine, is the placement of the author's own name within the inscriptions. If the inscription was a public means of marking achievement in Republican Rome, then the insertion of inscriptions that bear the poets' names may suggest a literary attempt to challenge the notion of public record, monumentality and authority; to proffer the intriguing possibility that every person's journey is a mark of achievement. And so we must keep in mind the period of time in which the inscriptional appearances are most frequent: a period in which ambitions of any kind were becoming increasingly tied to Augustus' good favour. It has been justifiably claimed that Roman love-poetry is, in no small part, a response to the shrinking arena of individual influence in a time of centralized power. I suggest that, although the inscription was not necessarily bound to the elegiac format (epic poems and lyric poems use them as well), and although the elegiac format was not bound to represent itself in inscriptional form, the frequent cooperation of elegiac poetry and poetic inscriptions derived from an impulse to textualize and codify the struggle for autonomy and artistic achievement in an age of increasing anxiety. So long as poets could use the promotional, self-aggrandizing opportunities that poetry provided, they saw fit to incorporate the monumental and the 'visible' within their poetic lines. In their world of escapist fantasy, unrelated to the complications of nation building and political ladder climbing, the inscriptions demand that attention be paid to small things. The elegiac movement and the poetic inscription are ideologically related, and ideally suited, to the methods of self-definition and innovation that formulate the poetic climate of the Augustan age.[11]

Theoretical concerns: ekphrasis and mimesis

The bulk of this study will concern itself with the placement of inscriptions within poems, and what purpose the inscriptions serve in their contexts to the narrative in general, to their characterizations and indeed to the very act of writing. What motivates the insertion of inscriptions into poems demands some examination. In the study of poetic aesthetics, particularly regarding poetic description, two important terms frequently arise: ekphrasis and mimesis. I will briefly examine why I think the former term is not applicable to the role of poetic inscriptions, and then develop to a greater extent why the second term is fundamentally relevant.

Is the inclusion of an inscription in a poem an ekphrastic act? Answering this question is made complicated because of the varying uses of the term ekphrasis throughout the history of literary analysis.[12] As we know, ekphrasis refers to the literary or narrative description of an artistic work, such as Achilles' shield in the *Iliad*, Aeneas' shield in the *Aeneid* and the relief on the Temple of Juno that Aeneas 'reads' and responds to in the *Aeneid*.[13] One goal of ekphrasis is to make the object appear before the mind's eye of the reader. Whether or not the purpose of such description is to elicit the interpretive faculties of the reader, to associate the object with some aspect of the narrative, to impress upon the reader a particular point of view, or to impress the reader with the considerable verbal artistry of the author – these are considerations that immediately complicate the notion of ekphrasis.[14] It is not my intention here to resolve these issues, but to examine whether or not ekphrasis operates in the inclusion of inscriptions in Roman verse. I prefer to speak of text over art, and as the following analysis will show, there are too many discrepancies between the uses of inscriptions within poetry and ekphrastic, set-piece narratives.

Is a poetic inscription a work of art? At first glance, the inclusion of an inscription in a poem is more akin to a literary quotation than a description, and surely one would not call the quotations of annalistic records that ancient historians used as primary sources ekphrastic moments.[15] It is likewise helpful to note the disparity between poetic inscriptions and typical artworks in narrative. An important qualification of set-piece narrative is that it markedly halts the movement of the plot in order to establish a mind's eye picture of a significant object. Yet Roman poets insert inscriptions that do service to the narrative, and form only a very brief interruption of the drama or none at all. Nor do they turn off the course of their narrative to describe a monument with an inscription on it, but instead they incorporate the inscription into the text, making it bear significant relevance to the surrounding text.[16] Like the inscription drawn by the finger of Yahweh on the wall before Belshazzar and his banqueters, the inscriptions in Roman poetry move along with the plot, their words are integral to it, and they provide potential for interpretation that can offer insight to the narrative and the characters.[17]

Regarding the notion of representation, in every instance of an inscription embedded in Roman poetry, the monument (or tablet or tree, etc.) on which the inscription appears is given little attention, save a few descriptive words. The locations of inscriptions are noted phrases like 'a small stone' and 'in marble'; the words of the inscriptions themselves are infrequently granted much description except for an occasional reference to size, 'in tall letters'; and the inscriptions are never embellished with artistic representations.[18] The reticence of the Latin poets to dwell descriptively upon the materials that hold the inscriptions, or the appearance of the inscriptions themselves, suggests that they should not be considered ekphrastic elements of the poems. Rather, tied formally as they are to the established practice of writing inscriptions throughout the empire, poetic inscriptions are carefully calibrated to resound within their narratives. They appear either as a result of the action within the narrative, or as proclamations of intention by characters who hope for possible outcomes. Inscriptions in Roman poetry do not appear and then disappear, nor do they change form. Indeed, much like real inscriptions in the Roman world, they are conceived as lasting texts, and their textuality conveys them permanence and significance.[19]

In fact if we consider Tara Welch's study done on the elegiac cityscape of Rome, we see what factors develop into a discussion of ekphrasis, and thus what factors are missing in the discussion of ekphrasis with regard to inscriptions (Welch 2005, 5):

> Propertius' techniques of focalization not only reframe Roman places in his audience's imagination, but also suggest a hierarchy of semantic influence:

> words may have power over images ... This relationship between words and images is similar to that which arises in instances of ekphrasis. While only one of the poems to be discussed [in her study] constitutes an ekphrasis *per se* [2.31], the other poems implicate both the poet and the reader in the interpretation of the places or monuments that are their subject ... Propertius' topographical poems are instances of ekphrasis with a twist: the places he describes are real works, seen and experienced by his audience in Rome. P.'s poems and the monuments they interpret engage each other via the reader/viewer ... These readers brought to Propertius' poems their prior experiences with the Roman places at issue, and took from the poet's works new ways of viewing Roman monuments.

There are no 'real works' among the elegist's inscriptions, and thus their depictions do not negotiate with the reader's viewing of actual monuments. Instead familiar types of inscriptions and all the conventions that they possess are brought into the poetry itself and given the opportunity to coalesce with the knowledge and experience of the reader. There is still a 'viewing' involved, a visualization of the monument and the words upon it, but with regard to poetic inscriptions there is no power of words over images, there is simply the power of words over time. If inscriptions are words given lasting presence, then poetic inscriptions are words meant to linger in the minds of the reader and render pre-eminence to their meaning over other words.

Considering these factors, I believe that mimesis is a considerably more helpful term to the purposes of this study. Traditionally defined as the representation of the natural world, especially human behaviour, in art and literature, mimesis is an association between life and art that makes the art understandable to its audience. Stephen Halliwell explains that mimesis in pre-Platonic terms is 'an idea of correspondence or equivalence – correspondence between mimetic works, activities, or performances and their putative real-world equivalents, whether the latter are taken to be externally given and independent or only hypothetically projectable from the mimetic works themselves' (Halliwell 2002, 15). Early in the formation of the concept of mimesis, Halliwell asserts, there is great interest 'in the effects of mimetic artworks on their viewers or hearers, [and in characterizing] the kinds of recognition, understanding, emotional response, and evaluation that such artworks can or should elicit in their audiences' (16).[20]

A duality appears, however, between mimcry of actual objects, true models, and the attempt to bring to life a set of characteristics that will remind the viewer of a type of thing, rather than a specific model.[21] Halliwell distinguishes the models as the 'world-reflecting' model and the 'world-creating' model (2002, 23). In the case of the former, representational art is a 'response to reality', and in the case of the latter, 'mimesis is the production of a "heterocosm", an imaginary world-in-itself, which may resemble or remind us of the real world ... but is not to be judged primarily or directly by comparison with it' (23).[22] Halliwell attributes this duality to Aristotle's thinking on the subject: 'the importance of Aristotle's understanding of mimesis rests on its "dual-aspect" function as a way of holding together the "worldlike" properties of artistic representation – its depiction, as he puts it (*Poetics* 9.1451a37), of things which *could* be the case – with its production of objects that possess a distinctive, though not wholly autonomous, rationale of their own' (152). That 'rationale', in turn, depends not merely on the intentions of the artist, but on 'the shared conventions, traditions, and possibilities of a culture. The mimetic status of certain objects is a matter of their having a significant content that can and, if their mimetic status us to be effectively realized, must be recognized and understood by their audiences' (153).

Poetry is a mimetic art in that it attempts to represent experiences, situations that are comprehensible to an audience, even if understood *not* to represent any real event. Invented inscriptions, I suggest, constitute a perfect marriage of the 'world-reflecting' and the 'world-creating' aspects of poetry, for they are reflective of Roman social practice and craft, yet they never quote verbatim any specific monument. Instead, they effectively elicit in the reader's mind comparison to the inscriptional *techne* that fills the Roman viewer's gaze (upon temples, monuments, tombstones etc.). More importantly, poetic inscriptions create links to human experience from poems in which they occur. Only within the confines of their 'heterocosmic' origins do the words of the inscriptions bear any meaning, but the inscription itself leaps off the page and draws connections between the observations made within the poem and the experiences of the reader with real, perhaps similarly conceived, inscriptions.[23] This study, in fact, is itself imitative of such studies that seek to explain the meaning and relevance of inscriptions in the Roman world. The understanding of a real inscription depends on archaeological context – on a tombstone versus a statue base, and, even then, in Pompeii versus Londinium. Similarly the understanding of an invented inscription depends on the character who 'writes' it, the themes that exist inside and outside the poem, the place it appears and the words it uses.

Reading poetic epitaphs will not inform us of Roman funereal practices, nor aid us in understanding the skills and instruments of stone carvers. Compare the imitative impulse of the inscription to the more ekphrastic passage seen in, for example, an architectural tour narrated in Pliny the Younger's epistles.[24] His descriptions, although slanted towards his own point of view of what is beautiful and pleasing, impart much information regarding the layout and significant expenditures in the construction of imperial Roman villas.[25] The mimetic act, by contrast, merely corresponds to what we know to be true; it does not translate the vision to our minds. Thus the poetic inscription provides the opportunity to imagine for ourselves the graphic nature of the text presented – to associate words with a context, and consider the meanings the words possess.

The mimesis implicit in the regular insertion of inscriptions into poetry is fundamental not only to understanding the nature of the particular poems that include them, but to discerning a new avenue for interpretation of Roman poetry in general. It is no small thing to suggest that Romans considered their poetic worlds to be reflective of the real world outside the poems. This very notion has required defence against strong opposition throughout Classical scholarship.[26] I embrace the second aspect of the mimetic tradition, namely its world-creating force. Therefore, no one will find me looking for Cynthia or Corinna among the ladies of Augustan Rome; yet it cannot be coincidence that Rome's cultural landscape appears in the poetry.

To show by reverse example, Tomis in Ovid's *Tristia* is often described in comparison to Rome. For example, when he speaks of spring's arrival at his outpost he formulates the scene in comparison to the verdant beauty of Italian spring (*Trist.* 3.12.15-26). Ovid does not invent a new vocabulary or re-establish aesthetic ideals to capture his experience. He portrays his Pontic environment and those who peopled it in contrast to his fatherland and compatriots, and he expresses the extremes of his experience in words used by Greek and Roman predecessors.[27] In fact Ovid's own poetic talent, he sadly reports in his later letters, begins to waste away from too long a separation from his homeland; he equates separation from Rome to loss of inspiration.[28] This may be a problematic claim considering the large number of poetic epistles he continued to compose (some of which contain really fascinating details about the tribes with whom he interacted), but as Betty Rose Nagle points out (Nagle 1980, 140), 'the self-depreciating themes in the poetics of exile ... are both conventional and strategic'.[29] The Roman poets found glory in reflecting the Roman milieu.

Textuality and orality

Another important aspect of the poetic inscription is its textuality. The reader of a poem is always, on some level, aware of the text before him, but the 'voice' of the narrator lulls him into thinking that he is hearing a story.[30] Of course this occurs in varying degrees related to genre, as Stephen Wheeler points out in his analysis of the fictional presence of the voice in the *Metamorphoses*, and is comparatively less prominent in Ovid's more text-invested elegiac works.[31] Yet even the elegiac poems were recited as well as read, and thus when we consider Roman poetry, we can never entirely eradicate the voice in the head of the reader. It is important to consider how a listener hearing a poem might catch onto different poetic techniques from those picked up by a reader reading a poem. When a poet uses alliteration, for example, it is noticeable first to the listener, secondarily to the reader; when a poet arranges words in chiasmus, it is likely to be more noticeable to the reader than the listener. To use a modern example, when William Carlos Williams places the divisions in the lines and stanzas of 'This is Just to Say', it is the reader who understands the perfection of those arranged words: 'the plums' to 'the icebox' to 'for breakfast' to 'delicious' to 'so sweet'.[32] The listener appreciates best the serpentine 'z, ss, ks, st, shuss and sw' that make the poem such a dazzling narrative of temptation; the serpent in the Garden could not have spoken better.

When the reader's eyes scan inscriptional lines, like (again) *SERVATA NASO CORINNA* his experience with the words is more immediate than the listener's. True, the listener can still conceive the image of an inscribed text. The reader, however, has less territory to cross: reading the inscription is the same act as reading real monuments. The text stands out as a written thing, different from the 'writing' of the poem itself. The reader can more easily conjure up the image of the surface upon which they lie. The text on a tombstone requires an internal vision of the character's final resting place; the text on a votive object evokes recent journeys to temples and shrines, and blends with the sentiments of frustration or contentment with a god's perceived actions (or inactions). Also, the inscriptions' mimetic representation of inscribed text reminds the reader of the process of seeing and reading (or not) marked graves, graffiti and the host of other 'readings' a man experiences as he walks the streets of his neighbourhood or through his city's forum. The nature of inscriptional text interrupts the reader's mode of reading and transforms it from the 'heard' voice of the poem's speaker, to something 'seen' in the landscape of the speaker's created world. Thus the poetic inscription is a mimetic representation of the textuality that, to some extent, governs the reader's experience with his own, real world, and with the imagined reality of the poem – a sort of hypertext.[33] Poetic text, as opposed to those familiar monuments, is always a location of hermeneutic potential, as we know. There is a difference between what a person understands when reading a tombstone on a friend's grave and what he comes to understand by reading a character's tombstone within a poem. The engagement of the reader in decoding the symbols and multi-layered references in a poem does not stop when an inscription is presented; rather such passages can become important clues in the process of decoding a poem.

This study does not pursue the entire corpus of inscriptions in Roman poetry; rather I have chosen to focus on the Augustan elegiac poets because they lived in an age where inscribed material was used in a significant manner to broadcast the accomplishments of the Augustan regime and make ties between that regime and the Republican past.[34] My analysis is particularly dependent upon three aspects of the age: the transformation of the political scene, the marked increase of monumental display for the purposes of advancing the new imperial political structure, and the unique position of the elegiac poet as an artistic celebrity. As I will show, the invented inscriptions that these poets create are very much a part of the ongoing dialogue between the educated Roman elite and the emerging imperial court.

Structure and arrangement

The material of this study is arranged by author primarily, and by theme secondarily, a structure that allows the patterns in an author's use of the inscription to become more evident. The first chapter summarizes the scholarship on Roman inscriptions, elegy, and their relationship, as well as aspects of Roman cultural practice that set apart the inscriptional text within Roman elegy as something not entirely owed to Hellenistic influences. Rome's political arena created an atmosphere of self-representation and self-monumentalization wherein the epitaph played a vital role in advertising particular aspects of a person's achievements. The transition from archaic metrical forms to Hellenistic, imported forms changed not only the format of inscriptions but some of their content as well. In addition, the pioneering elegiac efforts of Ennius, in concert with his role as eulogist to Rome's most illustrious men, imposed upon Roman elegy the task of communicating individual identity and achievement, as later reflected in the later literary-minded, elegiac movement. This chapter will also outline the various types of inscriptions that appear, and the significance of their representation within the work of the elegists.

The second chapter presents analysis of Catullus' elegies 65 and 68 to illustrate that these poems' notable theme of loss and grief, expressed as the loss of a brother, demonstrates the inextricable link between elegy and personal monument. In poem 68 in particular Catullus unifies his personal grievances with an erotic narrative. The repeated return of the author to his absent brother and the nature of his brother's burial, and also the repetition of particular expressions of grief, point the way for future elegists who will use aspects of the metre's epigraphic tradition to express loss and other sentiments as well. The chapter moves on to Propertius who likewise manipulates elegy in this way, but in a fashion that demonstrates an evolution of the genre. The poems that finish his first book (21 and 22) are epitaphic in nature (though they do not contain quoted inscriptions), and they feature reflections on homeland and loss. Their irrelevance to the collection's earlier, erotic preoccupations demonstrates the poet's care to highlight these epitaphic elegies as ones more suitable to the reflection of personal concerns. Yet Propertius opens up, so to speak, in Books 2 and 4, presenting a wide variety of inscriptions that reveal aspects of his own poetic identity and the characters of his literary world. Propertius' final and fourth book reveals an array of inscriptions that confront or concretize the characterizations he has portrayed. His final poem, a 'self-spoken' eulogy by an actual historical person, a woman close to the imperial family, raises intriguing issues about the nature of elegy. By momentarily returning elegy entirely to its original purpose at Rome as a eulogistic form, Propertius emphasizes the value of elegy as an artistic form that, by nature of its inherent textuality and its pragmatic utility, can represent the worlds of the author and the reader, the literary world and the real one.

Tibullus was in fact the very first of the elegiac poets (as far as we know since so little remains of Gallus' works) to quote an imaginary inscription: first upon a tombstone and second on a votive offering. Chapter 3 analyses the impact of these inscriptions on the poems in which they occur, for in each case Tibullus' inscription is a distillation of the poet's attitude reflected in the surrounding text. His self-authored epitaph (in poem 1.3) neatly displays the dilemma of the poet as a soldier in the service of Messalla, for the epitaph demands remembrance as a soldier rather than a poet. I will argue that such a poetic choice reflects a determination towards preserving Republican notions of citizenship and duty. Tibullus' second, votive inscription (in poem 1.9) succinctly articulates a transformation of the poet's attitude towards love, thereby re-directing the lover away from the frustrating idealism that permeates the collection towards a satisfying pragmatism that seeks the conditions of peace, *pax*, wherein love can more easily be attained and enjoyed. Tibullus' inscriptions become markers or signposts within the text to poetic attitudes and thematic development. Furthermore, Tibullus' inscriptions, in that they are original and unique, demonstrate relationships to previous elegiac publications, most notably Propertius' *Monobiblos* and Gallus' *Amores*. Tibullus is the first to see the literary gains in tying the literary elegiac form to its epigraphic tradition.

The fourth, fifth and sixth chapters treat the dominant themes that emerge from Ovid's frequent use of a variety of inscriptional types: epitaphs, votive inscriptions, *tituli* (namely triumphal dedications) and graffiti. As in the poetry of his predecessors, the type of inscription that Ovid uses reflects real-world applications of inscribed texts. It becomes clear that Ovid manipulates his reader's familiarity with these inscriptional formats to highlight aspects of his literary narrative and to draw increasing attention to his own role as author. Chapter 4 analyses the instances in which Ovid places his own name within several inscriptions to reveal anxieties about the position of the author, but also to highlight comic aspects. The subject of Chapter 5 is the *Heroides*, for there Ovid places several inscriptions (mostly epitaphs) in order to complicate the notion of authority and voice: the heroines speak for themselves more convincingly when they provide these kernels of final, fateful, self-representation. Additionally, Paris inscribes graffiti and Acontius leaves a votive inscription; each of these cases highlights an aspect of the intertextuality between Ovid's epistolary work and Callimachean elegy. Ovid's epic inscriptions are the topic of the sixth chapter, and here I will argue that, although the metrical format has changed, the passages maintain their authorizing purposes: Phaëthon's epitaph, Iphis' votive and Caieta's epitaph all emphasize significant themes in the narratives. Overall, Ovid's use of the inscription calls our attention to a variety of social forces that affect the way he presents his literary world – these social forces include the construction of gender roles, the somewhat unpredictable nature of the political power structure of the Augustan age, and the increasing encouragement from that power-structure to accept a new imperial narrative of success: to leave behind those things that cannot be recovered.

My final chapter provides my conclusions and the lessons learned from this exercise. Essentially this study argues that the elegiac poets learned their craft not merely from a preoccupation with Hellenistic literary techniques, but in tandem with an imbedded, uniquely Roman art of self-representation that is shown most vividly in the multitudes of inscriptions that the Romans produced to prolong the memory of their achievements. The elegiac poet harnessed that power of expression, usurped it in a fashion, and incorporated it within his poems to draw on the poignant and immediate effects that inscriptional text would have upon his reader. In the process, the elegiac poet developed a novel method of poetic expression, a mimetic textuality that resonated strongly in an age in which the parameters of achievement were being redrawn and the significance and the nature of memorial were being reconsidered.

1

Elegy and the Inscription

> How can the Roman senate and populace immortalize your great deeds with full honours by way of inscriptions and public annals, Augustus, when your reign and accomplishments extend to the ends of the earth?
>
> Horace, *Carm.* 4.14.1-6[1]

Suetonius' hyperbolic claim that Augustus transformed Rome from a city of brick to a city of marble (*Aug.* 28.3) points also to the fact that marble is a surface more conducive to inscription: its relative hardness renders letters more finely cut, and the light, delicate hues of marble create a much better backdrop for what is inscribed and then sometimes painted upon it.[2] As Horace makes clear in the passage above, an important manifestation of power in the Augustan age was the ability to post the written word, and as we know from the sheer amount of material evidence that still resides in situ, it became increasingly important at that time that public information was written on grander surfaces.[3] The elegiac poets of the Augustan age in particular usurped that powerful act of public writing and used it within their poems. In contrast with Rome's earlier poets, who wrote inscriptional-sounding epigrams or actual inscriptions for the glory of illustrious men, Augustan poets insert inscriptions to commemorate not heroes and statesmen, but characters in their poems, dramatic events in their poems, and, most importantly, themselves.

Latin inscriptions and Roman poetry

Because the primary focus of this study is fabricated inscriptions found in the works of the Augustan poets, principally the elegists, the goal of this chapter is to show common ground between the desire to erect inscriptions in public places and the desire to place 'inscribed' verses within poetry. Both desires emanate from a reverence for text and a yearning to commemorate the milestones of existence. The scholarship applied to Latin inscriptions over the last century and a half frames my exploration of invented inscriptions within their literary contexts, for its tendency to view the psychological and spiritual aspects of the Roman epigraphic legacy inspired my approach to seek the import of inscribed words within Roman poetry.

The study of real Latin inscriptions began in earnest in the mid-nineteenth century, and almost immediately related studies of poetic inscriptions emerged.[4] Soon after Theodor Mommsen began the *Corpus Inscriptionum Latinarum* in 1863, the compilation of poetic inscriptions by Franz Buecheler was begun in 1894 and supplemented by Einar Engström and Ernst Lommatzsch in 1912 and 1926 respectively. Simultaneously, thematic studies of Latin inscriptions by European and American philologists began with the debate between René Cagnat (1889) and Bruno Lier (1902) on the methods of composing epitaphs and the influence of Greek poetry on their sentiments. Studies then emerged that looked more to the sentiments themselves and what they told us about the people who left them on their graves.[5] The culmination of such analysis was, and arguably still is, Richmond Lattimore's rich comparative study between Greek and Roman epitaphs in 1942. Study of inscriptional evidence and its cultural relevance received fresh attention when Ramsay MacMullen (1982) published his provocative article on the epigraphic habit of the ancient Romans, answered in turn by J.C. Mann (1985). Both scholars suggest that Roman epigraphy is owed to a psychological need for preserving personal and civic identity, a phenomenon tied to *Romanitas*.[6]

Previous scholars had come close to such an assertion, typically in their studies of the poetic inscriptions made accessible by Buecheler's compendium. In 1935 Albert Purdie counted more than 2,300 verse inscriptions among the available catalogues of ancient epigraphy.[7] Comparing prose inscriptions to verse inscriptions, he wrote that the poetic ones bear 'a human breath that clings to them, something personal which is yet of all human experience' (Purdie 1935, 11). Henry Herbert Armstrong, in an earlier study, had noticed a unique sentimentality in Latin inscriptions: 'it was left for the intense autobiographic feeling of the Romans to develop such personifications to any extent' (Armstrong 1910, 222). He resisted the notion that Latin inscriptions and epigrams were entirely derivative from Greek: 'it seems much more probable that the thoughts expressed as well as the forms of expression were to some extent suggested by the Latin poets, at least for the thousand odd sepulchral poems written entirely in Latin' (1910, 260-1).[8] Even Lattimore cautiously observed that it is more indicative of the Latin prose inscription (than the Greek) to include the less formal biographical sketch, adding that in verse epitaphs, 'the manner of listing virtues and achievements may be characteristically Latin' (Lattimore 1942, 341).[9]

Built into the Roman notion of identity, as Roman philosophy of the late Republic clearly indicates, is the idea that actions prove a person's worth. Well-worded sentiments are noteworthy and a sign of cultural depth, but even Cicero, who quoted Greek poetry in his writings with great frequency, spilled far more ink on the need for actions that benefit the state than on the importance of turning a fine phrase or crafting the thoughts of mankind in metrical sublimity. Romans valued the capability of the inscription to summarize a person's life and career before they began to appreciate its capability for providing profound or whimsical reflections on the nature of life and death. From the tombs of the Scipios to the first elegiac verses of Ennius, there is evidence that the Romans treated the purpose and form of memorial with caution as they began to incorporate Hellenized forms into their traditional modes of honouring their dead. When we examine the inscriptions invented by poets, we will see that the impulse remains to use the inscription as a means of summarizing and emphasizing important action. Even the invented inscription in poetry owes as much to the Roman cultural milieu as it does to poetic motifs.

Several studies have analysed the appearances of invented inscriptions within Roman literature, the earliest of which is Arthur Stein's 1931 study. The majority of his work is dedicated to the various purposes that inscriptions serve in historical literature. Overall it is rare, he finds, that extant inscriptions are discussed in ancient literature, or that an inscription (extant or not) is discussed in more than one ancient source.[10] Often Roman writers criticize previous usage of a particular inscription because its information has been misinterpreted,[11] or they freely revise and summarize inscriptions in language that suits them.[12] The most frequent use of inscriptions, Stein asserts, is as mere references that suffice to support a particular historical point.[13] Just as we would not expect modern historians to use inscriptions to authorize events easily verified by other sources, the Romans, it seems, did not often rely on inscriptions to authenticate historical narrative.[14]

In the midst of these historiographic concerns, Stein makes an interesting observation: namely that despite the fact that inscriptions are little utilized in Roman historic inquiries, fictive or counterfeit inscriptions acquire definite meaning in ancient literature.[15] He calls invented inscriptions in Petronius, Horace, Ovid and Virgil a common motif, 'ein beliebtes dichterisches Motiv', which imbued the works with a literary character distinct from historical evidence (Stein 1931, 78). The practice of including fictive inscriptions was not limited to literary authors, however, considering the many false inscriptions identified in the problematic *Historia Augusta* (1931, 78).[16] Regarding fictive inscriptions, particularly epitaphs, Stein attributes to them all a parodic intention: 'die köstliche Parodie auf einer Grabschrift', and by way of example he provides the epitaph of Trimalchio in Petronius' *Satyricon* (1931, 57). Yet the *Satyricon* is satire, and Trimalchio a comic buffoon, and for that reason his epitaph is parody.[17]

When Stein addresses less humorous instances (e.g. the votive inscription for Corinna in *Am.* 2.13, and Hypermestra's last words in *Her.* 14) he quickly dismisses them as fantasy inscriptions of purely poetic purpose, and his lack of further explanation makes them lie uncomfortably with the surrounding parodic examples.[18] What should be said of Dido's epitaph in *Heroides* 7, or the epitaph that Ovid composes for himself in *Tristia* 3.3? Stein is silent about the other purposes these inscriptions might have. Further, he does not address the fact that different types of inscriptions appear in Latin poetry, not merely epitaphs, and how such generic choices might affect the way one reads both the inscriptions and the poems in which they appear. Thus the parallel assessments that Stein offers between works of vastly different periods and influences overlook the possible nuances of meaning within each, and the role that cultural context might play in each case, leaving much room for further interpretation of such passages. It is for this reason that I have chosen to limit the majority of my analysis to the Augustan age in particular, since the poets of that age are companions of a sort with respect to their common influences, their influence on each other and the period in which they operate.

Ewald Lissberger's 1934 study of poetic inscriptions tabulates epitaphic verses, phrases and words that he believes are borrowed from the poetry of Catullus, Tibullus, Propertius and Ovid.[19] He attributes the connection between epigraphy and previously published poetry to two main things: first, that elegy was intended as a poem of homage to a loved one, and so adapts easily and effectively to the epitaph or dedication; second, that verse denouement (*Versausgang*) and the distich-bound sense-break (*Sinneinschnitt*) of Roman elegy are useful to compact sentiments on gravestones (Lissberger 1934, 14-15). He provides tables and appendices showing the extent of the imitation of elegiac poets, and that the practice of borrowing was most common at Rome, but widespread throughout the empire.[20] Most significantly, he finds that Ovid's verses far surpass all other poets in the frequency of their appearance in the epitaphs on Roman graves, and credits such widespread imitation of Ovid's works to the broader themes of his poetry (love, abandonment, the anxiety of separation, and lament) and the rhetorical handling of the material (1934, 16-17). Ovid was poetically predisposed to expressing himself in a fashion that was memorable and quotable among the Roman populace – and it is appropriate to add that his corpus is quite extensive.[21] Aside from generic and rhetorical qualities, we should remember too that published verses, having already achieved a level of appreciation and authentication by virtue of their dissemination, would be, as they are today, material naturally considered appropriate to honour loved ones, particularly those verses that have moved people enough to read and acquire them.[22] Lissberger makes clear the influence and popularity of the Augustan poets and the marked relationship between poetic and epigraphic impulses; unfortunately his study does not investigate the invention of inscriptions by these same poets within their works.

Taking up where Lissberger leaves off, John Yardley addresses the problem of this assumption that bereaved families and epigraphers were purposely borrowing from the elegists: 'we know that the [inscriptional] genre existed with its numerous recurring *topoi* and conventional expressions in the time of the elegists and the decades preceding them … at least some of the turns of phrase and wording that we find recurring in later funerary contexts probably predated the elegists and were part of the tradition of funerary epigram before their time' (Yardley 1996, 268).

Yardley admits that there are some instances where bereaved families clearly borrow lines of published poetry, although he is more willing to attribute the similarity between poetry and epitaph to the widespread nature of Roman epigraphic culture that permeates all forms of writing; so much so as to influence poets as well as those who selected epigraphic texts.[23] Many poets, Yardley suggests, developed a language of mourning that reflected the epigraphic habit and demonstrated the cross-current of influence.[24]

I find it encouraging that although Yardley's analysis mentions the obvious tradition of Hellenistic epigram that influenced funerary epigraphy at Rome, he is willing to concede more significance to the Roman epigraphic habit, the saturation of Roman culture with the funerary monument, inscription and surrounding context.[25] This Roman emphasis is significant since it allows us to depart from the tendency in many studies of Roman poetry to assert Hellenistic influence on the evolving motifs of Roman verse to the diminishment of native traditions. Indeed the Hellenistic epigrams that circulated throughout Rome from the second century onwards take credit for the way poets often phrased their words.[26] But the impulse to include epigraphic texts within a poem is related significantly also to Roman modes of honouring individuals and to the Roman concept of a life proven through action. The inclusion of these epigraphic passages is often featured at a key point in the poem's narrative, often at the end, or often between major themes. In other words, the inscriptions themselves are significant elements of the narrative structure, and are not merely parroted, epigrammatic moments within the writer's poetic phraseology.

Studies that have already analysed the presence of epigraphic texts in Virgil's epic and the lyric poetry of Horace, for example, characterize them as 'epigrammatic' passages, tracing the lines of continuity between Roman sentiments and those found in Greek poetics. For example, the epitaphic passages for Palinurus and Caieta in the *Aeneid* have drawn a great deal of attention since they appear in Books 5 and 7 respectively in such a way as to form a frame for Book 6. Alessandro Barchiesi (1979) is the first to elaborate upon the epigrammatic nature of the lines spoken by Aeneas for Palinurus in *Aeneid* 5.870-1.[27] As he notes, this epigrammatic passage is later answered by another similar passage for Caieta in the beginning of Book 7 (1-4) that behaves less like a true epitaph, but, with words like *fama*, *honos* and *ossa*, evokes well the funereal context (1979, 10).[28] According to Barchiesi, these two passages form a frame for the 'book of death' (Book 6) in that they provide grounds for comparing Aeneas before and after the transformative events of Book 6. Aeneas evolves from a state of ignorance about his destiny and his whereabouts to a state of confidence and capability. When the hero realizes that Palinurus is dead in Book 5, he expresses grief and uncertainty that reflects his own bewilderment at where he is destined to go and how he will cope. After his experience with the world of the dead and his interview with his future-telling father, he confidently assigns the name of his dead nurse Caieta to the cliffs of Italy at the beginning of Book 7, an act that demonstrates his sense of ownership over all he surveys.[29] The hero, by way of his journey to the Underworld, gains a vision of the future and the determination to own his fate, and these epigrammatic passages punctuate that transformation.

Stratis Kyriakidis summarizes Barchiesi's argument and builds on it, developing this 'frame' into a significant narrative structure: 'Vergil uses the celebrated conciseness of this literary genre in order to present succinctly – epigrammatically one may say – Aeneas' and his own reactions not only towards persons dear to him but also towards the Italian land. The framing of book 6 by the two "epigrams" highlights these reactions and signifies the hero's psychological evolution before and after his visits to the Underworld' (1998, 53). Later Kyriakidis suggests that the voice that speaks the first four lines of Book 7, the second epigrammatic passage, is not that of Aeneas but of Virgil, who calls the reader's attention to the new programmatic direction of the narrative (1998, 77). Along with other aspects of the narrative (hymnal elements, the Homeric concept of *kleos*, etc.) the epigrammatic nature of the passage is responsible for grabbing the reader's attention to the dramatically new situation that unfolds for the hero: a situation stated explicitly in the new proem that Virgil provides (7.37-45).[30]

Martin Dinter (2005) expands the search for epigrammatic passages within the *Aeneid* and finds evidence that Virgil had several literary models in mind while adapting epigram to the epic context, specifically to the purpose of providing significant narrative structures. By looking first at epigrammatic tendencies in Homer's *Iliad* and demonstrating the ways that certain passages meet the criteria of epitaph,[31] Dinter goes on to say that Virgil's uses of 'embedded epi(c)grams … are part of a development of generic mixing, the absorption of the sepulchral epigram by subsequent forms of Roman poetry' (2005, 156). Catullus, as he points out, becomes a Roman model for the use of sepulchral epigram in Latin poetry: a model that all the later elegists show delight in applying to their works (2005, 156). Furthermore there is multiplicity in the way that Virgil 'dealt with this experimental and metapoetic epigrammatic heritage' (2005, 156). This is shown, Dinter claims, in the sub-categories of epigram within the *Aeneid*: sepulchral, dedicatory and a third category he calls metapoetic, in which epigrammatic lines in the poem answer to other poems.[32]

Nothing in these studies is incorrect, and Dinter is right to make distinctions between the various epigrammatic forms featured within the Latin literature. Yet there is room for further analysis: why is the Roman poet drawn so readily to the epigraphic impulse within his works, and why does it take shape with explicit reference to these different epigraphical types? To my mind, the impulse among the Augustan poets to reflect the Roman cultural milieu, as indicated in other kinds of interpretive models of the poetry (with respect to the city's topography, to decorative art, and to the political peculiarities of the period),[33] is a primary consideration in the interpretation of these passages and their role within the literature. Furthermore, the uniquely Roman cultural aspect of the epigraphic habit and its poetic reflection in the epigraphic text becomes more pronounced in the Augustan age. As we work our way beyond Virgil and epic to the elegiac poets, these subtle 'epigrammatic' passages that Virgil creates, often voiced by a character or the narrator within the body of the epic narrative, share the stage in the elegiac poems with explicitly stated inscriptions that are composed as if by a talented epigrapher, ready for carving upon an available surface. Their appearances are often introduced by words and phrases that draw attention to their graphic quality, such as *subscribam*, *adiciam titulam*, *inscribat*, or *taleque sub nostro nomine carmen erit*.[34] The elegiac poets have purposely moved from the incorporation of epigrammatic themes within their poetry to the construction of a Roman world where characters (and authors) apply their energies eagerly to the act of self-commemoration.

That desire to delineate text as a visual marker is seen first in Virgil, once,[35] but numerous times in Propertius and Ovid, and proportionately almost as often in Tibullus. The concentration of such 'visible' texts in the age of Augustus, I will continue to argue, is due as much to the explosion of epigraphic presence of the Augustan age as to the influence of Hellenistic anthologies. In the rest of this chapter I will examine the roots of poetic epigraphy at Rome and show that the Roman desire to write upon the landscapes of the city and its environs has much to do with this shift from poetry that merely evokes epigrammatic passages to poetry containing verse inscriptions.

Latin elegy, epigram and epigraphy

Latin inscriptions composed in poetic metre date at least as far back as the early third century BC.[36] Étienne Wolff links the origin of the funerary verse inscription at Rome to the desire of illustrious families like the Scipios to place on the tomb an abridged version of the person's eulogy (Wolff 2000, 55-61). The majority of the extant Scipionic *elogia* appear in Saturnian verse, a metrical form that lasted until the age of Cicero,[37] and whose inheritance from Greek poetics is still a matter of controversy.[38] Whatever its true origins, Jed Parsons explains why the Saturnian was a metre better suited to Latin of the late Archaic period, that is until the late third century BC when linguistic innovations made the accent structure of the language more fitting for increasingly popular new metres: septenarii, hexameters, elegy and the like.[39]

Nevertheless Saturnian inscriptions appear quite late. Despite the influx of useful, eulogistic Hellenistic forms like the elegy in the late third century BC, noble families such as the Scipios, the Mummii and the Vertuleii, as well as less illustrious but well-to-do families like those of Cicero's friend Atticus and the wealthy baker Eurysaces, chose the

Saturnian to commemorate their kin and themselves in the first century BC.[40] In addition, these epitaphs were quite readily visited and read by Romans of many ensuing generations.[41] The reason that Saturnians survive in inscriptions long after they are needed is, in all probability, that the Romans liked them – they saw them as traditional and were loath to risk placing on their eternal monuments something merely fashionable, that is, before the Greek metres were proven to have staying power. The reason may also be tied to the metre's capability to incorporate the types of inscriptions that Romans appreciated, a capability that, in their perception, at least initially, surpassed Hellenistic imports. By looking at some of the funerary inscriptions that pre-date the influence of Hellenistic metres, it is possible to surmise what qualities the Romans did appreciate in their lasting, commemorative monuments.

We are fortunate that the tomb-complex of the Scipios, one of Rome's most illustrious Republican families, remains preserved under a seventeenth-century farmhouse off the Appian Way, about 400 metres north-west of the Porta Appia. Even more fortunate are we to have the original sarcophagi from eight of the thirty tombs, the replicas of which lie within the tomb-site (the originals lie within the Vatican collections).[42] If inscriptions accompanied the burials, they originally appeared on the sarcophagi themselves, although today some of the reconstructions are displayed on the walls of the site. Inscriptions appear to mark the burial of both men and women within the tomb, and several men of the family receive epitaphs that consist of several verses and declare their achievements.[43] The text of the epitaph of L. Cornelius Scipio Barbatus, cos. 298 and cens. 290, appears in Saturnian verse (here with lines divided into Saturnian cola), *CIL* 1.2.7 (*CLE* 7):[44]

Cornelius Lucius	Scipio Barbatus[45]
Gnaivod patre prognatus,	fortis vir sapiensque,
quoius forma virtutei	parisuma fuit,
consol censor aidilis	quei fuit apud vos,
Taurasia Cisauna	Samnio cepit,
subigit omne Loucanam	opsidesque abdoucit.

Lucius Cornelius Scipio Barbatus was the son of his father Gaius, and was a man brave and wise whose beauty was equal to his virtue; he served as consul, censor and aedile among you all; he captured Taurasia, Cisauna and Samnium; he wholly subjugated Loucana, and took hostages.

Here also is the epitaph of L. Cornelius Scipio, son of the above Barbatus, cos. 259 and cens. 258 BC, *CIL* 1.2.9 (*CLE* 6):[46]

Honc oino ploirume	cosentiont R[omane
duonoro optumo	fuise viro
Luciom, Scipione filios	Barbati

consol censor aidilis hic fuet a[pud vos.
Hec cepit Corsica Aleriaque urbe,
dedet Tempestatebus aide mereto[d.

Most Romans agree that this one man, Lucius Scipio, son of Barbatus, was the best of good men; he served among you as consul, censor and aedile. He captured Corsica and the city of Aleria, and he gave a temple to the Storm-Gods because it was deserved.

As is evident in these inscriptions, the name, the achievements of civic virtue, the *cursus honorum*, the military conquests and the piety of the individual form the majority of poetic content. The phrases referring to the wisdom and beauty of the elder Barbatus echo Greek poetic sentiment, thereby making their composition before the mid-third century Hellenistic infusion of poetic forms into Rome unlikely, and we can therefore grant these inscriptions a *terminus a quo* of the late third century.[47] Noticeable also is the reference to the dead in the third person. Although one much later Saturnian inscription (to Marcus Caecilius in the age of Cicero) does address the reader,[48] the prevalent goal in this archaic poetic form is to highlight the name and the career of the individual;[49] poetic sentiments are given little or no attention. As Thomas Habinek writes, 'the epitaphs invite the reader to imagine the continuity of the Scipionic tradition, the allusions to a judging audience, either living or deceased, [and this suggests] that the force of tradition must be reinvented and reasserted in each succeeding generation, and, furthermore, that the reader is instrumental in the validation of that tradition' (Habinek 1998, 52).

Roughly a generation later, Saturnian inscriptions demonstrate more influence from Hellenistic poetic models, as is shown in the inscription of Publius Cornelius Scipio, an augur in 180 BC and one of the two sons of Scipio Africanus, *CIL* 1.2.10 (*CLE* 8):[50]

Quei apice insigne Dial[is fl]aminis gesistei,
mors perfe[cit] tua ut essent omnia brevia,
honos fama virtusque, gloria atque ingenium.
quibus sei in longa licu[i]set tibe utier vita,
facile facteis superases gloriam maiorum.
qua re lubens te in gremiu, Scipio, recip[i]t
terra, Publi, prognatum Publio, Corneli.

You who have worn the pointed cap of the *flamen* of Jupiter: death made brief all that was yours – your honour, fame, virtue, glory and talent. Had you been able to enjoy a long life, you would easily have surpassed by your deeds the glory of your ancestors. Therefore glad earth receives you, Publius Scipio Cornelius, son of Publius, into her bosom.

The poetic aspects are more obvious here:[51] joyful earth, the reception of the young man's body into the bosom of his land, the list of qualities that adorn his character, and even the second person address that speaks to the young man as if his spirit were alive to repeatedly perceive these praises, spoken aloud by the person who stops to visit the tombs and read the inscriptions.[52] All this indicates a notable shift from the drier, more career-driven inscriptions that represent, or attempt to reconstruct, the archaic form of funerary homage. Yet though the inscription is constructed more poetically to incorporate the role of the reader, poetic applications have not undermined the significant summary of actions that constitute the majority of the text.

The earliest Latin elegiac inscription, found also on a sarcophagus in a later addition to the Scipio tomb-complex, demonstrates a continuing development of poetic language and content in funerary homage. It dates to the late second century BC and commemorates the life of Cn. Cornelius Scipio Hispanus, a praetor in 139, *CIL* 1.2.15 (*CLE* 958):[53]

> Virtutes generis mieis moribus accumulavi,
> progeniem genui, facta patris petiei.
> maiorum optenui laudem, ut sibei me esse creatum
> laetentur: stirpem nobilitavit honor.

> I accumulated virtues according to the customs of my clan: I bore a son and I strove to achieve the deeds of my father. I earned the praise of my ancestors, so may they rejoice that I was born of them: (my) honour has ennobled their stock.

The dramatic nature of the first-person narrative draws the reader in to speak the words of the dead man, reincarnating him, in effect, for the seconds it takes to read his words. This practice of giving presence to the absent will play an important role in the elegiac poetry of the Augustan age. The man's name is not included inside the verses, but appears rather as a *titulus* above the verses, serving to introduce the reader to the identity before reading his biography.[54] The man's career, imbued with a sense of ownership by way of the first-person narrative, is more poetic than in the Saturnians where series of offices and cities conquered could be presented quite as lists, as seen in the earlier Barbati epitaphs. Even so, R.G. Tanner comments on the Saturnian nature of the hexameter lines of this elegiac inscription (Tanner 1961, 223). Among this treasure-trove of inscriptions, we see the slow evolution of expressions of commemoration. In keeping with the distinctly Roman desire to depict the honoured dead as men of action, Hispanus' poem is no generic sentiment of mourning: rather it gives special treatment to the man's biography, and allows the reader to understand the personal nature of his achievements and his pride in them. To corroborate the man's distinguished Roman career, the *titulus* appears as complement to the sentiments of the verses that follow.

As John Yardley points out, poetic *topoi* are conservative – one finds sentiments in Greece in the fifth century BC that are similar to those found in Rome in the Imperial period (Yardley 1996, 268).[55] The fact that our oldest known elegiac epitaph dates to at least forty years after Ennius was authoring his elegiac verses, during which time Saturnians continued to be produced (as they would for another hundred years), also suggests the conservative nature of Roman tastes in inscriptions.[56] The Scipio family displays old-fashioned preferences in the type of tomb-monument they chose to use (sarcophagi in rock-hewn tombs).[57] Their late adoption of the elegiac metre as the appropriate means of commemorating their family-members indicates the conservative impulses of Rome's old and important families.

Romans surely identified with the archaic language and format of the Saturnian, well adapted to encompass a man's career within its looser syllabic form. Perhaps they wished to avoid honouring their dead with poetic forms so new to their own culture, forms that had not yet established their place within Roman society.[58] In the century that followed the introduction of Hellenistic metres at Rome, the Romans found a way to preserve all parts of archaic inscriptional presentation while incorporating Hellenistic fashions that allowed for more exploration of sentiment and philosophy on their tombs. In the arena of self-commemoration the Romans continued to utilize a culturally unique format to honour their dead: they used both poetic and non-poetic lines to fully illustrate the breadth and impact of a person's life. This is a lesson which must not be forgotten, for although the centuries after the demise of the Saturnian saw an explosion of literary and epigraphic poetic forms inherited from Greece, the ancient Romans formulated their words and sentiments to express their own cultural experience. Even under the influence of Greek poetics, they found ways to alter the traditional form but not the function of inscriptional homage.

It was the great wave of Hellenic influence in the third and second centuries BC, after the wars in Greece and southern Italy, that brought Greek poetics to Rome and forever changed Roman modes of expression and commemoration. Étienne Wolff attributes the rapid spread and expansion of Latin verse-*elogia* to the availability in the second century of volumes of funerary epigram.[59] Our evidence attributes to Ennius the credit for introducing Rome to Hellenistic metres.[60] A Calabrian educated at Tarentum, he produced at least four epigrams still extant by way of various sources that represent the first examples of Latin elegy.[61] All four epigrams evoke inscriptions; the first two are literary epitaphs for Scipio Africanus, Vahlen (V) 19-20:[62]

> hic situs ille est cui nemo civis neque hostis
> quivit pro factis reddere opis pretium.[63]

Here lies the man whom neither friend nor foe could ever repay in kind for his accomplishments.

and V 21-4:[64]

a sole exoriente supra Maeotis paludes
  nemo est qui factis aequiperare queat.
si fas endo plagas caelestum ascendere cuiquam,
  mi soli caeli maxima porta patet.[65]

From where the sun rises over the marshes near the Sea of Azov can no one be found who can match (my) deeds; if it is fitting for anyone to climb to the region of the gods, the great portal of the skies lies open for me alone.

The third is an epitaph for himself, V 17-18:[66]

nemo me lacrimis decoret nec funera fletu
  faxit. cur? volito vivos per ora virum.[67]

Honour me not with tears nor accompany my death-rites with weeping. Why? For I fly still living through the lips of men.

The fourth is one that may not have been authored by Ennius, but its content is unmistakably inscriptional – probably meant to evoke a dedication on a statue or bust, V 15-16:[68]

aspicite, o cives, senis Enni imaginis formam.
  hic vestrum panxit maxima facta patrum.

Look, O citizens, at the shape of the appearance of the image of old Ennius. He penned the very great deeds of your ancestors.

It seems that Latin elegy in its infancy is drawn to the utilitarian aspect of the inscriptional epigram because it serves the useful purpose of honouring individuals, and Romans respond most receptively to those verses that honour great men.[69] Of all the epigrams that Ennius may have written, the ones preserved and deemed worthy of comment by later writers are those that evoke inscriptional writing. The first couplet (V 19-20), encapsulating Scipio's achievements with respect to friends and foes, creates a classic juxtaposition to which the elegiac verse is so aptly suited in its tight format of syntactically whole couplets. The longer epitaph for Scipio (V 21-4) grants the poet room to say more about the man's worthiness and to imagine him entering the gates of heaven, a sentiment granted further elaboration in Cicero's 'Dream of Scipio' at the end of his *De Republica*, and echoed with even more personal implications at the end of Propertius' fourth and final book of poetry.[70] The third epigram (V 17-18) gives us a poetic predecessor to Horace's *exegi monumentum* (*Carm.* 3.30) and provides early proof of the conceptual link between the permanence of words on stone and those in a text. Ennius clearly saw potential in the elegiac form for poetic self-commemoration – a poetic purpose that would come to fruition two hundred years later in the elegiac movement at Rome. Lastly, V 15-16, written probably by someone else for Ennius, admires the poet for his role in glorifying Rome's great men: a clear indication that Roman poetic efforts aimed at achieving purposes similar to those of epigraphic practice.

Despite their inscriptional style, we have no evidence that Ennius' epitaphs ever appeared on stone memorials or as dedications on statues.[71] As we have seen, the earliest known elegiac inscriptions in Latin date to later than 139 BC, more than a generation after the poet's death in 169. His practice of using the elegiac metre to memorialize the dead in a purely literary fashion suggests that he immediately appreciated the Hellenistic epigram as a literary technique containing many categories of expression, including the funereal.[72] It is not impossible to imagine that Ennius himself wrote some of the extant Scipionic *elogia* in Saturnian verse, electing to maintain the elegiac metre for literary purposes only.[73] At least it is likely to have occurred to him that elegiac inscriptions would make fine monuments to great men, since Greek elegiac epitaphs dated back to the eighth century BC.[74] However, given the conservative Roman preference for Saturnians on stone, and the emerging opportunity to write Rome's past in Hellenic verse-forms (as seen in Ennius' *Annales*), this early poet applied the imported metres to form new kinds of monuments to great men: ones not tied to stone and plots of expensive ground, but immortal forever 'through the lips of men'.[75]

Elegy and epigram were circulating quickly at Rome, however, if not immediately on the monuments of its best men. With it came other types of expression – ones not tied to such patriotic duties as honouring statesmen. Aulus Gellius reports the concerns of Cato the elder regarding the too frequent indulgence of Hellenistic entertaining pursuits. Amid a discussion of the word *elegans* and various opinions expressed in Cato's treatise on morals (the lost *Carmen de Moribus*), Gellius quotes Cato bemoaning the declining moral attitude among his contemporaries, a decline he connects indirectly to increasing literary concerns: 'once men paid more for horses than for cooks; once poetic artistry was not such an honour, and he who was studious in it or who dedicated himself to banqueting was called a flatterer.'[76] Gellius moves immediately from this statement by Cato to another from the same treatise and introduces it as an example of pre-eminent truth: 'human life is like iron; if iron is used it will wear out, but if it lies unused, rust will destroy it even so; likewise we see men worn out by training, but if you train not at all, inertia and lethargy do you more harm than exercise.'[77] Gellius clearly associates Cato's concern about his contemporaries, such as Fulvius Nobilior who took with him to his province several poets including Ennius,[78] with this maxim regarding the connection between a man's activities and his effectiveness. The connection that Gellius makes between artistic indulgence and physical weakness surely reflects an after-the-fact awareness among Romans that the new focus on artistic pursuits of the Republican period, enabled somewhat by the influx of Hellenistic material to Rome, was liable to do some detriment to the discipline and readiness of the elite.[79] Indeed, Kathryn Gutzwiller offers a description of the society that accompanied the light epigram in Greece – a youth culture preoccupied with ephemeral emotions and individuality rather than the traditional culture of hierarchy and tutelage (Gutzwiller 1998, 120):

> Instead of the communal sharing of emotional experience presupposed by old elegy, epigram depicts the particular and unique emotions that set apart and define individual selves. The lover of Hellenistic epigram seems younger than the lover of old elegy, and he chooses the sex and social status of his desired through personal preference alone. His feelings of joy or sorrow are not a communal experience that the other symposiasts share from time to time, but an emotional circumstance that hinders his participation in the conviviality of the moment and marks his alienation from group experience. Consequently, erotic epigram makes no attempt to instruct with lessons valuable beyond the immediate moment, but rather strives to illustrate the lover's interior emotional condition at a given point in time.

We cannot be certain to what extent this Greek atmosphere was achieved at Rome, and of course there are other ways to explain the beginnings of the elegiac movement at Rome without mentioning spiritual and moral decline, as many have shown.[80] In any case, within two or three generations after Cato, many epigrammatists lived in Rome and were friends or acquaintances of highly placed men like Q. Lutatius Catulus and Cicero.[81] Catulus, consul in 102 BC and friend of the epigrammatist Archias,[82] composed homoerotic verses in elegiac metre based on earlier works by Callimachus and Meleager.[83] The scene was set for the apolitical, erotic-elegiac movement of the late first century BC. Even so, the early attraction at Rome to epigram in the late third century BC, as evidenced by the early elegies of Ennius and the first funerary inscriptions that evoke epigram, derived from the rhetorical economy of the epigram and its unique ability to capture concisely a sentiment, expound a philosophical tenet, or praise individual achievements.[84]

The elegiac verse at Rome thus developed on a dual track. Providing a pithy medium for the inscriptional expression, it was used epigraphically at Rome from the late second century BC onwards and throughout the empire until its demise in the fifth century AD.[85] Its literary form, first demonstrated by Ennius and taking root in the elegies of Catulus, Lucilius and others, provided an attractive opportunity to artists interested in creating elegy that was not bound to sites and stones.[86] That form, influenced by Greek epigrammatists and the circulating anthologies of the period, and tending towards personal sentiment, satire and eroticism, was developing in elite Roman circles. The sympotic oral performance may have been its debut, but the elegy would soon bloom as a literary genre all its own,[87] experimented upon by Catullus, pioneered by Gallus, and brought to high artistry by Propertius, Tibullus and Ovid – though never too far removed from the arena of elitist amusement and titillation.

The embedded epigraphic text is a later addition to the elegiac form, and within the shorter, more compact narratives of elegy, it adds significantly to the narrative structure of a poem, as it does in epic. As I stated in my introduction, passages that are explicitly marked as graphic texts focus the reader's attention upon the act of reading; they comprise what Wolfgang Iser would typify as one of 'the many processes of focusing and refocusing that take place during the reading of the literary text' (Iser 1978, 113). Iser points to a variety of methods by which the narrative constructs what he calls 'spotlighting of textual perspectives' created by changes of perspective, or 'wandering viewpoints', within the narrative (1978, 114).[88] His conclusions about such literary strategies apply very well to the case of the epigraphic passage (1978, 116):

> In the time-flow of the reading process, past and future continually converge in the present moment, and the synthesizing operations of the wandering viewpoint enable the text to pass through the reader's mind as an ever-expanding network of connections. This also adds the dimension of space to that of time, for the accumulation of views and combinations gives us the illusion of depth and breadth, so that we have the impression that we are actually present in a real world.

The inscriptions in the poems that we will examine in the following chapters act as mimetic special effects, if you will, within their poems. They not only highlight aspects of character, action, authority and narrative, but they also create an important 'network of connections' between the ancient reader and the character – each of whom operates within a landscape full of graphic markers of commemoration and information. As suggested in my introduction, epigraphic passages serve as 'hyperlinks' between the character's fictional desire and the reader's real desire to install some record of his or her existence upon that landscape.[89]

Categories and characteristics

Several inscriptional types at Rome (epitaphs, votives, *tituli* and graffiti) have their counterparts in the types of epigraphic passages seen in Augustan poetry. This is evidence that as the poets considered cultural *topoi* for representation within their works, they looked at the entire epigraphic tradition at their disposal, and not merely the funerary epigram, which is naturally related to the elegiac metre. Certainly the presence of a votive inscription inside a poem about abortion, as in Ovid's *Am.* 2.13, may reveal intriguing aspects about the poet's attitude towards the event – even the way he words the inscription may indicate something important about how to read the inscription and the poem in general.[90] Furthermore, one should expect a votive inscription to work quite differently than an epitaph (or a graffito) inside a poem; indeed the purpose a type of inscription serves inside a poem may vary from author to author, from poem to poem.

Nevertheless, the types themselves exist in the material world that surrounds these poetics and must inform their function within the artistic world as well as the real one. Mimesis, to repeat my point in the introduction, relies on conditions located in reality and thus is grounded on experience. It is necessary to examine the cultural peculiarities unique to each type of inscription in order to better understand their place in the poetic text. Governing all of these considerations, of course, will be the relevance of context – for on the street as well as within narrative, context determines meaning. Below I provide the relevant passages from the Augustan poets, specifically those passages that best represent the poetic desire to recreate the epigraphic habit within the fictional narrative. I have categorized them by type of inscription, and I also provide summaries of the significances of these types in Roman culture.[91]

Epitaphs

To those who study Roman culture, epitaphs are, as Valerie Hope notes, an 'irreplaceable social record' (Hope 2001, iv). It is through their comprehensive study that we can discern statistics and figures, regarding diet, health, life expectancy, religious beliefs, familial and political associations, etc. (2001, 1). Yet the epitaph represents more than a statistical tool – its very existence tells us something important about the people who applied its use. Hearkening back to the assessment of an epigraphic habit operating in Roman society, Graham Oliver discusses the need to understand what he calls the 'epigraphic culture' at Rome, and to understand 'the degree to which a society was erecting inscriptions at any one moment or over a period of time' (Oliver 2000, 16). Richard Brilliant presents the problem within the context of the imperial practice of *damnatio memoriae*: 'the notion of survival in whatever form seemed to have a special urgency, given the extraordinary abundance of monuments dedicated to the preservation of the tokens of prior existence' (Brilliant 1999, 145).[92]

There is uncertainty regarding from what social conditions this 'urgency' might derive. MacMullen (1982) addresses the issue at length, but cannot distil particular reasons to explain varying concentrations of inscriptions in stone at various times. He finds that their concentration steadily increases throughout the empire from the time of Augustus to the reign of Severus, with decreases in usage occurring under Nero and

Domitian, and that then the concentrations fall off altogether into the third century. From this he generalizes that, 'apparently the rise and fall of the epigraphic habit was controlled by what we can only call a sense of audience' (1982, 246).[93] So long as people feel secure in the knowledge that there will be people to read and understand their tombstones, they leave a permanent record; when things look bleak, perhaps a sense of ennui sets in regarding the record of personal histories.

Henrik Mouritsen offers a slightly more nuanced perspective. He finds convincing evidence that most upper-class Romans of the post-Tiberian, Imperial period began to steer clear of the type of grandiose funerary monuments and necropoleis that still amaze us from the Republican and Augustan periods: the tomb of the Scipios, the pyramid of Sestius, and the tomb of Eumachia at Pompeii (Mouritsen 2005, 44-5). Mouritsen weighs the evidence of hundreds of funerary inscriptions to establish that the principal agents of funerary memorial were freedmen and those related to freedmen. Elite members of society in smaller towns like Pompeii, he finds, often chose to keep small burial grounds on their private estates.[94] Yet he offers a significant reason as to why elite citizens did not choose to commemorate themselves in the number and size of monuments being fashioned by their inferiors: such important men could rest 'safe in the knowledge that they would be preserved for posterity where it really mattered, i.e. on buildings, statue bases and public records in and around the forum' (2005, 54).[95]

Regarding the elite at Rome, Mouritsen suggests an additional reason as to why funerary monuments decrease in the Imperial period (2005, 55):

> [T]he new political order put a limit on overt senatorial competition and self-promotion ... [T]hroughout the imperial period we find a broad continuation of senatorial burials at a relatively modest level. This feature may perhaps be explained by the exceptional political circumstances obtaining in the capital. For with the rise of autocracy came a redefinition of the civic centre of Rome, which was no longer available as a field of aristocratic competition in the way it continued to be in the Italian towns. The Imperial monopoly over the central monumental spaces of Rome thus reduced the scope for senatorial self-commemoration and thereby indirectly contributed to the continued aristocratic presence in the urban necropolis. The senators were, literally, forced into the margins ...

This marginality was not acceptable, as we know, to many who thus died fighting and resisting Caesar and Octavian in the decades of the 40s and 30s BC; yet eventually even the proudest Romans learned to accept the new yoke of leadership that had appeared over their necks. Latin elegy not only appears, but positively proliferates at this crucial phase of transformation between the politics of self-determination and what Mouritsen baldly calls the 'autocracy' of the Imperial period. If security breeds public memorial, what does insecurity breed in poetry? In a period of such broad political and geographical transformation, the infiltration of epigraphy into poetry could be a sign that monuments of words, as opposed to monuments of stone, were perceived more likely to outlast the ravages of time.[96]

Regarding the content of Roman epitaphs, throughout the first half of the twentieth century there were many attempts to quantify epitaphic expression in order to learn the attitudes of the ancient world. Lattimore's aforementioned study examines epitaphs to determine belief structures (eschatology, religion, etc.) in the Greco-Roman world. What he finds is a multiplicity of beliefs and modes of expression that defy clear-cut categorization. His most compelling conclusions are those relevant to the Roman view of immortality in comparison with other cultures, and the poetic inscription in comparison to the far more common prose ones. Perhaps not surprisingly, verse epitaphs demonstrate greater sentimentality, something aptly attributed to the Greek poetic tradition that influences Roman poetics.[97] Prose inscriptions, by contrast, tend to express more distinctly Latin concerns: references to the *cursus honorum*, for example, and references to the *Di Manes*, the uniquely Italian concept of immortal spirits of the dead.[98] The Roman notion of immortality and the afterlife is ambiguous, however, considering the many inscriptions that deny the existence of an afterlife, or merely speak of Elysium as a place that is conceivable, but in which no faith is firm (Lattimore 1942, 62).[99] The concept as a whole, however, does seem to resonate more strongly under wider Roman influence than in previous periods: Lattimore finds that, 'no epitaph containing an unequivocal assertion of immortality is earlier than the fourth century BC. By far the greatest number comes from the Roman period' (1942, 53-4). Jocelyn Toynbee places more narrow chronological limits on the Roman notion of life after death: 'the bulk of our evidence, written and archaeological, for Roman afterlife ideas is not earlier than the first century BC' (Toynbee 1971, 34).

Purdie's earlier study focuses on Latin verse inscriptions of all types, and, with regard to epitaphs, also finds more evidence of a lack of theological continuity than any concrete belief system: 'Many of them are satisfied to employ formulae which witness to the traditional vague beliefs ... Scepticism and pure negation are the more common notes, although the higher influence of the mysteries and Neoplatonism is noticeable among the educated classes, who begin more and more to look upon death as the beginning of the life of the soul' (Purdie 1935, 39). When hopes of eternity are expressed, Purdie notes what achievements receive the most attention, and how they change throughout the course of Roman history. Republican epitaphs tend to dwell more on individual service to the state, while Imperial epitaphs boast more often the achievements of merchants and tradesmen.[100] He explains the change that develops from the first century BC onwards thus: 'the vast majority of the verse epitaphs belong to the classes who had no ancestors to take pride in: the great families, kept mindful of past and present splendour by the waxen effigies in their *atria*, yielded the epitaph to the humbler folk of the community as a weapon against oblivion after death' (1935, 60). Armstrong's study (1910) also supports this timeline. He finds that up to 100 BC, 'only those of senatorial and equestrian rank introduce autobiographic matter into inscriptions', while from that point until the end of the second century AD, 'with barely an exception, only the lower classes write their epitaphs and dedications in this way; finally, at the later date those of higher rank take up these forms, by this time wide-spread and vulgarized' (1910, 224). In addition, Lattimore finds that from the period of the late Republic onwards, Romans and Roman-influenced Greeks tend to focus on the non-military achievements of loved ones, and the hopes of loved ones to keep their memory everlasting (Lattimore 1942, 240-7).[101] Iiro Kajanto surveys the geographical distribution of epitaphs that mention eternity or perpetuity, and concludes that 'eternal memory was a genuine Roman idea', as opposed to one inspired by pre-existing cultures (Kajanto 1974, 68). Given the proliferation of the Latin epitaph referring to earth-bound immortality, to everlasting memory, from the first century BC onwards, there is sufficient evidence that there was a growing interest in preserving the name of the individual – more so than imagining the perpetuity of the person beyond the grave.

Most of these studies give priority to the wording of the epitaphs, and are little concerned with geographical or monumental context. Valerie Hope cautions against giving too much priority to the words of epitaphs without their monuments: 'such an interest may reflect the predilection of modern literate societies. The tendency has been encouraged by the traditional publication of epitaphs as disembodied texts; the words of the inscription are faithfully recorded and analysed whilst the context is not … But sometimes it is clear that the words of the inscription were only one element of the whole' (Hope 2001, 7).[102] Graham Oliver concurs: 'there is considerable danger if the inscribed monuments are divorced from the monuments on which they were cut. Methodological problems are deepened if the physical environment in which such inscribed monuments were viewed is ignored' (Oliver 2000, 18). Citing Greg Woolf (1996, 28), Oliver continues: 'the historian's tendency to treat inscriptions as a special kind of text needs to be modified, in other words, with a recognition that they are also a special kind of monument' (Oliver 2000, 18).

The monument that poets build for themselves is text – as Horace famously declares (*Carm.* 3.30.1-7):

> exegi monumentum aere perennius
> regalique situ pyramidum altius,
> quod non imber edax, non Aquilo impotens
> possit diruere aut innumerabilis
> annorum series et fuga temporum.
> non omnis moriar, multaque pars mei
> vitabit Libitiniam …

> I have built myself a monument more lasting than bronze and taller than the royal pile of the pyramids, that neither biting rain nor the raging Northeast Wind can demolish – or the onslaught of innumerable years or the passing of time. I will not die altogether, and much a part of me will avoid the goddess of Death.[103]

Given that Horace compares his poetic text to the monuments of great men, and given the role and importance of the epitaph in Roman society (at whatever sociological level they tended to be popular) for preserving the memory of the individual, we begin to understand the reasons why Roman poets often inserted them into their works.

Epitaphs are the most common type of inscription in the Augustan poets. The elegists contribute by far the greatest number of invented inscriptions.[104] Tibullus creates the first quoted (not merely evoked) epitaph at 1.3.55-6.[105] Propertius creates three 2.11.6, 2.13.35-6 and 4.7.85-6, and also provides several passages that evoke a funerary inscription: 1.7.24, 1.21, 1.22, 2.1.78, 2.5.28 and 4.11. By far Ovid outdoes them all, creating ten epitaphs: *Am.* 2.6.61-2; *Her.* 2.147-8, 7.193 and 195-6, 14.129-30, 15.183-4; *Meta.* 2.327-8, 14.143-4; *Fasti* 3.549-50; and *Trist.* 3.3.73-6. In addition he provides at least one passage that evokes the funerary inscription: *Am.* 3.9.67-8.

The place of these inscriptions within their poems can and should be subjected to inquiry; just as archaeologists seek to understand the context of a monument as well as what is written upon it, so too can literary interpreters apply the social context of inscriptions (or monuments and other material objects referred to within a poem) to explicate their purposes within the narrative, and to offer possibilities regarding what the poet means to highlight or emphasize by including them.

Votive inscriptions[106]

The votive inscription in general represents an exchange between the human and divine spheres; it represents proof of prayer, the power of belief and the integrity of an individual who keeps a promise. In the same way that written correspondence assumes and configures itself in response to an audience, so too do votive inscriptions configure an audience that encompasses both mortals and immortals.[107] Therefore, into this category I place all dedicatory inscriptions made to a god to serve as thanks, the fulfilment of a promise, or prayer. Votives are the second-most popular type of inscription that appears in the elegiac poets.[108] Tibullus composes a votive inscription at 1.9.83-4 and Propertius provides two at 2.14.27-8 and 4.3.72. Ovid again writes more than his predecessors combined with five total (*Am.* 1.11.27-8, 2.13.25; *Her.* 15.183-4,[109] 20.239-40; and *Meta.* 9.794).

Mary Beard has pointed out that the use of writing at the sites of shrines and temples is an important mode of identification and representation between worshipper and the divine. She speaks of graffiti, inscriptions on votive objects and priestly inscriptions as having 'symbolic functions' (Beard 1991, 38). Specifically, she attributes three such functions to the religious inscription: it defines the relationship between an individual and the divine; it constitutes an identity for gods and others who cannot speak; and it creates 'a hierarchy of religious power' (1991, 38). In explaining this notion of hierarchy, Beard points to the evidence that communication between gods and mortals, whether by oral (oracular) means or by written means, was a significant indication of the extent of the relationship between the mortal and divine spheres (1991, 38-9). Praying, non-literate offerings and other forms of homage certainly had their place, but in the ancient world, as Beard emphasizes, 'writing is necessarily connected with power' (1991, 58). Therefore, she concludes, even those who were illiterate understood the dynamic power of a literate society, the authority of written texts and the power of those who could manipulate words and symbols to create lasting records of their transactions and accomplishments.

Thousands of votive objects have been discovered throughout the ancient world, and the Italian practice of inscribing them is very old: votive inscriptions have been found dating as far back as the sixth century BC.[110] Even so, the available evidence demonstrates a considerable increase in the occurrence of inscribed votives, and an increase in the quality of objects dedicated, from the first century BC onwards in Italy. For example, a large category of votive objects from the fourth to the first century BC consists of terracotta anatomical models. Among thousands of such models dedicated to gods, Jean MacIntosh Turfa finds only five known cases of inscribed pieces (*ThesCRA*, v. 1, 363). Ingrid Edlund-Berry, in her study of twenty-five categories of votive objects from a similar period, also indicates the relative scarcity of inscriptions, adding that when they do appear, they tend to convey only the names of dedicants and deities (*ThesCRA*, vol. 1, 368). By contrast, Erika Simon, reporting on the vast array of marble votive objects that appear throughout Roman Imperial Italy, consistently finds inscriptions on the objects she studies (*ThesCRA*, vol. 1, 379-91). It was a product of the Imperial age that more and more wealthy citizens undertook to display homage to the gods with inscriptions on suitably expensive materials. With tabloid-like relish, for example, Dio Cassius reports the lavish shrine that Nero dedicated to the wife he murdered, Poppaea Sabina; on it he placed an inscription stating that the shrine was paid for by the women of Rome for the benefit of Sabina-Venus.[111]

What can be more expensive than a poem, given the amount of time and effort we can only imagine poets spending on their works? That votive dedications appear in poems suggests more than merely an imitative process, but also an authorial determination that poetic works, well-crafted, are worthy sites for reflection of the theological and moral universe. As I will show, the placement and use of votive inscriptions provide an equally dynamic relationship between text and audience, and the inscriptions carry into the poetic world explicit ties to a moral universe where human actions carry consequences and interact with divine will.

Tituli

More than the other categories of inscriptions, *tituli* lend themselves to a variety of poetic uses since they serve many purposes in Roman society: non-religious dedications on buildings, monuments and works of art; announcements in the public forum and on columns at crossroads and other heavily trafficked sites; and proclamations of victory on archways and on placards in triumphal processions. They may contain a few words, perhaps to honour an individual, or they may be many lines in length, as seen in the text of the *Res Gestae* (from the monument of Ancyra). They may be self-authored or dedicated by another; they may contain information of fleeting relevance, or they may hold value to countless generations. Once inscribed, however, *tituli* acquire permanence that can only be undone by destruction of the monument or by precise elimination of the inscription or words of the inscription. This practice, known as *damnatio memoriae*, became common enough in the Imperial period as members of ruling families vied for the throne or sought to hide the more shameful members of their circle, and an example of this is still visible today atop the Severan archway in the Roman forum.[112] We must remember that because all public record can be made subject to the whim of those with power over 'media', no inscription in stone is guaranteed permanence. Yet indeed there were worse things to happen to one's name, such as its being included in the proscription lists that led to the unjust execution of hundreds of Romans at various times in Rome's history.

In the Augustan age the *titulus* came to have added significance in the context of the large public forums being constructed for the featured (and selective) commemoration of the evolution of Rome from city-state to empire. *Tituli* were particularly instrumental in the Forum of Augustus as identifying inscriptions upon the so-called *summi viri*, statues of Rome's best men that lined the interior wall of the colonnades on either side of the forum's open space.[113] Pliny tells us that Augustus may have personally composed the *elogia* placed below the statues, although Paul Zanker offers mitigating circumstances that prevent such information from being taken literally (Zanker 1989, 212).[114] The names selected by Augustus for his forum and their arrangement within the complex may even have been inspired by previous poetic treatment of Rome's illustrious history, notably in *Aeneid* 6.[115] Moreover, we know that *tituli* of various types were frequent installations on temples, on statuary, on the new buildings of the Roman forum, on monuments, and within triumphal celebrations of Roman victories. There was enough of a surge of titular expression throughout the city to safely presume that poetic invention of such expression is in part a response to their presence throughout the Roman landscape, as seen in Ovid's *Ars* 2.744 and 3.812 and *Her.* 2.74, as well as in Propertius 3.23.24 and 4.2.59-64.

Context is therefore always significant in the case of the *titulus*, since the generic inscription (one not erected in dedication to a divinity or in honour of the deceased) can serve such a variety of purposes. In the cases with which the poets provide us, the inclusion of a *titulus* draws the reader's attention to a widely utilized means of conveying information in the Roman world, and thereby encourages the reader to take into consideration both its message and its significance within that context. For example, the placement of triumphal slogans at the end of the two lessons in the *Ars Amatoria* yields intriguing interpretations.[116] As the ensuing chapters will show, there are consequences that issue from a character's or an author's choice to put words on placards, columns or statues of the fictional landscape in which each operates.

Graffiti

The nature of graffiti has essentially remained the same over thousands of years – expressions of ephemeral relevance or whim etched upon a surface that was not necessarily intended for the purpose.[117] James Franklin suggests that most graffiti were written by the lower classes, and he identifies two main categories of graffiti: self-indulgent and informative.[118] The self-indulgent graffito depends little or not at all on whether or not it is read; it exists merely as a testament to the fact that someone was once moved to gouge letters upon a wall – whether it was to practise his or her 'a b c's or to write a line of poetry.[119] The informative graffito conveys information or a sentiment that others may want or need to read.[120] Such graffiti are found throughout Pompeii, and Franklin explains why: 'given the lack of alternative media for exchanging messages, informative graffiti seem to have been used more seriously and readily than they are today' (Franklin 1991, 88).

The case for narrative structures achieved by embedded graffiti in the poetry may seem scantier since graffiti occur only twice in the elegiac poetry, namely Ovid's *Heroides* 5.21-4 and 29-30 and 17.88. Even so, there are considerable literary precedents to keep in mind when addressing these instances, such as Acontius' inscription on trees for Cydippe in the *Aitia* of Callimachus (fr. 67 and 75 Pfeiffer). I will pose that the use of graffiti in Ovid's works may have less relevance to the cultural phenomenon, and have much more to do with poetology.[121]

Conclusion

In her study of Greek epigram, Gutzwiller discusses the significance of context with respect to the placement of epigrams within the anthologies, claiming that it provides a window of perception to the *personae* of individual authors. She likens this context to that of the remembered epigraphic verse in stone (Gutzwiller 1998, 7-8):

> the monument adorned by the epigram is no longer present but, like the banqueting hall as the site of sympotic epigram, must now be reconstructed in the reader's imagination ... So too, the placing of an epigram in a book grants the referents of that poem a certain indeterminacy of meaning. The reader of an inscription assumes the persons or events mentioned to be historically real ... The epigram placed in a book, whatever its intended purpose at the time of composition, gives meaning to its referents through exemplification: its subjects become types, presented, gemlike, through brief but specific details.

'Inscribed' verses within Roman poetry bear the same interpretability: what imagined reality does the poet create by inserting them into his verses, and how does that affect the poem's reading? As we have seen, Ennius used the epigrammatic form to create epitaphic verses free of a geographical context. By contrast, the Augustan poets reversed the dynamic evolution of epigrams from stone to text by recasting them as epigraphic intrusions upon the text. The epigrammatic tone of such verses highlights the activities of poetic *personae*, and the commitment of the poets themselves to the eternality of their work. In addition, the types of inscriptions used create a cultural framework in which these themes and events operate. In the coming chapters, the 'gem-like' qualities of the verse inscriptions will reinforce the themes of the larger poems where they reside. I have shown that it is not enough to say that shared Hellenistic origins or metrical structure explains inscriptional presence in Roman poetry – and yet this is precisely as far as previous commentators have gone in explaining these inscriptional passages.[122] The function of these passages extends much further than surrounding elegiac lines, and their strange textuality evokes the circumstances that attend real inscriptions in the Roman landscape, a cultural attitude that requires more discussion. I will approach each poetic inscription as if it too lies in situ, within the context of Rome's epigraphic culture, and the context of potential poetic aims.

2

Epitaphic Revelations in Catullus and Propertius

The early innovations of Ennius in the use of elegy for epigrammatic sentiments divorced from actual monuments and inscriptional contexts had a profound effect on the way that the later Roman elegists formulated their genre. It is not new to say that Roman elegy is intrinsically inclusive of a host of public and private concerns, but there is room to address the overlap between themes in elegiac poems and the topics of concern in the epigraphic tradition more specifically. As I will show in the earliest collections of elegies by Catullus and Propertius, the poets maintain a close link to inscription, monument and memory, while they simultaneously avail themselves of the literary traditions handed down from Hellenistic precedents. It is this Roman capability to associate poetic eulogy and individual achievement with the Hellenistic epigrammatic motifs that grants Latin elegy the potential to exhibit so many poetic typologies, and to achieve the expressionistic vivacity that accounts, in part, for the long-standing desire to find the 'truth' behind these poems.

In recent decades scholars have discouraged the practice of taking too literally the claims of the poems, going so far as to remove autobiographical considerations from their readings of the poems.[1] Dismissal of the ins and outs of the poets' relationships with their elegiac mistresses is one result. Who was Cynthia? Does it matter?[2] As many have shown, she and all the other elegiac mistresses are primarily phantoms of the poetic imagination: props around which the artist may stage a variety of vignettes, and through which he may launch into any of a series of narratives that will reflect his erudition.[3] One need not draw a schematic chart of a poet's life relating poem *a* to experience *b*.[4] Yet poets are human beings, not disembodied hands with pens attached. Even if the woman inside the poem is merely a reflection of personal anxieties, sociological projections and poetic ingenuity, it is still worthwhile to understand what inspires such characterizations. The rewarding aspect of interpreting Augustan poetry is that we have so many sources of information at our fingertips: from historical accounts to inscriptions to complete poetic works – the period is more translucent than any other in the ancient world.

Therefore let us consider the personal nature of Roman elegy, for I believe that the connection between epigraphic habits and elegiac poetry is due to two desires: a desire for self-representation and a desire to embed the poems in a Roman milieu, and create a level of realism within the plots and characters of the poems. Of course we must proceed with the understanding that when we discuss the nature of subjectivity and 'the personal' in ancient Rome, we are discussing something quite different from the modern notion of personal expression.

As Carlin Barton has shown, Roman men and women carefully constructed a variety of 'masks' (*personae*) through which they could function in different capacities: in the forum, at the homes of the rich and powerful, before one's extended family, before the household and even before one's spouse (Barton 1993, 114-16, and 2001, 56-64). There was the expectation on the individual to represent him or herself in the way surest to promote the dignity of the family. Thus 'personal expression' often related less to the feelings and beliefs of the single person than to the traditions and religious ties of the agnatic family, the wider *gens* and the Republic.[5] Individual accomplishment was a contribution to the greater good, and not merely a marker of personal success. We can more easily understand the wide gap that exists between Cicero's nobility in his various treatises or speeches and the wheedling attempts at diplomacy found in some of his letters when we grasp the significance of appearances (and audience) to the elite Roman.

As we know, *memor* is an adjective that means 'mindful' in the sense of keeping a mental impression of something. The impression that one leaves behind, *memoria* (meaning literally things one is mindful of) requires two interdependent agents in practically any society: the achievement of the individual to make oneself memorable, and the activities of a family or group to maintain a person's memory. In the Roman Republic the chief means of establishing individual achievement, and thereby remembrance, was a career in politics or the military or both. Elite families participated in establishing a person's memory by honouring the dead at the appropriate festivals, and in elite households by prominently displaying (always in private and occasionally in public) the person's mask, a literal 'impression' of the person's face. These masks (*imagines*) were featured in prominent parts of the private house, typically the *atrium*, and were incorporated into family rituals, most notably funeral processions for members of the *gens*.[6]

However, the forceful appropriation of a person's region or estate could deal a deadly blow to a person's potential for leaving a legacy. Once the connecting line between a man and his property was fractured, his standing in the community and his capability for maintaining his status rapidly disintegrated.[7] The land seizures that became quite commonplace in the periods of the Sullan and Marian proscriptions and throughout the second half of the first century BC (when veteran soldiers were granted settlements of other men's ancestral fields) drove a permanent wedge between many families and their historical settlements.[8] Lucius Sergius Catiline counted on the disillusionment of many inhabitants of Etruria who had been forcibly or circumstantially separated from their ancestral farms to support him in his bold plot to overthrow the government that, he felt, had granted him too few of its privileges.[9] Micaela Janan, in her analysis of poetry composed in the early principate, further addresses the erosion of civic identity (Janan 2001, 46):

> A long history of conquest meant that the Roman Empire was now a vast place, encompassing diverse races and cultures. Citizenship gradually became available to a broader and broader range of people within the Empire's borders, necessitating a profound shift in the conceptualization of 'citizen'. Rights are now vested in the person conceived as an abstract individual, rather than as an 'organic' member of a family, a tribe, a race. Yet the notion of citizenship never quite loses its 'organic' roots: the literature of this period frequently reflects upon the question 'who is a Roman?'... Alongside 'constructivist' answers to the question that would organize citizenship criteria around the individual's achievements ... circulate 'essentialist' answers based on some notion of an 'organic' relationship to the soil, to ancient customs, to the ancestors.

Meanwhile, the supreme honours of civic duty and leadership directed at the aristocratic and elite classes were beginning to erode. The triumph was granted only to members of the imperial family after 19 BC, and it was by means of this honour, as Werner Eck tells us, 'that members of the Roman ruling stratum derived the highest kind of boost to their image and gained specific social prestige' (Eck 1984, 138).[10] There were many resulting honours that derived from the momentary triumphal spectacle that were also no longer available to the Roman elite: the dedication of spoils throughout the city, the erection of triumphal portrait-statues and the erection of public buildings.[11] Augustus provided substitute honours, such as the *ornamenta triumphalia*, but the problem with such provisions was that they were not constitutionally ordained by the will of the people, but from the emperor: thus the civic power of these rewards was diluted by the nature of its source – favourites could win such honours alongside those who truly merited them.[12]

The fate of the poet Cornelius Gallus serves as an example of what could happen to those who too readily assigned themselves honours and memorials. He aroused the ire of Augustus and, as a result, the Senate by placing statues of himself throughout Egypt and inscribing his deeds on pyramids while he served in the region as first prefect.[13] The threat or certainty of a senatorial indictment led him to commit suicide in 27 BC. This is not to say that senators and other elite members of society did not continue to find acceptable ways to honour their deeds and memorialize themselves and their families. Indeed, Eck points out that it became increasingly fashionable at Rome and outside Rome for honorees not only to display their rank at the occasion of receiving their honour, but to publicize their entire *cursus honorum* as well: a fashion dictated in all likelihood by the statues of Roman heroes in the Forum of Augustus which displayed all the offices that each man held.[14]

The lists of accomplishments that men placed on their monuments and the late but duly granted 'right of three children' that was designed to honour mothers indicate how greatly the Romans desired benchmarks that could establish the success of the individual.[15] Augustus cleverly established new senatorial lines from the provinces and throughout Italy in order to provide more opportunity for the disenfranchised to find a place for themselves in the socio-political system. In addition the *princeps* established societies for freedmen who could thereby serve the emperor's political interests and obtain a stronger connection to the Roman system in which they longed to be a part.[16]

Therefore, as Eck points out, the population that took the most advantage of this new style of self-representation did not consist of the established Republican families, but by hosts of 'new men' who had lately entered the political system (1984, 151).[17] The medium of aristocratic self-representation continued to exist by way of community recognition, i.e. the dedicatory and honorific statues and inscriptions. Regarding funerary display, Mouritsen (2005) has shown that elite families seem to have purposely chosen not to build funerary monuments for themselves from the first century AD onwards, at precisely the time in which freedmen and other members of lower and servile classes were increasingly commemorating themselves in astounding numbers in marginal or liminal zones of settlements.[18] The reason Mouritsen provides for this development is that the political ruling class held its ground, so to speak, in civic centres with dedications and memorials that honoured its role in government (2005, 54-5). Furthermore, as Jane Fejfer points out, in the early Empire, space for honorary statues became restricted as imperial sculptural displays took possession of increasingly greater areas of Rome; municipal and provincial towns became alternative arenas of exhibiting ancestral pride (Fejfer 2002, 247-54).

Regarding modes of commemoration, therefore, there are clearly several forces at work upon those who lived during the great political and social upheaval of the second half of the first century BC. On the one hand the Roman political free agent must have lamented the loss of particular avenues of achievement and honour. On the other hand he must have acquired distaste for the increasing number of upstarts who took the opportunity of a reorganized body politic to distinguish their formerly ignoble families either through newly achieved political agency or through the newly available means of making vast fortunes. Added to this, he would also have noticed the continuous agglomeration of distinctions and honours adhering to the personage of the *princeps* and to the members of the imperial family. The competitive playing field of his ancestors, always tilted in the favour of the senatorial class, had now become broad and level, with the imperial family overseeing the plane from a lofty vantage point.

Where do the poets fit into this scenario? Are they members of the traditional elite, or did they exist among the ranks of upstarts? They must have considered themselves a finer part of the latter. The fact that they enjoyed the patronage of some of the most illustrious men of the aristocratic elite probably helped them to imagine themselves as members of the newly privileged generation. Nevertheless, each Augustan poet acknowledges his humble roots, the smallness of his pre-literary world and the newly acquired opportunities he enjoys by means of his literary talent. In that light, the elegists' particular care to place inscriptions into their poems can be seen in two ways: as a means by which they imitate their social betters by inscribing text in the public forum of their readership; and as a means by which they promote themselves not only as masters of text, members of the literate elite, but also as manipulators of and innovators upon those already established genres of inscriptional writing. If inscription holds meaning and significance in the real Roman world, how much more meaning and significance might it hold in a literary world where the author is sovereign?

This implementation of text as a means of leaving a record of oneself raises seemingly contradictory issues, however, when we consider elegy. The tendency for elegiac writers to write *recusationes*, lines or complete poems that defend their chosen themes and metre, is an indication that elegists are always conscious of the diminished status of their chosen genre in comparison with higher genres, epic in particular. That is not to say that the poets themselves believed that what they wrote was inferior poetry – there was not a Roman man alive who did not take seriously the need to accomplish something worthy of his name. Indeed these *recusationes* are rhetorically similar to *praeteritio*, a rhetorical pose of using indirect argumentation to convince an audience that the topic not being fully argued is worthy of consideration. Thus by stressing their poetic inability to write epic, and by introducing a host of circumstances that drive them to write elegy (most notably divine intervention or advisement), the poets bring attention to the qualities of elegy that may thereby attract a readership.

Even so, elegy's tendency to depict male speakers in attitudes of subjugation, weeping and uttering complaints, would have diminished the status of elegy for Roman audiences. Frank Copley's study on the paraclausithyron, for example, underscores the fact that elegiac poetry chiefly characterizes the mournful, locked out lover.[19] As we know, no respectable Roman man ever made a name for himself dwelling on his sadness, whatever its derivation. The accomplished Cicero had at least one friend eager to explain to him that his extended mourning for his dead daughter Tullia was contradictory to his philosophy and to Roman manhood.[20] We must suppose, therefore, that one of the problems with writing elegy was not just that it was not epic, but that it bore associations to activities that lay traditionally outside the sphere of proper male conduct.[21] Ennius, the inventor of Latin elegy, chose to pursue epic, drama and satire as more certain pathways to widespread admiration in his adopted country. The Roman poets of the early principate defended elegy because they had transformed it from something to be left to epigraphers and graffiti-artists; they preserved those qualities that made elegy a preferred medium of memorial while they added to elegy the craft of Hellenistic *poiesis*.

Another explanation for their persistence in defending the inclusion of elegy among Rome's great poetic forms is, ironically, its association with personal sentiment and its unique capacity for expressing the attitudes of the age. It is significant that all the great elegiac poets came from outside the city of Rome and were typically associated with landed families: Gallus hailed from Gallia Narbonensis, Catullus from Verona in northernmost Italy, Propertius from Umbria north of Latium, Tibullus probably from Tibur just outside Rome, and Ovid from Sulmona directly east of Rome. At least two of these men, Propertius and Tibullus, suffered at least indirectly from the land confiscations of 41-40 BC, and, perhaps more importantly, all of them lived in an age in which the character of Italy was rapidly changing to adjust to the imperial prominence of Rome. In a time in which so much was lost, in which so many connections were broken, the elegists saw a need for poetry that explored the variety of fractures that existed in society – between friends, between lovers, between people and their ancestral lands, and even the fractures and losses that occur within one person.[22] Only elegy could communicate so clearly the overlap of personal poetics with universal experience. What better medium could the ironically adept Romans have chosen to express lament over the fragmentation of self than that which had once been used as a monumental indicator of a person's achievements?[23]

So, though they apologized for it, these poets were aware of the power of elegy, and they saw the need to educate their readers on its new possibilities. For once in the history of Roman literature, the poets determined their content, their metre and their audience – they created art, and in doing so they re-established the limits of human expression. The elegiac landscape that Roman poets create is filled not only with the markers of their cultural erudition, but with the monuments they are compelled to make for the many things they and their readers wish to see remembered. Even in the initial elegies of Catullus we find expressions of personal loss and epitaphic phrases; in Propertius and Tibullus, and later Ovid, we find actual epitaphs and other types of inscriptional texts placed inside the poetry.

Romani Callimachi?

Given that so little of Gallus' elegies survive, the development of the elegiac book begins for us at Rome in 29/28 BC when a volume of poems featured as its first word the memorable name *Cynthia*.[24] The author of these poems was a man called, simply, 'Propertius' by commentators, copiers, imitators and admirers alike until the fourth century AD when the grammarian Donatus identified him as 'Sextus Propertius'.[25] He let his words promote him, and he let one word promote him more than any other: Cynthia. With his initial concentration on eroticism, and his later frequent self-associations with Callimachean poetics, Propertius seems to depart from older Latin elegiac applications, namely epigrammatic short poems and funerary poems on gravestones.

Nevertheless, only a generation earlier Catullus had begun to formulate the elegy into extended narrative poetry as seen in his experimental and influential poems 65-8.[26] In addition Cornelius Gallus, an older contemporary of Propertius, surely played a significant role in pre-figuring the shape of elegy, as Propertius himself attests at 2.34.91,[27] although we know very little about the precise nature of his influence, or even his style or content from the few remaining fragments.[28] We must look to Catullus, therefore, to find the foundation stone on which Propertius' elegies are constructed. Previous scholars have already done this to a considerable extent, but none have concentrated their observations on the epigraphic resonances in Catullus that find their way also into Propertius and later writers. My study will focus on Catullus' longer narrative poems 65 and 68 in order to demonstrate that his poetic preoccupation with grief and loss in these two elegies foreshadows a significant theme in later elegy, one manifestation of which is seen in the closing of the *Monobiblos*.

Clearly the most significant aspect of Catullus' elegies 65-8 is their length; they have respectively 24, 94, 48 and 160 lines. As we have seen up to that point, Latin elegy typically extended no longer than two or three distichs. Marilyn Skinner in her analysis of these unique poems notes 'the monumental configuration' of poems 65 through 68 a-b, and cautiously admits that their length is due to Hellenistic influence; more specifically the poems 'show conspicuous Callimachean features', a reference of course to Callimachus' lengthy elegiac *Aitia* (Skinner 2003, 29-30).[29] Nevertheless she is quick to add that there is inaccuracy in the depiction of Catullus as a Callimachean poet (2003, 30); in agreement with Skinner, I find in Catullus an ongoing negotiation between Callimachean poetics and Catullus' interest in capturing the Roman *mise-en-scène*. Let us review these Callimachean features. Poem 66 is a translation of Callimachus' *Lock of Berenice*. Poem 67 is a dialogue with a closed door that demonstrates, as Copley explains, a mix of the inherited Hellenistic paraclausithyron, the lament of the excluded lover, and the indigenous Italian *diffamatio*, that is, a song of adultery and cuckoldry.[30] Poem 68a-b draws upon diverse thematic elements, some of which are Hellenistic, but some of which are intensely personal and driven by expressions of loss.[31]

Poem 65 is the first elegy that appears in Catullus' collection; its theme is personal loss, its tone funerary. It is written as a letter to a friend named Hortalus, and claims to accompany a translation of a poem by Callimachus, presumably poem 66. Yet it is no mere prologue to a translation, but rather an excuse for the lateness of the translation that the orator Hortalus must have encouraged the promising young poet to undertake.

The reason he could not complete it sooner, he explains, is that he recently suffered the loss of his brother, and his mind has been filled with no other matter. Grief rather than poetry occupies his thoughts, he claims, and only with embarrassment does he release the promised translation to his friend's possession. It is not too long a poem, and so I present it in its entirety (65):

> Etsi me assiduo confectum cura dolore
> sevocat a doctis, Hortale, virginibus,
> nec potis est dulcis Musarum expromere fetus
> mens animi, tantis fluctuat ipsa malis –
> namque mei nuper Lethaeo gurgite fratris
> pallidulum manans adluit unda pedem,
> Troia Rhoeteo quem subter litore tellus
> ereptum nostris obterit ex oculis.
> [numquam ego te potero posthac audire loquentem?]
> numquam ego te, vita frater amabilior,
> aspiciam posthac? at certe semper amabo,
> semper maesta tua carmina morte canam
> qualia sub densis ramorum concinit umbris
> Daulias absumpti fata gemens Ityli –
> sed tamen in tantis maeroribus, Hortale, mitto
> haec expressa tibi carmina Battiadae,
> ne tua dicta vagis nequiquam credita ventis
> effluxisse meo forte putes animo,
> ut missum sponsi furtivo munere malum
> procurrit casto virginis e gremio,
> quod miserae oblitae molli sub veste locatum,
> dum adventu matris prosilit, excutitur,
> atque illud prono praeceps agitur decursu,
> huic manat tristi conscius ore rubor.

Although I am overwhelmed by incessant suffering and grief summons me from the Muses, Hortalus, and powerless is my mind (floundering in such misfortune) to produce the sweet children of the nine goddesses – for recently did the gushing wave in the swirl of Lethe wash the bloodless foot of my brother whom Trojan earth has crushed below the Phrygian shore and stolen from my eyes. Will I never again hear your voice? Will I never see you again, brother, more beloved than life? But surely I will always love: your death will cause me to sing your laments forever, as often as the Phocian nightingale sings under the shade of dense branches to mourn the death of her dead babe Itylus – but nevertheless, in the midst of such pain, Hortalus, I send you this translation of a poem by Callimachus so that you do not think that your advice has flowed from my mind and has been fruitlessly entrusted to the wandering winds, like an apple sent as the furtive gift of a lover that drops from the guiltless lap of the receiver; though it is placed under the girl's silken skirt, when she forgets and leaps up to welcome her mother, it is driven headlong on its downward course and is dislodged onto the floor, and a self-conscious blush spreads across her mournful face.

Though poetry is not on his mind, so he says, he beautifully and eloquently expresses his grief and his remorse in the very form he was clearly studying and preparing to master – the elegiac long-form.[32] Skinner points out the ruse and the opportunity for showcasing his artistry in Catullus' *recusatio*: 'disavowal of a given type of poetry is a subterfuge for expansion of the artistic repertoire; it is part of the lyric poet's efforts to invent a distinct authorial identity for himself by simultaneously distancing himself from and appealing to significant forces shaping the prior poetic tradition' (2003, 5).[33]

The question would then be: with respect to what 'prior poetic tradition' does Catullus stake his claim for originality? Skinner makes a compelling case that Catullus' elegies 65 and 116 form a ring composition that frames the other elegies, and she finds enough metrical and linguistic features in 116 to support a disassociation from Callimachean poetics and an association with Ennian epic (2003, 21-4).[34] Catullus, unlike later elegists, apologizes not for avoiding epic, but for transforming elegy from the preferred Callimachean mode into his own poetics, even if by doing so he approaches epic themes. In writing 65, therefore, Catullus demonstrates that he can compose elegy in Latin in a way that differs from Hellenistic precedents and that evokes something a lot closer to home than to the Alexandrian harbour.[35]

I agree with Skinner's analysis, but I would add that Ennian elegy also deserves credit for shaping Catullus' pioneering effort in 65. As I have shown, though Ennius possessed the opportunity to transform Roman poetics immediately, he chose rather to work within the conservative eulogistic tendencies of Roman poetry and apply his Alexandrian metres to historical epic and personal biography. In Catullus 65, despite its mythological allusions in lines 13-14 and 19-24, the dominant theme is clearly the poet's personal loss and the significance of a brother who died in the line of duty to family and state.[36] Indeed the poem includes lines similar to an epitaph (i.e. lines 5-8), and the epistolary, first person nature of the poem anticipates a reader, a third party whose eyes are drawn by artistry to consider the plight of the mourner. And when Catullus does address his brother in a dramatic, second-person apostrophe (lines 9-11), he draws attention to the deceased in a fashion much used in Roman epitaphs, as seen on the previously cited epitaph of Publius Cornelius Scipio, the augur of 180 BC (*CIL* 1.2.10; *CLE* 8; see p. 23).[37] Catullus thereby follows a tradition established by the first elegies of Ennius (at least those we know of) before he launches into Callimachean themes. As much as we see the Hellenistic influences on Catullus' conception of the elegiac poem, we see also that the traditional and well-documented Roman practice that honoured the dead with poetic inscriptions shapes the poem.

If the rest of Catullus' elegiac poems had all pursued the Callimachean model more closely, we might simply have viewed poem 65 as a poetic attempt, perhaps, to purge Roman conventions and make room for the serious application of Hellenistic themes. Yet Catullus does not convince us that this was ever his intention. Poem 68a reveals itself to be another consideration of grief. The poem focuses first on a friend's heartbreak but transforms into another lament for the death of his brother (68a.19-26):

> sed totum hoc studium luctu fraterna mihi mors
> abstulit. o misero frater adempte mihi,
> tu mea tu moriens fregisti commoda, frater,
> tecum una tota est nostra sepulta domus,
> omnia tecum una perierunt gaudia nostra
> quae tuus in vita dulcis alebat amor.
> cuius ego interitu tota de mente fugavi
> haec studia atque omnes delicias animi.

But the death of my brother, and its resulting malaise, has robbed all my passion. Oh brother stolen from me, wreck that I am, in dying you have shattered my complacency and made my entire estate a tomb, and with you have all my joys perished entirely, joys that your cherished love nourished when you lived. Suffering the loss of that love, I have abandoned the passions that consumed my mind and all the delights of my soul.

Shortly afterwards, in 68b, the dolorous atmosphere changes to sportive revelry in the delights of erotic accessibility since the poet has been granted a place to meet Lesbia at their own convenience. Nevertheless, the abrupt alteration leaves the reader with the impression that the poet indulges his passion to forget his woes. Description of their free encounters leads to a mythological vignette in which he compares the furtive arrival of his beloved (at their love-nest) to the arrival of Laodamia at the home of Protesilaus on her wedding night, a rather ominous transition. This was the husband she was destined to love more than life and doomed to lose as the first casualty of the Trojan War. We soon see to what purpose Catullus has taken us on this mythological journey to Troy: since that is also the site of his brother's death, his grief resurfaces (68b.89-100):

> Troia (nefas!) commune sepulcrum Asiae Europaeque,
> Troia virum et virtutum omnium acerba cinis,
> quaene etiam nostro letum miserabile fratri
> attulit. ei misero frater adempte mihi,
> ei misero fratri iucundum lumen ademptum,
> tecum una tota est nostra sepulta domus,
> omnia tecum una perierunt gaudia nostra
> quae tuus in vita dulcis alebat amor.
> quem nunc tam longe non inter nota sepulcra
> nec prope cognatos compositum cineres,
> sed Troia obscena, Troia infelice sepultum
> detinet extremo terra aliena solo.

Troy – wicked place! – the common grave of Asia and Europe alike, Troy – pitiless ash of men and all manliness – you have also imparted a wretched death to my brother. Ah, brother stolen from me, wreck that I am, ah, sweet light stolen from your wreck of a brother; in dying you have made my entire estate a grave, and with you have all my joys perished entirely, joys that your cherished love nourished when you lived. Now a foreign land possesses your poor corpse buried not among familiar tombstones near the ashes of your ancestors, but in faraway soil, in ominous Troy.

Clearly the memorial purposes of the elegy vie for equal time with the erudite aspects of poetic response and mythological re-creation. Catullus seems unwilling to surrender completely to Callimachean forms so long as there are personal experiences to relate. The funerary tradition of the elegy re-emerges in lines 92, 95 and 96, repeating the reference to his home as a tomb in lines 68a.22-4; this emphasis suggests an attempt to compose memorable text in lieu of the monument his brother rightly should have been bestowed. By giving these lines an epitaphic resonance, Catullus capitalizes on the irony of his situation: though a craftsman of words, circumstances keep him from rendering his brother an inscribed tomb (97: *nota sepulcra*), and the absent gravestone among familial tombs haunts his thoughts. The tragedy of a Roman *vir* separated in death from his ancestral ground becomes a theme all too familiar in the decades that pass between the composition of this poem (in 59/58) and the equally haunting line that Propertius composes in 28 BC for a kinsman (1.22.8: [*pulvis Etrusca* ...] *tu nullo miseri contegis ossa solo*).[38]

Even when Catullus finds his way back to love in the poem's final lines, we suspect that love is merely a recuperative for a tormented soul (68b.155-60):

sitis felices et tu simul et tua vita,
  et domus in qua nos lusimus et domina,
et qui principio nobis te tradidit Afer
  a quo sunt primo mi omnia nata bona,
et longe ante omnes mihi quae me carior ipso est,
  lux mea, qua viva vivere dulce mihi est.

May you be happy, Allius, you along with your sweetheart, and that house in which I and my mistress once played; and Afer who introduced you to us from the start, from whom first arose all my enjoyments, and she who far ahead of all is dearer to me than myself; my light, my life is sweet while you live.

The breathless quality of the polysyndeton (*et* ... *et* ... *et* ...) suggests a hyperbolic zeal. He states in lines 159-60 that his love is dearer to him than himself, and that she is his reason for living, but he is careful not to repeat what he said about his brother at 65.10, 'more beloved than life' (*vita frater amabilior*). That distinction may perhaps be a small one, but there exists in the funerary epigraphic tradition the frequent expression whereby the mourner wishes to exchange his or her life for the person buried at the site, or for the deceased to express happiness that his or her wish to die has come to be.[39] There is a compelling urgency among the bereft to consider the value of life in light of a loved one's passing. Although Catullus calls Lesbia *mea vita* twice in his collection, he never uses the same comparative *vita* that he uses in reference to his brother, suggesting that it is not she who holds ultimate control over his happiness.[40]

When he finishes his poem with these final distichs, he has transformed the elegy from something purely epigrammatic and from something Alexandrian into something uniquely personal and uniquely Roman.[41] Indeed in these four elegiac poems he has left a virtual map of topics and themes that later poets could use and further innovate. The first poem, being epistolary, paves the way for Propertius 4.3 and Ovid's *Heroides*. Poem 66 is a didactic exercise for all future elegiac usurpations of Callimachean themes and motifs seen throughout later elegy. Poem 67, set in Catullus' hometown of Verona, grants permission to include Roman and Italian topography as a setting for the elegiac theme, as seen most notably in Propertius' 2.23, 3.16 and 4.1a, and in Ovid's *Amores* 3.13 and throughout his *Fasti*. Poem 68 juxtaposes the pain of suffering with the ecstasy of love,[42] an irony that Propertius rightly codifies as the poet's dilemma in his first poem's first line: *Cynthia prima suis miserum me cepit ocellis*.

Catullus left the Latin elegy more thematically developed than he found it, and he added to it some of the Hellenistic aspects that would find more perfect expression in Propertius and Ovid.[43] No longer does the elegiac form have to be tied to the ephemeral and vague themes of epigrammatic poetry, but the focused schematic of a lover's, or a poet's (or a Roman's) experiences becomes the new mode of the genre. In later elegiac poetry, the insertion of actual inscriptions into the poems furthers the defiance of Catullus 65. What Catullus was content merely to allude to, namely the absent gravestone for his brother, the elegists will provide for themselves in consistent attempts, I believe, to negotiate between what they hope society will remember and what they fear society will forget.

Ardoris nostri magne poeta iaces[44]

The central concerns of Propertius' first book of poems are to highlight the erotic and Hellenistic aspects of the new medium, picking up where Calvus, Gallus and, to some extent, Catullus left off.[45] Nevertheless we find that many poems do not feature sexual eroticism, but focus on the complex issues that emerge in a personal relationship: sickness and death, abuse and betrayal, public life and festival.[46] Propertius, like the other elegists, responds to previous poems, alludes to previous accounts of legend and mythology, and reflects other aspects of his personal experience (the society in which he lives, his familial and social connections, etc.). Attitudes that appear more suited to comedy, to tragedy, even to epic, make appearances within the elegiac poem.[47] Some of this has been attributed to generic mixing, or, more accurately, to the implementation of a variety of generic themes within the elegiac rubric.[48] So it should not surprise that there are references to the epigrammatic, inscriptional aspects of Roman elegy throughout Propertius' first book as well. Sometimes these aspects reinforce his artistic identity, but sometimes they reveal the personal side of the Roman behind the Hellenistic mask.[49]

For example, in 1.6 Propertius refuses to accompany his friend Tullus abroad, preferring instead to remain home with Cynthia. He embraces his choice, devoting himself, as he says at 1.6.26, to *nequitia*, 'worthlessness', while acknowledging the diminution of his legacy, 27-8: *multi longinquo periere in amore libenter, / in quorum numero me quoque terra tegat*, 'many have freely perished in a drawn-out affair: as one of their number let earth also cover me'. In 1.7 he more aggressively defends his choice to write *nostros ... amores* (5), pointing out that those who have experienced love admire his work, as will his friend Ponticus if Love ever pays him a visit. As he draws the poem to a close, he writes that all young lovers will one day speak admiringly of him, 1.7.23-4: *nec poterunt iuvenes nostro reticere sepulcro / 'Ardoris nostri magne poeta iaces'*, 'and young men will not be able to resist saying over my grave, "you lie dead, great poet of our passion".' Propertius predicts his legacy as one he himself brings about by means of his text, and he undermines the humbler prediction of his reputation in the previous poem.

Later in a series of three poems about the absence of Cynthia (1.17, 18 and 19),[50] Propertius dwells on his funeral twice. In 1.17 the shipwrecked lover imagines with self-pity how his funeral might have been observed with Cynthia in charge, 19-24. He mentions a tombstone, but says nothing of an epitaph (1.17.20: *ultimus et posito staret amore lapis*). Most importantly he emphasizes Cynthia's role in the obsequies (1.17.21 and 23: *illa ... donasset ... / illa ... clamasset*), and makes her the one who speaks the usual wish of devoted survivors, 24: *ut mihi non ullo pondere terra foret*, 'that the earth lie lightly upon me'. Poem 19 renounces fear of death, so long as Cynthia preserves her love for him. Thus as the poems of the *Monobiblos* progress, concerns about the poet's literary reputation give way to hopes that what the poet has represented be granted the weight of truth – that Cynthia may turn out to be the love he continually exhorts her to become. This structure imbues the artist with extraordinary powers: he not only secures for himself a transformation of cultural reception whereby he becomes a beloved poet rather than a wastrel, but he transforms the fickle *puella* into a devoted wife – a fantasy he continues to pursue in his second book. At the end of this unique collection, Propertius presents two poems (21 and 22) that reveal something about the poet himself, and nothing at all, it seems, about the erotic drama of the other pieces. But before we analyse these two epitaphic poems, we should take note of poem 20, the Hylas poem.

In commentaries, poem 1.20 often receives praise for its graceful treatment of the Hercules-Hylas myth found in previous Hellenistic treatments (Apollonius of Rhodes, 1.1182-1272 and Theocritus 13).[51] More significantly, however, poem 1.20 features address of one poet by another, and the legend it tells expresses loss that results not from the hard-heartedness of a lover, but from the usurpation and rapacity of others. Hylas is a carefree, beautiful youth loved by Hercules. While exploring the woods near the cliffs of Mysia (in north-west Asia Minor) where the Argo has harboured, the boy narrowly escapes the forceful advances of the sons of the North Wind. After that he comes upon a placid pool surrounded by flowers and fruit-trees. When he dips his hands into the pool to drink the water, the tree-nymphs below who have instantly fallen in love with him grab hold of his arms and pull him into the pool and take possession of him. Hercules cries out the name of his beloved squire to find him, but hears only the echo of his call reverberating among the hills. Propertius ends the tale with this warning (1.20.51-2): *his, o Galle, tuos monitus servabis amores, / formosum Nymphis credere visus Hylan*, 'Warned by these events, oh Gallus, you must protect your love, you who have been sent to entrust your lovely Hylas to the Nymphs.'

I suggest that the Hylas poem serves as a structural segue between poems of Cynthia's absence (17-19) and the ensuing two poems that construct epitaphs for a lost homeland. Poem 20 provides a point of direct communication between two poets, for surely all agree that the addressee, Gallus, must be the poet Cornelius Gallus.[52] The communion between Propertius and Gallus is established in 1.20 within the context of allusion to Hellenistic precedents, for both poets, we assume, serve elegy in a way that honours the foregoing artists of the relevant genres: bucolic poetry, epic, elegy and epigram. At the same time these two poets have carved out something unique in their new elegies: a focus on the personal, erotic and subjective narrative.

The Hylas narrative is a warning against losing sight of love (51: *servabis amores*). I argue that Propertius means not merely the object of desire (woman or man), but the love of writing, its concomitant powers of transformation and representation, and the monuments to self that one creates thereby. Gallus would have remained alive with Propertius to enjoy the fruit of his literary success had he not lost sight of what inspired him and not been drawn into the fatal maw of politics and empire-building.[53] The biting winds and the grasping nymphs form allegory to the political forces that occasionally succeed in usurping and tearing down beautiful things.[54] Poem 1.20, placed where it is, becomes a warning that Propertius also directs at himself as he attempts in the two poems that follow to trace the relationship between himself and his past. The talented poet can write personal and subjective narratives safely within the code of elegiac constructs; but when approaching autobiography and the sadness of real loss and disillusionment, the poet knows he is on unstable and treacherous ground. When the past is being reinvented, it is dangerous to dwell on past events.[55] Propertius attempts it anyway, and in doing so brings elegy temporarily back from Alexandrian artistry to its epigraphic roots and its monumental purposes.

In fact the first of these epigrammatic poems, 1.21, could very well serve as an epitaph, as commentators have noted.[56] Yet it is not an epitaph for the poet – like the one suggested at 1.7.23-4 – it is for a compatriot of Umbria, the region where he was born and raised. The epitaphic poem captures the last words of a soldier dying from wounds received from brigands. He speaks to a passing comrade-in-arms who turns out to be the brother of his betrothed. The dying soldier, whose name we discover in the next poem is Gallus, asks the passer-by to get home safe so that his family may have cause to rejoice and so that he may inform his sister that Gallus has died.[57] He ends his appeal by asking that the sister treat any bones that she finds on the mountain as if they were his. In short the poem expresses a dying man's last hope that he may receive the honour of the remembered dead, despite the irony and anonymity of his demise. It is a poignant appeal that seems to sit uncomfortably among the preceding poems about erotic longing and desire.

Propertius addresses a dark chapter in his autobiography and that of his hometown region (1.21.7-8):

> Gallum per medios ereptum Caesaris ensis
>   effugere ignotas non potuisse manus;

> (Let her know) that I, Gallus, rescued as I was from the swords of Caesar,
> was not able to escape thuggish hands.

The lines refer to the conflict that beleaguered his home region: the Perusine War of 41 BC. The irony of these lines is of course that he escaped the war with Octavian to be killed by brigands.[58] The word *ereptum* even suggests that mercy was applied in his case, as we know that many fighters were released after the surrender. The brief allusion still manages to suggest the universal dread that would accompany any conflict with the armies of the recently adopted Caesar.

This issue is driven home with greater force in the book's final poem, 1.22, a poem that also achieves epitaphic resonance:

> Qualis et unde genus, qui sint mihi, Tulle, Penates,
>   quaeris pro nostra semper amicitia.
> si Perusina tibi patriae sunt nota sepulcra,
>   Italiae duris funera temporibus,
> cum Romana suos egit Discordia civis,
>   (sic mihi praecipue, pulvis Etrusca, dolor,

tu proiecta mei perpessa es membra propinqui,
  tu nullo miseri contegis ossa solo,)
proxima supposito contingens Umbria campo
  me genuit terris fertilis uberibus.

> Of what sort and where are my family origins, and who might my household gods be, Tullus, you always inquire on account of our friendship. Perhaps you are familiar with the Perusine tombs of my fatherland and the graves of Italy brought about by difficult times when Roman Discord harassed her own citizens. (For this reason, Etrurian dust, you are a chief source of grief to me, for you have allowed the limbs of my kinsman to lie strewn about and you do not cover the poor man's bones with any soil.) Nearby, fertile Umbria, which lies tangent to this low-lying plain, raised me upon its nurturing earth.

Propertius notes the association between his birthplace and its tombs in lines 3-5. More particularly he explicitly emphasizes the Perusine War, although here he does not mention Augustus' involvement. In lines 6-8 he creates continuity between this poem and the preceding poem by mentioning a kinsman who sounds very much like the Gallus of 1.21. Whereas Catullus remonstrated with Troy (68b *Troia nefas*!) and spoke of the sad lot of his brother buried in foreign soil (68b.99-100), Propertius' kinsman lies unburied on ancestral lands – an utter degradation of the hope that ancestral lands will serve as a resting place. Instead these lands cause suffering since they have failed their essential task (*mihi praecipue, pulvis Etrusca, dolor*). Propertius does finally get around to praising his native land, saving for last a description of Perusia and the hills of Umbria as a rich and fertile place (10: *me genuit terris fertilis uberibus*). Yet he more extensively reveals the sad and morbid associations that emerge with thoughts of home. Perhaps he took a risk in doing so; it could have been viewed as an unnecessary reminder of past grievances to refer to one of Octavian's campaigns in this light; indeed, other than in poem 21, he appears nowhere else in the first book.[59]

Thus the poet brings his work to a close with two poems that essentially create an epitaph not merely for Gallus, but for Perusia and the region of western Etruria on the borders of Umbria, a land that in 41 BC became something other than it had always been: no longer the home of the proud Etruscans, but a part of Rome. Furthermore, if Janan (2001, 36-41) and others are correct that the Gallus throughout the *Monobiblos* is really meant to be the elegist Gallus, then much of the book becomes an extensive monument to the craft, love and bravery of another poet whose political circumstances would soon force him to eternal silence.

I believe that by ending the collection with these two epigrammatic poems, Propertius returns to the original and pragmatic purpose of elegy, that is to say, inscribed epitaphs, in order to reveal that his poetic capability is not necessarily devoted to a world of erudition and fantasy. As we saw above, Propertius made a point of addressing death and his legacy in poems that are otherwise dedicated to various aspects of a problematic love affair. The concerns of the love-poet, these poems and passages suggest, are more than erotic fluff, and more than the allusive concerns of the so-called *neoteroi*; they are universal to all who have visited the extremes of emotional experience. Propertius demonstrates that he too has experiences that extend to the socio-political world in which he and all Romans play a part. Thus Propertius leaves his reader with the sense that something greater than Cynthia is responsible for his world-view: that *Romana Discordia* (1.22.5) left him mindful of the consequences of recent events and political shifts. Cynthia, for all her guile and elusiveness, is no dreadful Roman legion.

Breve in exiguo marmore nomen ero[60]

In Propertius' second book of poems some of the same concerns resurface and poetic inscriptions play a more significant role. The collection's prologue piece is addressed to Maecenas, the celebrated patron of the arts and friendly supporter of Horace and Virgil as well. Aspects of the poem are typical of its recusatory purpose: naming the passion that holds him to his present course (lines 4-16), denying that he has the wherewithal to write about legend and historical actions (lines 17-42), and aligning himself with his favourite Alexandrian predecessor Callimachus (line 40). Indeed, the poet states, each person can only achieve according to his capabilities and his fortune (lines 43-70). Then as if to deflect any further *invidia* towards his chosen career, Propertius admits the limitations that his choice will put upon his legacy: he paints the picture of his own death and the appearance of his tomb, including the inscription upon it (2.1.71-8):

> quandocumque igitur vitam mea fata reposcent
>   et breve in exiguo marmore nomen ero,
> Maecenas, nostrae spes invidiosa iuventae,
>   et vitae et morti gloria iusta meae
> si te forte meo ducet via proxima busto,
>   esseda caelatis siste Britanna iugis,
> taliaque illacrimans mutae iace verba favillae:
>   'Hoc misero fatum dura puella fuit.'

> Whenever it happens that death claims my life and all I will be is a brief name on a narrow marble slab – if by chance, Maecenas, oh enviable hope of our generation and ample source of pride to me alive or dead, the road happens to take you close-by my tomb, halt your British chariot with its engraved harness, and shedding a tear speak such words over my silent embers: 'A hard-hearted woman was this man's end.'

Propertius' reference to a 'brief name on a narrow marble slab' points to the lack of titles and political offices that will appear on his tomb.[61] The poet acknowledges that contrary to the traditional notions of success for men of his rank he will gain only the distinction of his name.[62] Yet the fact that he writes this in the first poem of a new book that follows on the heels of a previous, successful volume implicitly suggests that Propertius has merited distinction already for his literary works. Furthermore, he hopes that Maecenas will attend his funeral and visit his grave.[63] Despite his claims of occupying a lower station than the great statesman, the poem reveals the poet's hopes that his work will make him memorable.

Before Propertius conceives this monument of remembrance, visited by Maecenas, he weaves into his *recusatio* references to prior historical events that again raise the spectre of that former devastating event that altered his homeland. When he lists the achievements of Augustus he dwells foremost on the civil war campaigns, and immediately comes back to the topic of the Perusine War where he closed his first book of poems (2.1.27-9):

> nam quotiens Mutinam aut, civilia busta, Philippos
>   aut canerem Siculae classica bella fugae
> eversosque focos antiquae gentis Etruscae.

> For as often as I would sing of the tombs of our citizens, Mutina or Philippi, or of naval warfare resulting in Sicilian flight and the ruined hearths of the ancient Etruscan race …

The reader familiar with Propertius' first book might well remember the plaintive line 22.6: *sic mihi praecipue, pulvis Etrusca, dolor*, and infer corresponding sentiment with the recurring mention of that event. Certainly the phrase here, '*antiquae gentis Etruscae*', evokes the destruction of not merely a town, but a very old and noble race of people. Notice too that he speaks not of walls and ramparts brought low, but *focos*, domestic and religious hearths overturned. Given the significance of the ever-vigilant cult of the *focus* at Rome, the cult of Vesta and the other ancient traditions associated with the sanctity of the domestic hearth, Propertius implies that a harsh and impious destruction was brought upon his region. In later lines he mentions the foreign conquests of Augustus, but in these initial lines he draws attention to the fact that Octavian's proving grounds were primarily on Italian soil and his first casualties created civil-war tombs (*civilia busta*). By contrast, Augustus did his best in later representations of himself to conflate several years of civil war to the Battle of Actium. His naval victory over Antony and Cleopatra began to overshadow the other more violent conflicts that came before 31 BC.[64]

Propertius' poetic monument wilfully includes epitaphs, as it were, not only for himself and his literary creations, but for his homeland and for those events of recent memory that might more comfortably have been forgotten. In fact the implied repetition of *canerem* (27-8) evokes Catullus' claim that he will always sing the grief of his brother's death (65.12: *semper maesta tua carmina morte canam*). Coupled with Propertius' recusatory denial that he can sing of such historic *topoi* lies the implication that if he were to approach such topics, he would be compelled to sing the events brought upon Perusia, and those are verses Augustus might not like to hear sung.

Poem 2.11, a six-line epigram that Lawrence Richardson (1977) dubs in his introduction to the poem, 'a perfect epigram', answers to the epitaph in 2.1 by drawing attention to Cynthia's dependency on his poetry, illustrating thereby the mutual relationship that exists between author and subject, or author and text:

> Scribant de te alii vel sis ignota licebit:
>   laudet, qui sterili semina ponit humo.
> omnia, crede mihi, tecum uno munera lecto
>   auferet extremi funeris atra dies;
> et tua transibit contemnens ossa viator,
>   nec dicet: 'Cinis hic docta puella fuit.'

> Let others write about you, or then again let you go unknown to any: let him praise you who sows his seed in barren earth. Believe me, the black day of your last rites will carry your gifts with you to your final resting place; and the traveller will pass by and note not your remains, nor will he say, 'This ash was an accomplished girl.'

Richardson notes the epitaphic quality of the last line, and adds: 'Propertius in threatening to break with his mistress knows that he will be withdrawing her chances of immortal fame … [That] she appreciates and savours the fame his poems bring is implicit in the epithet *docta* in the last verse' (1977, 244-5).[65] While Richardson is right about Cynthia's character, it is crucial also to see that Propertius is not merely writing to threaten a mistress into compliance with his wishes. In writing this epigram and in ending it with an epitaph, Propertius draws attention to the nature of *fama* and to what is at stake if one does not write. The final lines of both 2.11 and 2.1 pertain to the memory of the deceased. In 2.1, the epitaph at the end serves to justify his poetic choices – if Maecenas will pay him this honour, then he will not have pursued his literary career in vain. In 2.11, Propertius clarifies the stark situation for Cynthia – her memory is entirely in his hands, despite the fact that she writes poetry herself (1.2.27-30 and 2.3.17-22). The only way her talent will survive is through his poetry. In 2.1 the poet regards himself a friend, or at least a client, of the great Maecenas; in 2.11 he informs Cynthia that her only hope of patronage lies in him.

In fact in 2.5 the poet threatens to write the following about Cynthia if she will not alter her flighty ways, 28: *Cynthia, forma potens: Cynthia, verba levis*, 'Cynthia, a powerful beauty: Cynthia, capricious in word.'[66]

Commentators have suggested that the phrase *levis verba* refers to her ability to keep a promise or even mean what she says. However, there is also the idea that the words she writes are trivial, light and unimportant. This seems to me to justify the threatening nature of the words that follow, i.e. lines 29-30: *quamvis contemnas murmura famae, / hic tibi pallori, Cynthia, versus erit*, 'although you disregard the murmurs of gossip, this line, Cynthia, will make you pale.' His threat to undermine her poetic labours in line 28 makes the choice of *versus* in line 30 more meaningful: 'here is a verse to wipe out all your verses'.

The idea that a woman is dependent on a man to preserve her memory is common enough in Roman culture. Even among the tombs of the Scipios, though the women buried there were of high birth and were probably quite accomplished as the wives and mothers of great statesmen, not a one receives more than merely a name and a patronymic. This is not to say that women did not receive the honour of epitaphic verses to commemorate them on their tombs, but these verses were commonly formulated with respect to their roles as wives and mothers.[67] Since Cynthia is both an object of love and the process of writing about that love, since Cynthia is also *Cynthia*, i.e. Propertius' poetry, then the reason that she appears in all four books of his poetry (even after, as some have suggested, the 'real' affair had ended)[68] is that once Cynthia becomes a recognizable commodity intertwined with the poet's *fama* and his literary legacy, she must continue to exist.[69]

Later in 2.34.93, after matching poetic loves with their creators (Lesbia with Catullus, Lycoris with Gallus) he places Cynthia's name at the head of the line and his own name in the genitive at the end (93-4):

> Cynthia *quin etiam* versu laudata Properti,
> hos inter si me ponere Fama volet.[70]

> Cynthia (will go on) glorified in the verse of Propertius, if Fame shall be willing to place me among these predecessors.

By this juxtaposition of her name to his, it is apparent that Cynthia's and the poet's fame are interdependent, and furthermore he leaves little doubt, by explicit use of the genitive (*Properti*), who possesses authority over whom. Such conflation of the beloved and the poetry inspired by her leaves the poet at a great advantage whereby he can discuss his *puella* in an erotic fashion and suggest the intimate and necessary bond between him and his work. As I will show in Chapter 4, Ovid achieves this same end by linking Corinna to himself in an intriguing fashion in the *Amores*.

After considering his funeral in the hands of one of Rome's most influential men in 2.1, and his control over Cynthia's memorial in 2.11, Propertius considers his own funeral again in 2.13. After writing 16 lines on the ecstasy of being with Cynthia, he takes a dark turn and commands her to oversee his funeral.[71] He explains with great detail what should occur, even providing the epitaph he would have Cynthia place upon his grave. He wants none of the trappings of funerals of noblemen (i.e. the parade of masks, the ivory-posted bier, the perfumes); rather he wants his volumes of poetry to accompany his funeral;[72] lastly he wants Cynthia to make a show of her grief. He tells her to tear at her hair and clothes, walk unadorned and half-dressed, call out his name repeatedly and give him one final kiss before his body is burned. Then he asks her to plant a laurel tree that will cast its shade over a small stone that bears this message (2.13.35-6):

> et duo sint versus: QUI NUNC IACET HORRIDA PULVIS,
>   UNIUS HIC QUONDAM SERVUS AMORIS ERAT.

> And let two lines be inscribed: 'He who now lies here as gloomy dust was once the slave of a single love.'

Here we see the first occurrence in his poems of an epitaph explicitly composed for the tomb. Thus Propertian elegy departs from epigrammatic, inscriptional adaptation and mimetically absorbs the experience of composing and reading public inscriptions.[73]

The wording of the inscription is significant with respect to its memorial purpose. By configuring himself as the 'slave of a single love', Propertius adjusts his role in the poetic narrative away from the role of victim that he created in 2.1. In the manly world of 2.1, where real men wage wars, Propertius' lot is lamentable – he becomes the victim of a *dura puella*, and his achievements, in comparison with his great contemporary Maecenas, are unremarkable (2.1.72: *et breve in exiguo marmore nomen ero*). There Propertius apologetically represents himself as a man capable of more but lost to the seductive powers of the demimonde. Considering his social position and his connections, however, he is anything but a *servus* in 2.1, and perhaps to make such a claim to Maecenas would have been reprehensible. In the lover's world of 2.13, in contrast, he is an active participant in his own narrative of seduction. Far from recusing himself, Propertius embraces his choice and his abject status even more boldly than he did in poem 1.7 as we saw above. There is little honour perhaps in the word 'slave', but Propertius defiantly suggests that the originality of his chosen vocation, and primarily its poetic expression, will make him as famous as Achilles (2.13.37-42):[74]

> nec minus haec nostri notescet fama sepulcri,
>   quam fuerant Pthii busta cruenta viri.
> tu quoque si quando venies ad fata, memento,
>   hoc iter ad lapides cana veni memores.
> interea cave sis nos aspernata sepultos:
>   non nihil ad verum conscia terra sapit.

> The fame of my tomb will become known no less than had the grave mound of Achilles been stained with gore. You also, whenever you approach your final hour, remember to come white-haired by this path to my mindful stones. In the meantime be careful that you not spurn my ghost: this wakeful earth is capable of finding out the truth.

The phrase *horrida pulvis* in line 35, within the epitaph, finds intriguing correspondence to Achilles' *busta cruenta* in line 38. How can this be? Propertius has purposely rejected the warrior's world in favour of the lover's. Yet as later lines reveal, the correspondence between him and Achilles has more to do with the nature of their gravesites than their living activities. We cannot be certain what was written on Achilles' tomb, but what tradition remembers is that the Greeks sacrificed Polyxena, the virgin daughter of Priam, in order to satiate the spirit of the dead hero, hence his 'gory tomb'.[75] Propertius actually imagines Cynthia returning to his gravesite to die, and the placement of her dying body upon his tomb correlates to the dead Polyxena. Given the nature of their relationship it is unlikely that Cynthia will meet his demand for steadfast devotion, as the threat in lines 2.13.41-2 implies. Yet in his desired obsequies, similarly portrayed in the first book (1.17), Cynthia becomes essentially a devoted Roman wife who carries out the wishes of a dead husband and makes public her grief and her commitment to his memory. The tragedy of Polyxena's situation becomes irony in Cynthia's, but in each case a woman has been coerced, one by violence, another by fantasy, into the service of a man's aggrandizement. Just as Achilles' death demanded the sacrifice of a woman to satisfy his spirit's honour and bloodlust, Propertius' last wishes indulgently demand that Cynthia become something other than she is for the sake of the poet's satisfaction.[76]

In the poem's final lines, Propertius expresses the overall futility of these coercions; once the poet is dead, he cannot write anymore (2.13.57-8):

> sed frustra mutos revocabis, Cynthia, Manis:
> nam mea qui poterunt ossa minuta loqui?

> But in vain will you call on my soul made silent, Cynthia, for how will my shrunken bones be able to answer?

No response to Cynthia means no new lines to praise or admonish her.[77] Again the poet reminds Cynthia that her fame extends only so far as the poet's output. More than that, once she loses him, for all her talent and cleverness, she cries out into an empty wilderness. Actions may speak louder than words, but unrecorded action is lost forever: text creates memory and he controls the text. He is the slave of love, and Cynthia is the slave of the text.

Propertius' inscription seems humble outside the context of the poem in which it appears: its beginning is only part of a line of verse, he does not include his name or his status as artist, and he calls himself a slave; but it should be taken as a part of a larger narrative that extends throughout Book 2. The epitaphic lines in poems 2.1, 2.5, 2.11 and 2.13 are sequential attempts to fashion, or pose, the authorial identity – is he a victim? an angry artist who uses his pen to avenge his wrongs? Is he a slave and not his own man? Is he all these at once, or do new phases of experience bring new attitudes towards love? Perhaps all these potential revelations are merely performances created to entertain the reader with their nuance and cleverness.

I believe that the appearance of epitaphic, inscriptional text within these poems amounts to a codification of this elegist's aims. The slave of love is not a man of politics, war, land or family – he is a new man fashioned by artifice and ingenuity who must, by necessity, seek to provide an alternative to the existing categories of Roman manhood. Propertius' lonesome plea to Maecenas to visit his grave in 2.1 expresses the hope that at least one man from those traditional categories will acknowledge him and save him from the obscurity that other men like him have suffered. Cornelius Gallus may appear to be the key figure whose example, by his recent indictment and death, serves as a warning to the love-poet, but we must remember that Gallus was a soldier and politician who wrote poetry. Indeed, as we will examine in greater detail in the next chapter, Tibullus' first book of poems pre-dates this second book by Propertius, and in that poetic debut Tibullus includes mention of his own military service, coupling his poetic identity to one firmly established in the sphere of traditional Roman activities. Propertius is asking for leniency because the only thing he chooses is poetry. Propertius is marching on lonely ground. His poetry, his chosen metre and the quantity of his work form a challenge to the Roman notion of manhood, career and duty. Propertius carefully and subtly builds his monument of words by providing a variety of perspectives to his reader in order to gain his legacy at last.

Hic carmen media dignum me scribe columna[78]

Propertius' fourth book of poems presents a variety of dramatic shifts from the artist's previous poetic purposes, and for this reason scholars have recently provided many intriguing and new interpretations of this collection.[79] The words that perhaps best describe its themes are aetiological, Callimachean and circumspect. Eroticism is a low priority in the poems of Book 4: far from presenting an ideally romantic or purely male-centred view of the poet's existence with Cynthia, Propertius undertakes to represent some of the harsher aspects of male-female interaction in seven of the eleven poems. Poem 3 depicts the sorrowful state of a Roman matron who waits at home for her man's return from campaign with Augustus. Poem 4 depicts the treasonous behaviour of Tarpeia who, though she betrayed her Vestal vows and Rome, acted for love. Poems 5, 7 and 8 deal with Cynthia, and although some in the past have considered Cynthia a less essential figure in this book, these three Cynthia poems that do appear perform two crucial functions. They frame the book's masterful centrepiece 4.6 – a poem about Actium that features the victory of Apollo over Cleopatra – and they provide Cynthia's previously elusive, objectified characterization with a realistic context vis-à-vis the harsh economic conditions of the unmarried woman in Roman society.[80] These three poems in particular, in addition to the other two mentioned, go to significant lengths in deconstructing the typical male-centred perspective of the elegiac narrator.[81]

Yet Cynthia is absent in an unusual place; she does not appear in the final poem of Book 4.[82] Propertius ended Books 2 and 3 with poems about Cynthia, but he finishes Book 4, and his career as far as we know, with poem 11, which speaks the mind of an illustrious, married woman. This *matrona* named Cornelia speaks from the grave in an extended epitaphic passage that reveals despair over circumstances that threaten to diminish her memory. This poem reiterates some of the concerns that emerge at the end of the *Monobiblos* where Cynthia is also absent: i.e. the gap that lies between the elegiac pose of aloof artistic representation and the elegiac interest in recording memory and capturing personal expression. As I will show, Propertius' final book of poems continues to consider the implications of death, legacy and text, but in a way that seems to override the previous preoccupations with the artist's own status. Throughout Book 4 other 'voices' join in and provide their own narratives of history, of suffering and of self-representation. In four cases, these narratives coincide with inscriptional passages that I see as attempts to codify memory, and to establish memorial.

Quoted inscriptions appear in three poems in Book 4. Poem 2 closes with a dedicatory *titulus* that appears on a statue of Vertumnus and honours the artist who masterfully depicts the god in a way that suggests multiple forms. Poem 3 closes with a celebratory, votive *titulus* to no god in particular that a Roman matron, called Arethusa in the poem, promises to erect at the Capene gate if her husband returns safely.[83] In poem 7 Cynthia returns from the dead to chastise her lover for his neglectful mismanagement of her funeral and his careless mistreatment of her possessions and slaves. Near the end of the poem, she provides him the inscription she wants placed above her tomb. In addition to these three, Cornelia's poem (4.11) could be read as an extended epitaph as several commentators have suggested, thereby making the entire poem a potential inscription. In every case the inscriptional passages provide coded links to significant aspects of the author's evolving display of self-representation: as artist, as lover and as citizen.

4.2.59-64

In 4.2 the dedication on the statue of Vertumnus gives praise to the artist who is, within the poem, Mamurrus, the fabled bronze-smith of the eleven shields made to match the one that dropped from heaven during the reign of Numa (4.2.59-64):

STIPES ACERNUS ERAM, PROPERANTI FALCE DOLATUS,
ANTE NUMAM GRATA PAUPER IN URBE DEUS.
AT TIBI, MAMURRI, FORMAE CAELATOR AENAE,
TELLUS ARTIFICES NE TERAT OSCA MANUS,
QUI ME TAM DOCILIS POTUISTI FUNDERE IN USUS.
UNUM OPUS EST, OPERI NON DATUR UNUS HONOS.

I was once a maple sapling hacked up by a hasty carving-knife, a pauper-god in a welcoming city before the time of Numa. But let not Oscan earth bruise your skilful hands, Mamurrus, moulder of the brazen form, who was capable of casting me for so many discernible purposes. One work it is, but granted to it are multiple honours.

The transformative properties of the god Vertumnus, however, are not conveyed merely by ecphrastic descriptions of the statue, but also by the marvellous linguistic artistry of the poem. The repetitious punning of the root-forms of a Latin verb that implies 'changing' or 'turning into', *verto, -ere*, (*VERT* and *VERS*) in a variety of words throughout the poem is evidence of the linguistic efforts that the poet applies to characterize the god more firmly as one who undergoes the physical changes he describes. Jeri Blair DeBrohun has taken the poet's efforts at depicting mutability a step further by showing that parallels exist between the transformative Vertumnus and the poet himself, 'who can assume and discard identities with ease because his existence outside the poem is faceless and formless. Vertumnus therefore represents the perfect medium between the poet and any role he wishes to assume or create' (DeBrohun 2003, 173).

The inscription at the poem's end grants emphasis to the artist of the marvellous statue, which makes Propertius identifiable not only with the statue, but also with the admired artist. The inscription to Mamurrus is homage to those who by their skill render such nuance and mutability within their medium that it performs a variety of *personae* (personalities, faces, characterizations) for the viewer. Propertius continuously impresses and sometimes befuddles his reader with the complexities of Cynthia and her depictions. Poem 1.3, for example, has received enormous attention for the way in which a sleeping Cynthia becomes a sort of statue that grants the lover licence to consider her in a variety of appearances or guises, and in a variety of scenarios as well.[84]

Propertius' identity within the poems is also mutable, but he grants more attention, I believe, to his identity outside the poem. Throughout his works he establishes that his Roman identity, his 'personal' identity, is contingent on his poetic reputation, or more accurately his poetic reception. The gravestones that the poet considers throughout his prior collections provide one way of working out the artist's negotiation with his legacy. This dedicatory inscription in 4.2 suggests to the reader and to those who question his artistic integrity as a writer of *that kind* of poetry that he has earned his place among the greatest craftsmen of Rome. Furthermore, this subtle analogy between himself and a significant Roman artisan reinforces the notion that Propertius has been writing for his people all along. In conjunction with his claims of being a *Romanus Callimachus* (4.1a.64), his artistic focus has not been on a faraway place or on themes too erudite to be comprehended. He has fashioned a Roman collection for Romans to love and make their own. The inscription for Mamurrus suggests that there is a historicity and a Roman context to the man behind any artistic mask. Although Propertius makes manifest a variety of poses and expressions within his work, there is someone behind all that who seeks, who deserves, public acknowledgement for his artistry. By means of the inscription in 4.2, he demands that all this artistry be recognized for what it truly is.

4.3.72

Poem 4.3 depicts the Roman matron Arethusa writing an epistolary elegy to her husband Lycotas who has joined Augustus in extra-provincial campaigns to Bactra, [China], Moesia, Britain and India.[85] The impossibility of such deployment in such a wide variety of places lends hyperbole to the complaint. The list may simply illustrate the extent of the area over which Rome has military influence, though others have drawn more elaborate conclusions from it.[86] This cartographic catalogue also suggests that Arethusa is uncertain as to where her husband actually is – clearly a possible scenario in a time in which mail directed home from soldiers was often not possible. Like the epistles in Ovid's later *Heroides*, Arethusa's missive is in the dead-letter-office of a poetic collection. It is not an epistle for the eyes of her husband, but an attempt to shape her own view of what war does to family. I agree with Maria Wyke's analysis that this poem provides an opportunity for the poet's reader to consider the vantage point of the unsung hero of long campaigns and the victim of circumstance – the long-suffering wife at home.[87]

As DeBrohun points out, 'Arethusa's plight often resembles that of an *exclusus amator*, the 'soldier' of the elegiac world' (2003, 150). Like Propertius who apologetically avoids military action, Arethusa is a lover at home who is sceptical of the value of the fight beyond Rome's borders and is much more focused on the fight within – in her case, to keep faith in her husband and her marriage.[88] Like Propertius' *amator*, Arethusa is a jealous lover. She first directs her animus at her husband's chosen life: it seems that he prefers army-life to domestic bliss. She also reveals her fear that her husband is unfaithful, 69: *incorrupta mei conserva foedera lecti!*, 'keep untainted the promise of my marriage bed!' The next line reveals her essential position, 70: *hac ego te sola lege redisse velim*, 'on this condition alone would I want you to return'. If he returns to her faithful to their vows, she promises to erect a votive inscription, 72: *SALVO GRATA PUELLA VIRO*, 'a grateful girl (erects this in appreciation) for her safe-and-sound husband'. Propertius' inclusion of an inscription in this non-funerary context at the letter's end offers a dramatic ending in two major respects.[89]

First, the inscription provides an interesting juxtaposition of *puella* to *vir*. Throughout Propertius' poetry *puella* has typically meant a mistress, usually Cynthia, and *vir* or other words associated with spousal commitment have often been used by the poet ironically either to suggest the status he longs for in relation to Cynthia or to refer to the status society requires of him with some other more appropriate woman.[90] In my earlier discussions of poems that feature the poet's funeral, I showed that the poet repeatedly engages in fantasy by transforming Cynthia into a good wife who makes a show of mourning her lost love: especially in 1.17, 1.19 and 2.13. In 4.3, although Arethusa and Lycotas are legally married and their relationship is sanctioned by society in every sense, the playing field of their intimacy has been made uneven by Lycotas' absence, and thereby the relationship engages in the same economic exchange of promises and threats that drive the advantage to one side or the other in Propertius' affair with Cynthia. Arethusa is driven to use her piety as a bargaining chip for Lycotas' fidelity. Her promised thanks to the gods will only be erected if her husband comes home safe, and she only wants him home if he has been faithful to her. Her inscription becomes a promise based on a threat – if the gods do hear her prayers, then Lycotas had better behave himself; after all, the excessive manifestations of her piety in lines 55-62 do suggest that she has made the gods her allies. The semantic arrangement of the inscription is important. The words *grata puella* are embedded within the phrase *salvo viro*. The emphasis of herself in the phrase suggests that her place in this domestic scenario is more important than his. Her gratitude depends on the safe return of her husband, but that, as we know from her letter, depends on his fidelity. The context of the surrounding letter reveals the veiled threat that lies within such a seemingly innocent declaration of thanks to the gods.

Secondly, Arethusa's promise in return for her husband's fidelity is text posted in public at the Capene gate. The votive nature of her inscription amplifies her dependence on the gods to ratify her bargain – it lends her veiled threat the power of a higher authority. Yet since we know that her letter is meant for our eyes, and not for her husband's, the place of that divine authority has been subtly linked to our own righteous approval of her cause. By placing her votive inscription in the letter, she begs the reader to nod in agreement with her position – thereby making the reader a demi-god whose judgment contributes to the moral universe of the jealous and wounded lover. How many times have we seen Propertius promise to wield or revoke his public poetic craft to bargain with Cynthia? Clearly, commemorative or poetic text as contingent on perceived right action develops as a frequent *topos* in Propertian elegy. Arethusa's promised inscription is therefore a unique feminine usurpation of the power of text to bargain, albeit within a male-authored text, with a potentially unreliable husband, and to bargain with a society that typically takes the husband's side. Furthermore, if Arethusa's complaint will draw the sympathy of the reader, it necessarily draws animosity towards imperial motives that demand so much absence of fathers and husbands from their families. Propertius once again builds a subtle case for the prosecution against policies that challenge the traditions and institutions of Republican society. The votive inscription therefore plays a role in capping off the complaint with a touch of comprehensible and poignant realism.

4.7.85-6 and 4.11

Two female speakers in Book 4 fashion their own forms of inscriptional remembrance. The poems that represent the words of Cynthia (4.7) and Cornelia (4.11) are best discussed in concert, for they both represent the voices of dead women who speak from their graves to the men who have survived them.

Poem 4.7 is the lover's account of a night spent in the company of Cynthia's ghost. Believing herself a victim of one of Propertius' slaves, a man she calls Lygdamus (35-6), she returns from the grave to indict her lover for neglecting her funeral (23-34), and for taking on a new mistress too soon (39-46).[91] She demands that he re-locate her tomb near her birthplace, plant ivy over it (the plant associated with poetic art), and mark it with a column upon which he should place an inscription (4.7.79-86):[92]

> pone hederam tumulo, mihi quae praegnante corymbo
>   mollia contortis alliget ossa comis.
> ramosis Anio qua pomifer incubat arvis,
>   et numquam Herculeo numine pallet ebur,
> hic carmen media dignum me scribe columna,
>   sed breve quod currens vector ab urbe legat:
> HIC TIBURTINA IACET AUREA CYNTHIA TERRA:
>   ACCESSIT RIPAE LAUS, ANIENE, TUAE.

> Place ivy upon my tomb, to bind with its swollen clusters my soft bones to its twining tendrils; where the fruit-giving Anio lies upon its irrigated plain, and where ivory never loses its lustre[93] – a blessing of Hercules – here write me a worthy couplet posted upon a column, brief enough that the hasty traveller from the city may read it: 'Here in Tiburtine earth lies glorious Cynthia: my praise, river-god Anienus, increases your stature.'[94]

Cornelia's poem, 4.11, could be viewed as an extended inscription, as commentators have pointed out.[95] The most inscriptional moments of the poem are its opening lines, lines 35-6 and its closing lines:

> Desine, Paulle, meum lacrimis urgere sepulcrum:
> panditur ad nullas ianua nigra preces;
> cum semel infernas intrarunt funera leges,
> non exorato stant adamante viae.
>
> 4.11.1-4

> Cease, Paullus, from weeping over my tomb: the black portal is opened for no prayers; when once the shades of the dead have entered the jurisdiction of the world below, no roads remain to any called back;

> iungor, Paulle, tuo sic discessura cubili:
> in lapide hoc uni nupta fuisse legar.
>
> 4.11.35-6

> Thus departing am I joined, Paullus, to your bed-chamber: on this stone will it be read that I was married to one man alone;

and lastly

> moribus et caelum patuit: sim digna merendo,
> cuius honoratis ossa vehantur avis.
>
> 4.11.101-2

> Even heaven has opened for virtue: may I be worthy of meriting that my bones be conveyed to my honoured ancestors.

I will begin my analysis of these four passages by quoting a useful insight that DeBrohun offers in the concluding epilogue of her study on Propertius' fourth book of poems (DeBrohun 2003, 242):

> [D]eath, like aetiology, is manipulable as a topographical subject as well. Graves and tombs are themselves monuments, and sepulchral epigrams may be seen akin to dedicatory inscriptions. In poem 4.7, Cynthia is very much concerned with her own inadequate funeral and, specifically, with the establishment of an epitaph that will memorialize her as she desires to be remembered (85-6). In 4.11, Cornelia's attempt simultaneously to establish and to elude full closure of her life includes a suggestion of appropriate wording for her own epitaph (35-6) … [B]oth death and aetiology are associated closely with closure and 'fixity', as the *aetion* itself affixes a specific meaning to a particular site. Yet both may also be seen as representative of a kind of immortality, as a gravesite with its inscribed stone, like a temple, and like a poetic collection, may outlive its own generation to be visited and read again and again.

DeBrohun eloquently states what my analysis here also demonstrates: that the poet's use of inscriptions is a reflection of his own quest for immortality through his works. There is common ground between the poet's self-referential inscriptions and these women's inscriptions, and this is the key to understanding why the poet shifts from the voice of the elegiac lover and glory-seeking poet, still manifest in poem 4.1, to that of lonely and forlorn women who fear primarily that they are misunderstood and underestimated.[96]

Propertius has identified similarities between his own predicament as an elegiac poet in an imperial court that appreciates epic and the predicament of women who traditionally have had to accept the crumbs of responsibility and praise that they are granted. Roman women's histories were not typically part of wider collective memory; their accomplishments were not granted the notice they deserved; and their influence upon the writers of their age was frequently reduced to sexualized, objectified attributes.[97] Even though Propertius is a part of the system that perpetuates the notion of woman as erotic cipher, Propertius can nevertheless also see that her treatment is not always fair. Perhaps it was the intense focus of the erotic elegy upon this rather silent population that eventually inspired Propertius to transform his voice to a woman's. Thus we have these experimental poems in which women's voices raise similar concerns regarding memory and record.

In 4.7, Cynthia's 'self-authored' epitaph mirrors in some respects the claims made by the poet in the first poem of the collection (4.1a.63-6):

> ut nostris tumefacta superbiat Umbria libris,
>   Umbria Romani patria Callimachi!
> scandentis quisquis cernit de vallibus arces,
>   ingenio muros aestimet ille meo!

> Just as Umbria takes pride in my books – Umbria, fatherland of a Roman Callimachus! – may whosoever spies her towering citadels from the valleys below appraise them by my talent!

Both the poet and Cynthia draw direct lines of linkage between themselves and their birthplace (*Tiburtina ... terra*), and both claim that their reputations do service to improve the status of their homelands – Propertius' fame exalts the citadels of Umbria, Cynthia's fame increases the banks of the Anio. Additionally, when Cynthia demands this couplet, she refers to it as *dignum*, and her request follows a demand that he burn all the poems he wrote about her beforehand, 77-8: *et quoscumque meo fecisti nomine versus, / ure mihi: laudes desine habere meas*!, 'and please burn what verses you wrote in my honour: do not keep my praises!' She clearly means that the simple, dignified epitaph should substitute for all the poems he wrote about her. Her words follow from the idea that she wants to be free of his poetic power entirely.

Can it be that lines 77-8 suggest that Propertius has received praises meant for her – have Cynthia's (i.e. some woman's) poetic skills played some role in shaping his very collection? I admit it seems very unlikely that Propertius would make such a suggestion, given his evident preoccupation with his poetic *fama* and his frequent attempts, as seen prominently in 4.2, to link the artistry of his work closely to himself. Yet the accusation hangs there without much development, and the emphases of *laudes* and (especially) *meas* in accord with the juridical sense of *habere* to refer to legal ownership suggest her attempt to recover what is rightfully hers. The word *dignum* in line 83 professes Cynthia's personal aesthetic: she wants her monument to express only her own accomplishment in her own words, for once.

Alternatively Propertius is allowing the reader to infer that his poetry has taken on a life of its own, beyond his own artistic aims and efforts. This literary woman, this *docta puella*, whose own *fama* has come into existence by the poet's talent, has grown tired of seeing his name increase in stature because of her presence in the poetry, or because of the poetry itself. She resents the fact that Propertius promoted himself through her, and – like Mary Shelley's later Frankenstein monster – the creation has returned to destroy the legacy of the creator. It is a short-lived rebellion, however, as Propertius indicates in the next and last poem he would ever write about Cynthia. In 4.8, the power balance has been restored: Cynthia is jealous over the lover's dalliances with other women and her last words in the poem express her desire to rest eternally with him in a single tomb: the problematic metamorphosis of Cynthia into a domesticated *uxor* seen throughout the collection has finally been resolved. This does not cancel out her protest in 4.7 however, for her demands there are too compelling. Perhaps Propertius could not resist raising this tantalizing issue – that his elegiac efforts are intrinsically unjust – in any case, it seems he purposely chose to move past it quickly.

Cornelia's poem (4.11) reveals a slightly different kind of anxiety from that expressed in 4.7. Cynthia is anxious about the way that her poet has represented her; Cornelia is fearful that her meagre record will not stand the test of time. Unlike Cynthia (who may have been loosely based on a woman or women that Propertius knew), Cornelia actually existed. She was the daughter of Scribonia and Publius Cornelius Scipio (*cos.* 38 BC) before Scribonia married Octavian. She was therefore the older half-sister of Julia, Augustus' only child.[98] She was married to L. Aemilius Paullus Lepidus (*cos. suff.* 34 BC and *cens.* 22 BC) and died in 16 BC.[99] Propertius amplifies the historicity of her person by revealing these personal anxieties.

Going over the achievements of her life, mostly due to her paternal family's recognition, she admits that it is only through her children that she will achieve any lasting remembrance, 4.11.69-70: *mihi cumba volenti / solvitur aucturis tot mea fata meis*, 'my ferry disembarks with a willing passenger since so many of mine will increase my lot'. The quality of her virtuous, blameless life to which she refers throughout the poem, she marks, will be measured by society with respect to her lasting marriage. The line in which she makes this claim explicitly mentions the words *uni nupta* as if they will certainly appear on her tomb (36: *in lapide hoc ... legar*).[100] Cornelia's emphasis on this formulaic manner of praising women seems a protest that for all her mothering, for all her many virtues, and all her efforts to make lasting these final words, her mere act of staying married will distinguish her in the ages to come.

Propertius' Cornelia deals an effective coup de grâce, however, in the poem's dramatic finale. In line 101, she points out that the heavens have a tendency to admit those whose virtues are profound (*moribus et caelum patuit*). This reference to the heavens opening is an allusion to an epigram that Ennius wrote for her ancestor, Scipio Africanus, a century and a half before (V 21-4):[101]

> si fas endo plagas caelestum ascendere cuiquam,
> mi soli caeli maxima porta patet.

> If it is fitting for anyone to climb to the region of the gods, the great portal of the skies lies open for me alone.

As the poets have clearly written, heaven is the destination of those who have earned that place by their deeds. Cornelia hopes that heaven regards merit more than gender as she finishes her poem claiming a place among her ancestors (101-2: *sim digna merendo, / cuius honoratis ossa vehantur avis*).[102] This reference to Ennius links this *laudatio* to a long tradition of poetic eulogy of society's most distinguished elite.

By finishing his elegiac corpus with this poem, Propertius returns elegy to this original purpose, but does so in a fashion that can hardly be called purely Hellenistic, or even Ennian. This lengthy final poem meanders through a decidedly elegiac range of Roman topics (from grief to mythology to teleology to family pride and devotion to structure of the Roman household) but ends in the very place where elegy once began. Propertius has capped off his collection with an Ennian flourish that reminds his reader of the progress the elegy has made in the hands of a *Romanus Callimachus*. Furthermore his final poem returns the elegy to its original Roman function: to honour great individuals whose lives were spent in service to the Republic. Looking back over his collection after reading 4.11, the reader may see that all the erotic fantasies of Cynthia, the subtle socio-political commentaries and the expressions of self-monumentalization in his poems are Propertius' innovations on this Roman impulse to characterize what resonates with true experience.[103]

Conclusion

When elegy entered the Roman milieu, it was first applied to activities that Romans already valued, primarily to praising Rome's best men. When Latin elegy next appears a century later, in Catullus, its capacity for eulogy remains, but with a difference. Catullus writes elegy that evokes the memory not of generals or aristocrats, but of his brother, a man important, perhaps, only to him. Catullus reveals a preoccupation with monuments when he repeats his lament for his brother in three places, and in the last place explicitly mentions his absent monument among the tombs of his ancestors. Those lines in poem 68b become his brother's monument. Catullus may not have considered himself an elegiac poet (his apology in 65 suggests he was only experimenting with a new form), but he, like Ennius, must have understood the potential of the medium for building monuments of words.

Propertius' poems also capitalize on the inscriptional capability of the metre as he poses a variety of scenarios regarding the nature of his literary legacy. He imagines what people will say about him over his tomb: Maecenas' words of regret, his readers' passionate admiration, and Cynthia's disconsolate weeping. In his most experimental book of elegies he includes three inscriptions, each of which in its own way contributes to the understanding of the poem it accompanies. But most significantly, at two important leaving-off places, at the ends of his first and fourth books of poetry, Propertius composes the poems that most transparently reveal the memorial aspects of the genre. In these funereal epigrams for a kinsman and a homeland, and in an extended inscription for a female descendant from the Scipios – perhaps the most splendid representatives of Rome's Republican legacy – Propertius utilizes the elegy to memorialize those whose voices were lost to an entirely new generation of Romans in the age of Empire. Augustus' Rome was surely a thing of beauty to the eye, and his empire was undoubtedly a cause of relief and security to many thousands, perhaps many millions throughout the Roman world, but the personal and the private narratives of the past were not yet ready to give up the ghost – and in Propertius' elegies they found a voice.

3

Tibullan Inscriptions: Between Self and *Persona*

In the previous chapter I explored the inscriptions that Propertius placed in his elegies, but chronologically he was not the first to place inscriptions within his work, a practice he did not adopt until his second book of elegies. Tibullus, whose first collection of poems appeared immediately after Propertius' first book, was the first elegist to include an invented inscription within a poem. He does not merely use language reminiscent of epitaphs, as seen in Catullus and in Propertius' first book, but actually composes single distichs as inscriptions – and he does so in two places: the first appears as seen upon his tombstone in 1.3; the second appears as a votive inscription to Venus at the end of 1.9.

In order to stay true to a strict chronology of the elegiac genre, I chose to discuss Propertius before Tibullus in the structure of this study. Propertius' poetic debut drew significant inspiration from the body of long elegies by Catullus, as well as the books of poems by Gallus. Therefore the development of elegy in Propertius' first book, particularly the epigraphic qualities of the genre, merited prior consideration. As this chapter will indicate, Propertius' early elegies affect Tibullus' formulation of the genre, and effect Tibullan responses to Propertius' preceding poems.

As shown in the previous chapter, Catullus demonstrates in his long elegies a desire to memorialize his brother, and in each case the grief he expresses seemingly interrupts his self-introduction as an elegiac poet in 65, and the erotic narrative of 68a as well as a mythological correlation in 68b. Yet these so-called interruptions show themselves to be crucial to the process of introducing the metrical genre, for they bring to the fore the notion that the elegiac poem was intrinsically associated with personal histories, and that the epigrammatic and epigraphic history of the genre, combined with the Roman epigraphic style of memorial (poetic even in its archaic manifestations), made Catullus' elegiac experiments an intersection of generic (Alexandrian) and epitaphic (Roman) concerns. Since we see those same concerns surface in the poems of the *Monobiblos*, then we can say with greater conviction that Propertius is approaching elegy in a way that is not entirely Alexandrian, and that he too is incorporating the epigraphic tradition of his own culture into his experience with the elegiac genre. Nevertheless, he did not insert quoted inscriptions within his verses as Tibullus did immediately afterwards. Why did it not occur to him to do so? Or was the inclusion of inscriptions too mundane, not poetic enough? I would presume the latter, but this can hardly be proven. I can merely postulate that Propertius clearly saw potential in the practice after it appeared in Tibullus and manipulated it many times. I would also submit that Tibullus incorporated the inscriptions into his poems as a means of bridging the gap between common practice and poetic expression. In doing so, he made the epigraphic tradition more vivid and more essential to his elegies in order to captivate the Roman reader.

This chapter will demonstrate that Tibullus, though deeply immersed in the Hellenistic poetic style,[1] finds himself drawn also to the indigenous, Roman elements of the elegiac tradition – namely that close association the Romans made between poetic verse and memorial.[2] Tibullus' inscriptions are hints that his poetry abides alongside a real world of socio-political consequences, and the inscriptional passages that he composes serve as bold, Latin-elegiac responses and challenges to Propertius' first book as well as other elegiac predecessors. In turn, by way of response to Tibullus' first book of poems, Propertius' inscriptional purposes in his later books (discussed previously in Chapter 2) become all the more clear.

The works of Tibullus are quite different from those of Propertius. Even though Propertius was probably an influence in Tibullus' poetic career, the two demonstrate quite different dispositions and literary aesthetics;[3] it may better serve to speak of these two authors in terms of their interaction than their influences of one upon the other.[4] Quintilian remarks, in supreme brevity, that Tibullus wrote elegant and polished verses, though 'there are those who prefer Propertius'.[5] Francis Cairns has justifiably taken this to mean that Quintilian preferred Tibullus (Cairns 1979, 4); but it also suggests that in a world of critical perspectives, few readers enjoyed both elegists equally: the two poets appealed to different sorts of people.[6] Some Romans perhaps preferred Propertius' obscure mythological retellings, well-drawn characters and erotic verve, while those who viewed poetry as a clever exercise of erudition preferred Tibullus' word-craft and generic play.[7] As erotic objects Delia and Marathus are not nearly so compelling as Cynthia, the *dura puella* who dominates the Propertian collection. No Propertian narrator, however, quite captures the humorous irony of the situation in Tibullus 1.4 in which lascivious Priapus becomes the teacher of gentle seduction.[8]

The poets show further differences in the ways they represent Roman society. Propertius takes more risks than Tibullus – there is little doubt that the final two poems of his *Monobiblos*, as I indicated earlier, are indications that the plan of unifying everyone under Rome has caused great loss to many.[9] Tibullus on the other hand tends to discuss the demands of Roman society only in relation to himself, as if his lack of love for soldiering was merely an aesthetic choice. Perhaps readers somewhat disillusioned with their current age enjoyed Tibullus' poetic expressions, while those who mourned a previous age altogether found in Propertius an expression of their regret.[10]

Cairns reveals another dichotomy that governed the Roman reception of the elegiac output: on the one hand he supposes that all poetic patrons wanted to be part of 'a movement which was consciously emulating and surpassing, in Latin and within two generations, the greatest achievements of five centuries of Greek literature' (Cairns 1979, 229). On the other hand he grants that these patrons 'wanted poetry written by Roman citizens within a context of civic involvement' (1979, 32). This leaves a lot of room for literary preferences to move to one side (literary aesthetics) or the other (representation of the civic status quo). Each of the two poets engaged to different degrees within these areas of representation and provided what their audiences appreciated.

Tibullus published two books of poems,[11] and the second appeared immediately after the young poet's death – he was only in his thirties.[12] The cause of his death is unknown, but the tragedy of a young man cut short at the beginning of such a brilliant literary career inspired Ovid to commemorate his life and his talent with a poem, *Am.* 3.9. Tibullus' first book of poems has been declared his great success, demonstrating a structure that continues to delight scholars with its ingenuity and complexity.[13] The book exhibits a structure that places emphasis on the erotic episodes (first with the *puella* Delia, and then with the *puer* Marathus) in such a way that an intriguing meta-narrative emerges. The poet's programmatic stance, presented in the first poem, values what he considers to be the simple life: one that values rusticity and love and views the two as complementary and mutually compatible. By the same token, the poet-lover eschews military and political involvement, for such affairs interrupt the constancy of love's presence and they disrupt the agricultural cycle that demands vigilant maintenance.[14] By way of the various episodes that occur in poems 2-3, 5-6 and 8-9, however, the poet becomes disillusioned with his version of ethereal, literary love, and ends the book with an ode dedicated not to love, but to peace (*Pax*) (1.10).[15] Love is described in this poem not as an inspiring goal that takes the lover outside social norms of behaviour (the typical stance in elegy), but as situated well within the confines of domestic rusticity. The compatibility of Love and Agriculture in 1.1 is reformulated to Peace and Agriculture in 1.10. Love remains in the final poem, but as a powerful and sometimes unwieldy force that can disinterestedly incite and quell violence. In the lines that appear near the poem's end, a married couple engages in an angry dispute and a physical brawl. Love in this mundane setting has the potential to become a source of anxiety to those involved.[16] Peace becomes the backdrop for success in all areas, including amorous attachment, whether in the poet's ethereal world or in the life of the everyday citizen.

In addition to this erotic meta-narrative, amid this almost philosophical (and sometimes comical) exploration of the qualities of love, Tibullus punctuates his work with two genre poems, 1.4 and 1.7.[17] These genre poems, as Eleanor Winsor Leach points out, allow Tibullus to expound upon his personal *ars poetica* (Leach 1980, 82). Those poetics fall in line significantly with Hellenistic traits, particularly in the first genre poem. In poem 4, Priapus acts as narrator and *magister amoris* for the benefit of someone named Titius, though it is left to the Tibullan *amator* to impart the lesson that Priapus offers to his unreceptive friend.[18] The poem's Hellenistic qualities include the erotodidactic nature of the narrative, the delayed introduction of a key character (Titius appears in the final ten lines of the poem), and other ironic surprises whereby 'the reader is forced to re-assess the situation presented in the elegy' (Cairns 1979, 175).[19] In addition, the Roman character of Priapus is coated with an Apollonian gloss; Leach points out that although in the Roman Priapean tradition Priapus is an ungainly god whose exaggerated physical endowment(s) reflect a coarseness of thought and base intentions, Tibullus' Priapus becomes a 'sophisticated Alexandrianizing poet' (Leach 1980, 89). Therefore if poem 4 is a genre poem, and the majority of that poem is spent dressing up Roman cultural aspects to espouse Alexandrian tenets, then it is clear that early on in his poetic collection, Tibullus' interest lies in establishing direct lines between his Roman craft and Greek poetic tradition.

Yet the poet seems also to enjoy challenging the Alexandrian quality of the fabric he weaves. Poem 1.7, the second genre poem, is panegyric addressed to Messalla, Tibullus' patron, and the general under whom he served during a campaign in the East that led to Messalla's notable victory in Aquitania.[20] As Leach points out, 'the choice of Messalla as addressee gives added complexity to the poem introducing a note of Roman reality into the literary situation' (1980, 86). This 'reality' is strategically placed, Leach argues, for similar to the fourth *Eclogue* of Virgil in which prophecy and dynasty reverse 'the Vergilian divorce between politics and poetry', Tibullus' seventh poem makes him a participant in the glory of Messalla, not as soldier on campaign with the great general, but in 'the part he now plays in reconstructing and celebrating [Messalla's deeds] in verse ... The poem becomes a vehicle for the joining together of many opposites. Imagination and history combine in the colorful record of Messalla's military progress' (1980, 90). The poet's former dismissal of military life and his preference for a life devoted to agriculture and love are not entirely compromised by 1.7, but in this poem Tibullus has acknowledged the special place that Messalla holds in the Roman world. As we know, such honorific poetry does not lie outside the purview of poets like Callimachus and other Alexandrians who also wrote elegiac verses in their poems for the benefit of monarchs.[21] Even so, the intrusion of the Roman notions of hierarchy, career and patronage enter strangely among so many poems that have dealt almost exclusively with the pursuit of love and the lover's various failures.

The inscriptional passages in 1.3 and 1.9 play a part in blending the real with the unreal: in mixing the literary world of Hellenistic poetics with the Roman realities visited upon anyone who takes up a poetic career in that vital period. The first significant trait of these two imagined inscriptions is that each of them contains the name of the poet – the only appearances of Tibullus' name within the entire collection of poems. In fact, Tibullus' bold inclusion of his name twice in his first book may be a direct response to the coded nature of Propertius' self-introduction in poems 21 and 22 of his *Monobiblos*, published one year before Tibullus' first book of elegies appeared. As I showed in the previous chapter, Propertius associates himself, in 1.21 vaguely and in 1.22 more explicitly, to a homeland that has received rough treatment in recent decades, and the poet poses indirect criticism to its treatment by manipulating the rhetoric of grief and epitaphic memorial when he discusses it. Propertius never names himself however, and thereby he avoids too deep an association between himself and the verses that might be construed as protest. Tibullus, by contrast, does not baulk at naming himself, and the reason why is worthy of examination. Therefore in the following sections I will examine poems 1.3 and 1.9 with regard to the ways these poems respond to the Roman elegiac tradition, and with special attention to their inscriptional formulations.

Hic iacet Tibullus

In poem 1.3, Tibullus depicts himself as a sick soldier, alone on the island of Corfu (ancient Corcyra – he calls it Phaeacia), left behind by his regiment since he cannot accompany them in his condition. Fearful of impending death, the lover first asks his commander Messalla and his cohort to remember him well; he chides death for its greedy grip on him; then he mourns that no women are present to see to his funeral – not mother, nor sister, nor Delia.[22] Then the poem turns to thoughts of Delia – how she mourned his leaving; how he delayed his departure; and the prayers she made to Isis. Then he speaks to Isis himself, promising Delia's gratitude for protection, but vowing his own pious thanks to his household gods (his paternal *Penates* and his ancient *Lar*). Then the poet turns his thoughts to the golden age of Saturn when men tilled the soil and never left home seeking booty and expansion of territory through war as they do in his age – the age of Jupiter. This leads him to compose his own epitaph (49-56):

> nunc Iove sub domino caedes et vulnera semper,
>   nunc mare, nunc leti mille repente viae.
> parce, pater: timidum non me periuria terrent,
>   non dicta in sanctos impia verba deos.
> quod si fatales iam nunc explevimus annos,
>   fac lapis inscriptis stet super ossa notis:
> HIC IACET IMMITI CONSUMPTUS MORTE TIBULLUS
>   MESSALLAM TERRA DUM SEQUITURQUE MARI.

> In this age under the mastery of Jupiter do slaughter and carnage always occur, even on sea; now there are a thousand paths of sudden death. Spare me God-father: no false-sworn oaths plague me with guilt, nor have I spoken impious words against the sacred gods. But if now I have already fulfilled my allotted years, see to it that a stone stands over my bones with these inscribed words: 'Here lies Tibullus consumed by a pitiless death while he accompanied Messalla on land and sea.'

After dictating his epitaph, Tibullus begins to consider the afterworld: he expresses the hope that Venus will guide him through Elysian fields, since he has been such a loyal disciple. Elysium looks a lot like the poet's preferred world in poem 1.1, a place of love and natural bounty. He then goes on to narrate the sights and figures of Hades or the underworld (at 67 he calls it *scelerata sedes*) including Tantalus, Tityos, the Danaids and, uniquely, those who have challenged or have flouted his dedication to love (1.3.81-2): *illic sit quicumque meos violavit amores, / optavit lentas et mihi militias* (let there also reside in that place whosoever has done damage to my love, or has wished me lengthy duty abroad).[23] The poem ends with an abrupt address to Delia (1.3.83: *at tu casta, precor, maneas*) in which the poet asks her to remain true and tirelessly await his return. The final lines express his last wish that he might one day appear before her and they might be reunited. The fact that he asks *Lucifer* (the morning star) to bring this joyous sight to him does suggest that he hopes to recover and return home: a somewhat abrupt reversal of all his preparations for death and the afterlife.

Tibullus' epitaph has received a great deal of attention, particularly regarding the fact that Delia does not appear in it.[24] David Bright notes that Tibullus leaves a soldier's epitaph, not a lover's, and this may perhaps be a reflection of the Odyssean allusion made implicitly by the reference to the island where he lingers as Phaeacia instead of Corcyra and the attempt to transform Delia into a diligent Penelope (Bright 1978, 32-3). In accordance with heroic concerns, Tibullus' 'thoughts turn to the survival of his name ... [and] what men will say after his death' (1978, 26). In addition Bright calls the inscription the 'only fleeting contact with the present reality' within a poem in which the speaker's 'thoughts move through a world of recollection and vision' (1978, 19). Cairns sees the epitaph as 'the centre-piece of the elegy' since it highlights and combines the theme of loyalty to Messalla with that of the poet's fear of death in a foreign land; around this epitaph, he claims, 'other structural aspects become clear' (Cairns 1979, 46).[25] These 'structural aspects' vary to some degree depending on the scholarly interpretation, but most agree that the elegy revolves around the epitaph in an attempt to negotiate between the past, the present and the future, for in those unreal dimensions does the poet's fantasy align with possible realization.[26]

The inscription therefore represents an intersection of activity between

Tibullus the poet and Messalla, one of Rome's greatest generals of the Augustan age. If poem 1.7 is a dose of reality in the midst of Hellenistic and erotic concerns, then the inscription in 1.3 is likewise an attempt to identify the poet with a significant historical *persona* and moment. As Bright suggests, by bringing Messalla into his epitaph, 'the world of Tibullus is enriched, endowed with a higher value, by its involvement in the world of such a personage' (Bright 1978, 65). The Tibullan *persona* of lover exists in the poetry the author creates, while the author himself is a participant in many of the activities that mark the success of a Roman citizen. The inscription is a revelation of Tibullus' personal concern that it be remembered that he too was a fully participating Roman man. While poets like Propertius would later focus on concretizing their literary identities in a society that failed to value the poetic exercise as fully as it might, Tibullus served Rome by way of some traditional routes, in the manner of Gallus and Horace before him.

Indeed the viewpoint of the experienced soldier can be valuable to the production of poetry. As recent centuries have proved, it is often the soldier who becomes the most eloquent spokesperson to articulate the violence and the horrors of war and advocate the pursuits of peace.[27] This latter activity was Tibullus' concern, and for that he is well remembered; but concern that his civic duty also be acknowledged gives us the words of 1.3.55-6.[28] Tibullus' epitaph in 1.3, the first composed by any elegiac poet, comprises the most autobiographical, the most real, account of the author's life, particularly in comparison to the other 'self-revelations' in a genre in which the 'reality' of events and persons is difficult or impossible to pin down.[29]

Tibullus' concerns for self-representation become all the more apparent when we compare his epitaph to that first created by Propertius. When Propertius responds to Tibullus 1.3 with an epitaph and a near-epitaph in his second book, he is careful how he configures his poetic posture.[30] Probably in response to Tibullus' self-memorial within the context of his service to Messalla, Propertius represents himself in relation to his patron Maecenas. In 2.1 he intimately connects himself to this other great Augustan general, much in the fashion of Tibullus 1.7, and asks Maecenas to visit his grave and say these words over it (2.1.77-8): *Huic misero fatum dura puella fuit.* Yet later, within the context of a funeral led by Cynthia (2.13), where Maecenas is absent, he refers to himself as 'the slave of a single love' in his first quoted epitaph (36: *UNIUS HIC QUONDAM SERVUS AMORIS ERAT*). To speak of slavery in 2.1, within the context of his relationship with Maecenas, would be unnecessarily humiliating.[31] His imagined epitaph in 2.13 therefore emphasizes his poetic pose as a slave of love, a strategy that keeps the author close to his poetic aims, as R.O.A.M. Lyne has suggested.[32]

Propertius, therefore, is unwilling to let down his poet's mask even when he brings Maecenas into the activities of his poetic world: the final lines of 2.1 express Propertius' hope that his work will make him memorable among Rome's greatest men. In contrast to Tibullus' choice to step momentarily out of his poetic *persona* when he fashions his epitaph, Propertius remains 'in character'. This may reflect Propertius' unwillingness to compromise the integrity of his poetic *persona*; that is, to stay true to the elegiac boundaries that he has set for himself and his themes. If elegiac poetry was going to earn respect in the Roman culture of politics and war, then poets had to demand that their art receive validation from Rome's leading men.

Surely a patron such as Maecenas would have appreciated the clever way that Propertius dignifies him in 2.1: he rides gallantly to the poet's grave in a Celtic chariot, the booty of Roman conquest perhaps, but more probably a fashionable 'light gig' of the period.[33] His ostentatious presence makes him a fitting participant in the passionate drama that drives the erotic elegy, a drama in which the opposite poles of luxury and simplicity are forever in contention. Perhaps the reputations of Messalla and Maecenas as contemporaneous patrons of poetry even established a slight literary rivalry between the two. Propertius 2.1 may mean to place Maecenas in a role more significant to the poetry itself in response to the primarily military role that Tibullus had assigned his patron in 1.7 and at 1.3.55-6.

Both Maecenas and Messalla were known to have contributed to the success of Augustus' rise to power, though Messalla was by far the more accomplished commander and statesman; Tibullus' Messalla is one whom even poets accompany over land and sea.[34] Yet we also know that Messalla was a later convert than Maecenas to Octavian's camp. Maecenas fought with Octavian at Philippi and was one of his most intimate friends.[35] He was also one of the wealthiest and most luxury-seeking Romans of his generation. Perhaps in response to Tibullus' advertisement of his patron's allegiance to Rome and his many manifestations of his sense of duty, Propertius attempts to configure Maecenas as a man of the new generation, one indeed much like himself, whose distinction comes not merely from these traditional paths of honours, but from highly developed aesthetic values. This was not an attitude that resided comfortably among Republican Roman *mores*, as I explained in my first chapter, but it was one that more and more Romans became willing to adopt in the age of Augustus, an age in which one's proximity to the imperial family began to matter more than ancestral ties or civic accomplishments.[36]

Tibullus' form of self-representation in his epitaph in 1.3 is significant for it embraces that older, more traditional form of identification, namely one's association to important campaigns and great generals.[37] The inscription suggests that Roman cultural forces were so strong that even Tibullus, a poet imbued in the Alexandrian style, either did not conceive of his own epitaph outside the norm of Roman commemorations, or did not think it appropriate to conceive it in any other way. Propertius clearly felt free, afterwards, to respond to Tibullus' more traditional associations between himself and Roman culture with an epitaph that kept him, as I suggested, in poetic character, but he was not the first to compose an epitaph in elegy, and his epitaph must stand in response to Tibullus' innovation.

There is another direction in which we should consider the meta-poetic response: with regard to Tibullus' responses to the *Monobiblos*. As we know, Propertius published his first book of elegies a year earlier than Tibullus. Lyne points out many Propertian / Tibullan exchanges, including the comic and bourgeois aspects of Tibullus' funereal considerations in comparison to the anxiety-ridden poems of Propertius, as seen in the contrast in tone between Tib. 1.1.55-60 and Prop. 1.1.19.5-12 and 19-24: 'Tibullus washes away Propertian *Angst* on a tide of tears, confidence, and security. The devotion of Delia at Tibullus' funeral is not in the slightest doubt ... Acute Propertian anxieties are replaced by smug Tibullan confidence: this is surely funny' (Lyne 1998, 529). With respect to Tibullus 1.3, Lyne sees nearly the same forces at work: '[Tibullus] exhibits a more bourgeois and sentimental concern than expressed by Propertius, and the poem holds out the prospect of a happy outcome ... We can see here further amusingly complacent glances at Propertius' funeral agonizing in 1.17 and 19 – and, also, at his tougher stranded condition in 1.17' (1998, n. 40).

Although I appreciate the potential for comic ribbing between Latin elegists, there are aspects of poem 1.3 that make its funereal concerns slightly more than witty repartee. The inscription in 1.3 occurs within the context of the poet's problematic relationship to Jupiter – the god whose age has replaced the golden age of Saturn (49-50). In the lines just preceding the passage quoted beforehand, Tibullus writes this of that golden age, 47-8: *non acies, non ira fuit non bella nec ensem / immiti saevus duxerat arte faber*, 'there was not argument, wrath or war; nor had the craftsman of savagery with his ruthless skill produced the sword.' In Jupiter's age, by contrast, war and carnage are everywhere. Tibullus crafts a delicate situation in which he offers criticism of the age of Jupiter, and yet seeks from the same god protection over his soul and his body (*parce, pater*).[38] The use of *pater* in 51 certainly points to Jupiter as father of gods and men and to the Roman context in which Jupiter was quite literally located at the 'head' of state on the Capitoline Hill. The association between the head of state and the king of gods was certainly transferrable to the unique sort of power wielded by Augustus who was granted permanent proconsular *imperium* in 27 BC, the same year that Tibullus' first book appears.

It was not Augustus' choice to associate himself closely to Jupiter (he aptly selected Mars and Venus instead), but long-standing tradition associated the triumphant *imperator* with Jupiter on the day of triumph. The significant martial and political powers that Augustus held made him a human reflection of the power of Jupiter over the heavens, as Ovid would make explicitly clear a generation later in a passage in his *Metamorphoses*

(1.204-5). This is not to say that lines 47-8 should be construed as a direct confrontation with Augustus, his policies or Roman military expansion in any specific way. Nevertheless, the possibility exists that Tibullus' disavowal of the military life is a particular response to the escalated military involvement of Rome's leading men in domestic conflicts in the years preceding 27 BC. Tibullus is not so daring as Propertius, however, to criticize openly the treatment of a particular area or to discuss a particular campaign like the Perusine War.[39] Yet in these lines of poem 1.3, Tibullus offers a general (even gentle) protest to warfare that does not entirely exclude Augustus from implication in the agency of troubled times.

The delicate balance that Tibullus maintains between criticizing and seeking help from Jupiter is one that, I believe, is stabilized by use of the inscription. Its inclusion dramatically performs the lover's and the poet's death since to read the epitaph is to imagine the desolate shore on which it sits, the rotting corpse thinly covered with foreign soil, and the cause that brought this solitary soldier reluctantly so far from home (*Messalam sequitur*). We may recall how effective was Catullus' grief in poems 65 and 68 in which he mourns his brother, buried in Phrygian soil, far from his ancestral tombs. Tibullus leaves an inscription that suits his historical reality as client of a great general, not the lover's 'reality', and thus he names himself. Far from viewing the inscription in 1.3 as a smug, bourgeois expression, I see it as a means by which Tibullus can respond with greater confidence to Propertius' subtler self-identifications, and do so without offending his patron and his patron's lord.

The care with which both Propertius and Tibullus craft their poetic *personae* in relation to their more illustrious contemporaries cannot be denied. The inclusion of the inscription in Tibullus 1.3, besides providing a mitigating presence in a potentially controversial situation, allows Tibullus to go one step further than Propertius in establishing himself through his poetry. Again we are drawn to the original elegiac purpose as determined first by Ennius and re-articulated in Catullus – namely its utility in poetically honouring Rome's great citizens, or, in this later age, in creating memorials unjustly withheld by circumstance.

Resolutus amore Tibullus

Poem 1.9 marks the transition of the poet-lover's attitude from one that esteems above all else love and simplicity to one that newly appreciates the social condition that fosters these enjoyments, namely Peace. In 1.9 the poet expresses exasperation with a male lover, Marathus, whose entanglement with a privileged household has diverted him away from the Tibullan lover. Tibullus reveals that the boy is accepting gifts from an older man in exchange for his attentions; at the same time he is sleeping with the man's young wife while stringing along the increasingly more disillusioned poet.[40] By the poem's end the poet has determined that he must bid farewell to Marathus, for how can he continue with a lover who will value his purse over his heart? He claims that he will find another male lover and that this will make Marathus regret how he treated him. To cap off the poem, he composes the votive inscription that he will place on a golden palm and dedicate to Venus in celebration of casting off the mercenary boy (1.9.77-84):

> blanditiasne meas aliis tu vendere es ausus,
>   tune aliis demens oscula ferre mea?
> tunc flebis cum me vinctum puer alter habebit
>   et geret in regno regna superba tuo.
> at tua tunc me poena iuvet, Venerique merenti
>   fixa notet casus aurea palma meos:
> HANC TIBI FALLACI RESOLUTUS AMORE TIBULLUS
>   DEDICAT ET GRATA SIS DEA MENTE ROGAT.

> Have you been so bold as to sell the enjoyments that are (by rights) mine to others? Are you mad to render my kisses to people other than myself? Then you will weep when another boy shall tie up and possess me and shall rule proudly in your former kingdom – but then your suffering would delight me. Let a golden palm, hung for deserving Venus, make known my advantageous outcome: 'Tibullus, released from a false love, dedicates this to you and asks, goddess, that you may think kindly of the giver.'

Commentators have remarked that the dedicatory inscription is a common elegiac motif, with possibly earlier references to votive inscriptions occurring in Horace's *Carm.* 1.5.13-16 and 3.26.1-6.[41] Yet another influence on Tibullus was undoubtedly the elegist Cornelius Gallus, and one of the few fragments we have of his poems includes a possible reference to leaving votive offerings in temples: fr. 2.2-5 (Courtney):[42]

> fata mihi, Caesar, tum erunt mea dulcia quom tu
>   maxima Romanae pars eris historiae,
> postque tuum reditum multorum templa deorum
>   fixa legam spolieis deivitiora tueis.

> Then, Caesar, will my destiny take a pleasant turn when you become a vital part of Roman history, and, after your return, I shall 'read' many gods' temples made the richer for being hung with your trophies.[43]

There is some controversy as to whether Gallus' words *templa ... legam* refer to reading inscriptions on temples or reading about temples enriched by Caesar's victories. Edward Courtney interprets the phrase in the former sense, and he supports this idea by referring to Cicero's *sepulcra legens* at *Cato* (*De Senectute*) 21, to Martial's *marmora ... legis* at 10.63.1-2, and to an actual inscription: *CLE* 1552 B 20: *monimenta legas* (1993, 266). If we look at later poems, we note that Propertius uses *lego* at 3.4.16

to refer to learning about something through reading inscriptions: *et titulis oppida capta legam*. In Ovid's *Heroides*, furthermore, Helen writes of her experience 'reading' her own name written in wine upon the table by Paris, 17.87-8: *legi sub nomine nostro / quod deducta mero littera fecit, AMO*. *Lego*, therefore, is frequently associated with the act of reading inscriptional texts, and while the phrase *lego templa* may have no Latin precedent in the sense of reading inscriptions on temples, as the first commentator of the fragment points out,[44] it is suggestive of such a process.

R.G.M. Nisbet and P.J. Parsons prefer not to assume reference to words inscribed on those temples; instead they suggest that the speaker in the poem finds information about these temples in historical sources (I shall read *of* temples made the richer ...).[45] This raises a question, for although Gallus does indeed mention histories in the previous distich, he does not make a secure connection between the histories he one day will read about Caesar, and the textual evidence of Caesar's largesse. As we can see in the passage, Gallus distinguishes two periods of time: one in the future when history records Caesar's successes (*fata ... erunt ... dulcia quom ... Romanae pars eris historiae)*, and one in the very-near-future when Julius Caesar returns to Rome and bestows his prizes upon the city (*postque tuum reditum ... legam*). It was common practice, as we know, to accompany gifts of spoils with an inscription to explain time, provenance, and of course the dedicator. Ovid makes this perfectly clear when he encourages his pupils in the *Ars Amatoria* to leave his name on their dedicated spoils, 2.744 and 3.812: *inscribat (inscribant) spoliis NASO MAGISTER ERAT*. More importantly, Augustus provides a very tangible example of the Roman practice of commemorating in inscriptional form the act of enriching the religious infrastructure at Rome when he records his own magnanimity in his own lengthy epitaph, the *Res Gestae*, meant to be read on bronze obelisks outside his tomb on the Campus Martius.[46]

I concur with Courtney: Gallus is making a distinct reference to reading inscriptions dedicated in temples throughout the city. Therefore this formulates an important elegiac reference to the act of leaving dedicatory inscriptions in Rome that predates the inscriptional passages in Horace and Virgil. To reinforce my presumption that Tibullus is borrowing from Gallus the idea of utilizing the dedicatory (or votive) inscription, there are verbal similarities in his poem to the language of Gallus: the word *fixa* appears in both, in a similar position – at the beginning of a pentameter line that bears structural similarities in both authors. Compare Gallus' *fixa legam spolieis deivitiora tueis* with Tibullus' 1.9.82: *fixa notet casus aurea palma meos*, and some intriguing parallels come to light. Each author follows *fixa* with the verb (Gallus uses the future that could be subjunctive; Tibullus uses the subjunctive); each author follows the verb with a noun that is modified by a possessive pronominal adjective at the end of the line (*spolieis tueis* and *casus meos*); between these noun-adjective pairings, each author then inserts a word that agrees with *fixa* syntactically: in Gallus' case *deivitiora* and *fixa* both modify *templa* that appears in the previous line, while in Tibullus' case the *aurea palma* is what *fixa* modifies. Moreover, the lines we have of Gallus' fragment repeat the future tense throughout (*erunt, eris, legam*), and in Tibullus the future tense dominates as well with an eventual lapse into the jussive subjunctive (*flebis, habebit, geret, iuvet, notet*).

Furthermore, Gallus' lines call attention to the fact that Julius Caesar is re-shaping the topographical and political landscape of Rome by means of the available paths of self-promotion, one of which involves saturating the city with evidence of his accumulated wealth. Tibullus, as much as a decade later, goes so far as to compose the votive inscription that he himself will offer to Venus, the particular protector of the Caesarian clan, on a golden palm that is also a symbolic token of military victory. Tibullus has therefore usurped the power of the dictator and has placed within his poem an indication of his own capability of cultivating divine power to suit his affairs. It is of course ironic that Tibullus applies all this effort merely to righting the wrongs done him by a lover, and all the more ironic that he imagines himself the victor when he admits that he will achieve his ends by being 'bound' by some other lover (79: *me vinctum*).[47] Tibullus is no Julius Caesar, but he will put his largesse to good use to achieve his ends. There may, in fact, be a subtle comment here on the questionable nature of gods that accept golden gifts in return for deeds that bring misery to many but success to the man with an open purse.

Indeed, there is irony in the type of gift that Tibullus dedicates to Venus. Given that the poet makes the claim of poverty early in his work,[48] and given that he castigates his lovers in this and other poems for greed and a desire for gifts in return for love, it is odd that he gives to the goddess of love a token of gold, a payment of sorts, for her continued aid on his behalf.[49] What is the difference between 'paying' Venus to look favourably upon a lover (which thereby, one hopes, makes love's acquisition all the easier) and paying a person to bestow that love upon him? It seems that Tibullus has trapped himself in a seeming contradiction. The poet has come to a crossroads in his attitude towards love: the idealism of previous poems begins to transform to this more cynical view of love as something that can be manipulated. Thus if we allow this inscription, like the one in 1.3, to intrude real-world activities upon the fictional world of the poem, then the votive inscription imitates the processes that real Romans used to alter something in their lives, to authorize the decisions they make. This appeal to divine aid suggests a radical shift in the lover's state of mind: rather than suffer silently the tortures of a cruel or indifferent lover, the Tibullan *persona* desires to change the direction of his erotic pursuits towards easier targets – towards a person whose love is more easily obtained with the help of Venus and a modest purse. He can turn his back on Marathus and on Delia if they will continue to interfere with his new objective: peace – the theme of poem 10 and the final poem in the first book.

Lastly, the inscription in poem 1.9 serves to establish the link between Tibullus and Venus, a relationship that reflects the traditional association between poets and gods. Others have already demonstrated the extent to which Hellenistic poets selectively evinced a pose of piety.[50] The Roman poets borrowed this pose effectively, referring to themselves often as *vates*, or prophets, singing the inspired words of gods. Cairns points out ways that Tibullus displays this quality also, such as praying to the rustic deities that govern his chosen environment (particularly in poem 1.1). Additionally, as we saw in 1.3, the poet carefully negotiates his position with Jupiter by pointing out the purity of his words and intentions. In several other places too Tibullus addresses Venus and makes her his ally in the cause of requited love.[51] So the inscription serves that purpose of concretizing the relationship between the poet and his divine protector.

At the same time, the poet's changed attitude is evident in the inscription, whereby he is willing to deal with the gods by the route available to everyday Romans, namely sacrifice and homage. Instead of claiming a special relationship with Venus based primarily on his role as her spokesperson, a craftsman of inspired words of love, he makes a simple and utterly mundane request from the goddess that she repay his devotion with a little bit of tasty revenge. With a few ounces of gold, so it seems, he cancels out all his lofty erotic pursuits, the very devotion of his poetic soul, in order to finally gain the upper hand and see Marathus unhappy. Similarly, in an earlier poem when he seems ready to say good-bye forever to Delia, he tells her that if she continues acting as she is, one day Venus will look down from heaven upon her, aged and alone, and bid her heavenly entourage to reflect on the way events turn out for those who revile love's call (1.6.83-4: *hanc Venus ex alto flentem sublimis Olympo / spectat et infidis quam sit acerba monet*).[52] Therefore when the poet ends his poetic relationships with his lovers, he does so by using the goddess as witness to the closure. The inscription in 1.9 mimetically reproduces the permanence and meaningful nature of real inscriptions that record transactions between mortals and gods, and provides an element of finality to the lover's decision to change his focus from love to peace in the ensuing poem.

Conclusion

The two inscriptions in Tibullus' poetry, one an epitaph, one a votive inscription, both reveal their author's engagement not only with Hellenistic sources but with the Roman elegiac movement situated as it was in the unique cultural environment at Rome. The epitaph in 1.3 indicates the poet's anxiety that the full compass of his service and experience receive notice. His last words, intended for his tomb, declare him a loyal (if reluctant) soldier who dutifully follows his commander and patron on land and sea. Tibullus thereby combines the poetic theme of love, abandonment and hopeful nostalgia – notable Greek and Hellenistic poetic themes – with the Roman notion of a course of honours that distinguishes the individual as a participant in the business of the *patria*. His epitaph is a reflection, I believe, of the Roman practice of making monuments a reminder of civic action and political involvement. Even in his Odyssean context on 'Phaeacia', the poet-lover does not forget to mark his tomb with the distinctions he has earned. He will not be like Catullus' unfortunate brother, buried among unfamiliar tombs.[53]

The votive inscription in 1.9 conveys the artist's exasperation not only with Marathus, the deceitful boy, but with love in general. His willingness to make a monetary transaction of sorts with Venus for her favour suggests that the poet-lover has come to understand the value of what he earlier deemed as love's corruption. The circumstances that have made the poet-lover suffer in every attempt to achieve his idealistic love affairs have brought him to the realization that he may actually fare better if he joins in the mundane practice of seeking petty (even mean-spirited) pleasures by coming to Venus not as her *vates* or her poetic servant, but as a man with money to spend. The votive inscription also evokes a Gallan reference to reading dedicatory inscriptions on temples that result from the victories of Julius Caesar. The purpose in referring to Gallus' lines, I have suggested, is that the poet is borrowing for his own petty purposes the grandiose activities of someone like Caesar. Gallus wrote of Caesar leaving his spoils throughout Rome's temples in return for victory and, ironically, the establishment of peace at war's end; Tibullus writes of leaving a token of victory as his final act in a succession of failed love-affairs, and just before he embarks on his new religion in poem 1.10 – one that values peace, *Pax*, above all else.

Tibullus was indeed a widely admired elegiac poet, and his stylistic influence is noticeable particularly in Ovid; many have discussed this. What has gone with relatively little comment all these years, however, is the fact that Tibullus added to the elegiac poem these passages that overtly cross over from the more remote and aesthetically pleasing sphere of the Alexandrians to evoke the everyday activities of Romans who looked to text as a means of leaving a record of their service, their piety and, as in Tibullus' case, their names.

4

Naso's Inscriptions

In the works of Ovid's elegiac predecessors, epigraphic moments inside a poem provide new avenues for interpretation. Some inscriptional passages, particularly those evoking or serving as epitaphs, provide the poets with the opportunity to reveal aspects of their own personal identification: as a member of a family (Catullus 68), as an Italian (Propertius 1.22), or as a soldier (Tibullus 1.3). Sometimes the epitaph is used to render presence and even permanence to a literary fiction. This was Propertius' response in his second book of elegies to Tibullus' rather forthright self-identification as a soldier and dedicated citizen in 1.3. Propertius, by contrast, remains in character as the injured lover even when he imagines his patron Maecenas coming to his grave in 2.1, and again in 2.13 when he imagines his obsequies overseen by Cynthia. The epigraphic qualities that the poets incorporate into their elegies, therefore, begin to disassociate from aspects of personal autobiography. Even Tibullus, whose first application of the quoted inscription was directed towards self-representation – the epitaph in 1.3 – creates a votive inscription in 1.9 that names him again, but is pertinent not to biographical concerns but to the thematic structure of his elegiac book, suggesting that the poet's attitude about love has altered.

Most of the passages we have considered to this point have been funereal: only Tibullus 1.9 and Propertius 4.2 and 4.3 incorporate other types of inscriptional text. Yet, as I have demonstrated, these other types are no less capable of cementing the attitudes of the poem – whether votive or dedicatory, these inscriptions harness the magical power of the written word in a way that readers would well have understood from their own experiences with inscribed texts.[1] In the following three chapters I will examine Ovid's use of the poetic inscription, for Ovid surpasses all his predecessors in the number and application of the inscribed verse: he creates not only epitaphs, votives and dedicatory inscriptions, but also triumphal *tituli* and graffiti – creating a total of eighteen inscriptions, although two are repeated in two places.[2] These types evoke a cultural context in the spirit of which the inscription must be analysed. We cannot doubt that Romans approached different types of inscriptions with different expectations and that they participated in a varying levels of reverence or celebration relative to the inscribed texts they observed. It was my original intention to divide Ovid's inscriptions into categories of type, but themes emerge from Ovid's inscriptional applications, and so I have chosen three to explore.

This chapter will discuss the ways in which Ovid repeatedly uses his own name in his inscriptions, exploiting the use of name that Tibullus so successfully applied in the very first elegiac inscriptions. This practice of naming himself draws inexorable lines of thought between the sentiments of the poem and some aspect of Ovid's creative process. In one instance, when Ovid writes his own epitaph while languishing in exile, we may note the return of elegiac, epitaphic self-representation that was perhaps less obvious in Propertius 1.22, but no less poignant. The fifth chapter will explore Ovid's concentrated use of the inscription in the *Heroides*, for seven inscriptional passages appear in those epistolary works, and patterns of characterization emerge that merit analysis. The sixth chapter will address Ovid's other literary inscriptions, particularly those that appear in his epic, the *Metamorphoses*, for I concur with those who see Ovid's epic as an extension of his elegiac pioneering. The aims of the epic inscriptions are closely related to the aims of those in the *Heroides*: they focus on female characterizations and make significant statements about the potential role of inscribed text as anathema to persistent grief and lack of power.

What's in a name?

Any time the male elegiac poet uses his own name, we must consider what the poet may communicate in the space between the fictionalized elegiac world and the world in which the poet lives and draws his inspiration. Indeed, as Barbara Boyd points out, 'Ovid creates a close identification with the narrator-poet who carries his name ... [Thus] the dominant plot of the *Amores* is to carve out a distinctive role for himself in the Roman poetic tradition' (Boyd 1997, 165). Two inscriptions in the *Amores* allow for a convergence between the fictional construct of the poetic narrative and 'real' expressions of hope and purpose from characters within the poem, and, by extension, their creator. In the *Ars Amatoria* Ovid also names himself '*magister*' in the triumphal inscriptions he demands of his pupils at the end of each of the two lessons in his erotodidactic work. It is a daring move for it inextricably links Ovid the author to the provocative material he has created, and it emphasizes an added level of personal responsibility for all that the lessons contain. Furthermore, the precise repetition of the inscription and the inscriptions' triumphal context brings to the fore issues of audience and raises the possibility of a humorous scenario in which the self-proclaimed *magister* is laughing in his sleeve at his readers. Lastly, Ovid writes his own epitaph in the *Tristia*: the context of the inscription and its tone clearly demonstrate the poetic manipulation of inscribed text to formulate a monument of words and to render textual permanence amidst the fleeting fictions of a poetic world.

Both of the relevant passages in the *Amores* are votive inscriptions. As we know, there were many ways in which text was used for religious purposes: '[such] dedications were inscribed, prayers were recited from book-rolls, complex magical spells circulated in written form' (Harris 1989, 218), and of course votive inscriptions were left by the thousands at cult sites across the Roman empire. I argue that by insinuating the pragmatic and realistic functions of seeking divine aid, via inscriptions, into his poetic world, Ovid provides the reader with familiar, iconic modes of authorization. There are no authorities like the gods; and the elegiac poet frequently capitalizes on a pose of religious piety to sanction his works, receiving and putting into writing the voice and will of a divine power. As we saw in Tibullus 1.9, the presence of the votive inscription not only validates the lover's altered attitude towards Marathus, but also suggests an alteration in the poet's attitude towards Love in general: a shift that becomes clear in the re-articulation of the lover's 'religion' in the ensuing, last poem of the collection. In *Amores* 1.11 and 2.13 the *amator* of the *Amores* prays and leaves votive offerings that potentially extend beyond the narrative's sealed environment in which problems float away at the stroke of the poet's pen. The suggestion that 'Naso' depends as much on divine providence as his readers – that the inexplicable and unsolvable dilemmas that befall the human condition are his too – allows the reader to identify more closely with him.

FIDAS SIBI NASO MINISTRAS

In *Amores* 1.11, we see the attempts of the *amator* to foster written correspondence between himself and Corinna; specifically he wants a hand-written invitation to her bedchamber. He solicits the aid of Corinna's hairdresser, Nape, to help him convey his messages. He demands that she pressure her mistress to write back as soon as possible. In the closing verses, he writes that if the tablets come back with one precious word – the imperative '*veni*' (24) – he will wrap his tablets with laurel and offer them at Venus' shrine, along with the inscription (1.11.27-8):

> subscribam VENERI FIDAS SIBI NASO MINISTRAS
> DEDICAT, AT NUPER VILE FUISTIS ACER.

> I will inscribe, 'Naso dedicates to Venus you servants faithful to himself that were, but recently, merely maple-wood.'

Am. 1.11 appears as a diptych with poem 1.12,[3] and the situation that the latter poem relates does not match the *amator*'s hopeful fantasy (*veni!*). Instead of being invited to share Corinna's bed, he receives the reply that his lover is not available, 1.12.1-2: *tristes rediere tabellae / infelix hodie littera posse negat* ('my sad tablets have returned, and the unhappy message upon them says that today a meeting is not possible'). After receiving this message, he flies into a rage and throws his tablets onto the crossroads to be crushed under some wagon's wheels (13-14: *proiectae triviis iaceatis, inutile lignum, / vosque rotae frangat praetereuntis onus*). He then goes on to imagine that the maple-tree from which the tablet was fashioned must have served as a site of a lynching, must have been cut to enable a crucifixion, and must have once shaded birds of ill-omen: owls and vultures (17-20). The lofty praises in 1.11 turn to revulsion; the laurels of 1.11 and the thought of using the tablets as a votive offering are forgotten.

The votive inscription in *Am.* 1.11 that Ovid's lover presents at the shrine of Venus is imagined, anticipating the favourable reply that Corinna might, but does not, send. Ovid names his *amator* (and himself) in an inscriptional verse, and he places the name, 'Naso', among the words 'ministers faithful to himself'. The lover's identification is incorporated within the instrument of his success: these 'faithful ministers' here refer to writing tablets within the specific situation of poem 1.11. When we consider Ovid as poet of the *Amores*, we remember that writing implements are the medium by which his fame is secured, and his lasting memory assured.

Indeed, Ovid has a history of personifying not just his letter-tablets, but also his books and their component epistolary parts, even granting them the agency to represent their author.[4] The humble epigram that begins the condensed edition of the *Amores*, the *epigramma ipsius*, is one such example of the author's use of his texts to mediate between himself and his audience.[5] Much as a playwright in Roman theatre allowed his characters to curry praise and applause for the author 'behind the scenes', Ovid's epigram humorously defends the text's new appearance:

> Qui modo Nasonis fueramus quinque libelli,
> tres sumus; hoc illi praetulit auctor opus.
> ut iam nulla tibi nos sit legisse voluptas,
> at levior demptis poena duobus erit.

We of Naso, who recently had been five books, are now three; the author has preferred this arrangement to that one. Granted, you may have had no desire to read us before, but with two books removed the penalty is easier to bear.

The five *libelli* that have been reconfigured as three call themselves *Nasonis*, 'Ovid's', and they compliantly refer to their author who prefers this new arrangement of poems. The power of the author, as this epigram makes clear, applies not only to the production of verse, but to its arrangement as well. Ovid's craft and involvement in the publication process receive emphasis here as he sanctions his texts and promotes himself.

The votive inscription in *Am.* 1.11 likewise illustrates an interdependency between poet and text, lover and tablets: and what grand tablets they are made to be. The laurels with which he adorns his 'conquering tablets' (25: *victrices tabellas*) explicitly show that the power of words is equivocal to or greater than the power of the sword. The overarching theme of *militia amoris* in elegy tends to borrow from the military sphere in articulating its successes, as the first two poems of the *Amores* amply demonstrate.[6] Thus Ovid's 'crowning' of his books in laurel, the leaf used to crown the triumphant general in processions, indicates the extent to which he associates his seductive victories with martial victories, and the agents of his will, his *generals* so to speak, with his writings. In the centre of this verbal arrangement sits '*NASO*', the governing, imperial presence of the author whose hand has made it all possible.

The other words in the inscription deserve comment too, for each word is literally loaded with ironic significance. The word *ministra* can implicitly refer to a maidservant as well as to the tablets. As we do recognize, there is another important character in the dramatic pairing of these poems: Nape, Corinna's hairdresser, and Ovid's secret agent. Ovid paints quite a picture of her capability and her willingness to serve his needs (*Am.* 1.11.1-14):

> Colligere incertos et in ordine ponere crines
> docta neque ancillas inter habenda Nape
> inque ministeriis furtivae cognita noctis
> utilis et dandis ingeniosa notis,
> saepe venire ad me dubitantem hortata Corinnam,
> saepe laboranti fida reperta mihi,
> accipe et ad dominam peraratas mane tabellas
> perfer et obstantes sedula pelle moras.
> nec silicum venae nec durum in pectore ferrum
> nec tibi simplicitas ordine maior adest;
> credibile est et te sensisse Cupidinis arcus:
> in me militiae signa tuere tuae.
> si quaeret quid agam, spe noctis vivere dices;
> certera fert blanda cera notata manu.

Oh Nape, tamer and arranger of unruly hair, best of slave-girls, learned and useful in the duties of the furtive night and clever at passing along missives, often have you urged my fainthearted Corinna to come to me, often have you proven yourself true to me in my distress; accept these inscribed tablets and take them to your mistress in the morning, and industriously block all hindering delays. Your veins are not made of stone, nor your breast of iron, nor are you simple-minded, at least no more than your station warrants. I believe you yourself have been on the receiving end of Cupid's bow: in looking out for me you protect the standards of your own campaign. If she asks what I am up to, you will say that I live in hope of a single night; the wax inscribed by my flattering hand takes care of the rest.

Despite the fact that most of the narrative of 1.11 is dedicated to the lover's instructions to Nape (Ovid develops her character as experienced and capable), the praise and laurels rendered go to the poet's own handiwork – his 'conquering tablets'. Thus the use of *ministrae* in the inscription, referring to the tablets, pointedly marks the absence of any credit given to Nape. As we know, slaves typically made up the invisible work force that sustained the Roman economy. Credit due to their efforts was rarely given, and even within households where male slaves occasionally had the opportunity to serve men of high rank as scribes or tutors, the precise nature of their duty, or the extent to which they competently exercised their duties, receives mention only rarely: Cicero's praise of and concern for Tiro is surely the exception, and not the typical case.[7]

Slave-girls, in particular, receive almost no mention among writers of history or treatises. Stock characters in comedies, slave-girls are commonly the love interests of freeborn young men, and these young women usually end up being freeborn themselves, their identities humorously having been lost or confused at a younger age. A much more realistic and brutal portrayal of the lot of a slave-girl's existence is found in the pair of poems *Am.* 2.7 and 2.8. Here the *amator* speaks of a relationship ('affair') between himself and Corinna's hairdresser, Cypassis. As Sharon James (1997) has shown, the relationship was one rooted primarily in the total subordination intrinsic to Roman slavery and the total availability and exploitability of a slave's body, and was, therefore, not an affair but rape. James discusses at length the silence of the slave, for that silence allows the lover to have unimpeded access to her (1997, 72). She adds, in the case of another slave-girl who appears at *Ars* 1.358-91, that the slave's silence 'is to be only partial, for she is also to be required to tell the lover of her mistress' doings. Thus the *praeceptor*'s advice [to his male audience] is that the lover coerce her into both silence and speech, always to serve his own interests' (1997, 73).

Although there is little support for the claim that the *amator* uses Nape in 1.11 in the same fashion as he does Cypassis in 2.8, nevertheless the descriptions of the two slaves in the two poems have strong similarities.[8] For example, the lover's opportunistic exploitation of the slave, as messenger or sexual tool, requires him to identify her virtues, at least those pertinent to her utility. Compare 1.11.4: *utilis et dandis ingeniosa notis*, and 2.8.4: *apta quidem dominae sed magis apta mihi*. Nape is 'useful' and 'talented' (and at 1.11.2 she is 'learned'); Cypassis is emphatically called 'suitable', for both her mistress' demands and his own. An important component of their virtue is that they show loyalty towards the *amator*, and here a key distinction emerges between them: Nape has demonstrated that loyalty (1.11.6: *fida*), but Cypassis in 2.8 has not. Her failure lies not in the fact that she has spoken against the *amator*, but that she blushed when accused by her mistress of bedding her lover (2.8.16: *vidi te totis erubuisse genis*). The *amator* expects such self-control in a slave who is 'well-versed' merely in 'furtive pleasure' (2.8.3). Half a century later, however, the younger Seneca explains that to control a blush is an impossible task even for well-versed public speakers.[9] The expectations of the female slave are intriguingly similar to those on the lover's tablets in 1.11 – that they represent him faithfully and that they bring him sexual success; yet the tablets are granted greater appreciation and privilege than the slave.

In *Am.* 1.11 Nape is commanded to speak for the poet, using only his own words of course (13: *dices* 'you will say'; 15: *dum loquor* 'while I speak'; 19: *iubeto* 'you must order (Corinna)'. In addition, her duties include closely watching her mistress for signs of pleasure or consternation that she can report back to the *amator* (17-24):

aspicias oculos mando frontemque legentis:
  et tacito vultu scire futura licet.
nec mora, perlectis rescribat multa iubeto:
  odi, cum late splendida cera vacat.
comprimat ordinibus versus, oculosque moretur
  margine in extremo littera rasa meos.
quid digitos opus est graphio lassare tenendo?
  hoc habeat scriptum tota tabella, 'veni'.

Make sure that you watch her eyes and forehead as she reads my message: it is possible to know what will happen by reading even a calm expression. Without delay, once she has read it thoroughly, order her to write back in volume: I hate it when the plain of wax lies empty and untouched. Make sure she writes in a small, orderly fashion so that my eyes are made to wander all the way to the edges of the tablet. But why should her fingers be made weary by too much writing? Let the whole tablet hold only this word: *Come*!

Nape is expected to be not only a messenger, but an interpreter of body language and a stand-in for the *amator* himself, explaining the poet's love to Corinna and directing her as she writes her reply. Even though the lover makes it plain in line 14 that his 'message will take care of the rest', it is clear that Nape is still required to make Corinna's reply fitting for the occasion: the logistics of wording and writing style are the responsibility of the *ministra*. Yet, when the time comes for praises and honours, all is given to the tablets. The slave-girl is made silent – speaking only the words that the poet tells her to say – and invisible because her actions are given no merit in the poet-lover's anticipation of his own success. Thus he makes the entire episode that has not yet occurred a conquest of his own making, with himself and his tablets in the centre of the triumph; meanwhile Nape recedes entirely into the background where she, like all slaves, quietly waits for her next assignment.[10] The invisibility and absence of Nape in the inscription of 1.11, and the total self-absorption of the lover with his literary handiwork receives full complement in the equally noticeable absence and silence of Corinna in 1.12. When the poem begins, the lover receives his tablets back bearing a message that Ovid reports to us in indirect speech (2: *infelix hodie littera posse negat*). Rather than provide, verbatim, Corinna's answer, Ovid silences the elegiac mistress.

The rest of the poem portrays the lover's anger at his tablets. Throughout his tirade he expresses no sentiment of either satisfaction or dissatisfaction with his mistress over her negative response: she receives no comment of any kind. This is so despite the fact that in other poems, lovers are wont to denigrate their mistresses for valuing money and security over the eternal fame of their poet-lover's verses.[11] Corinna is simply ignored when her hand commits to wax a negative reply to a poet's invitations. Since all is written by the poet, there is no sense in attributing to her hand any authoritative textual document; even the given quote '*veni*' in *Am.* 1.11 appears as a word that he would have her produce, not her own words; it bears no reality. The absence of Corinna, the love-object, in the rant of 1.12 occurs also in many places of the *Amores*, a situation that has inspired much previous scholarship to examine the sparse nature of the Woman's role in elegiac poetry.[12]

The love affair, it seems, is not really with Corinna, but with the tablets and thus with the poet's own creation. The text that Naso creates is truly his faithful servant, and its failure to bring him what he desires, namely a night of sex, causes him to lose his temper, an episode that reveals the power that he has invested in his writing. The narcissistic nature of the lover's relationship with his writing makes its failure all the more monstrous (to him), for what power does he wield if he cannot persuade through writing a weak and silent woman to do his bidding?

The placement of such high value upon and trust in the lover's tablets plays out also in a phrase in the inscription created in 1.11. The lover describes his tablets as *nuper vile acer*, 'but recently common maple-wood'. The use of *nuper* suggests a transformation, but to what? The obvious answer is that, as a votive offering, the tablets have been transformed from utilitarian tool into something profoundly divine and appropriate as a gift to Venus. But what makes them appropriate as a gift to Venus is what is written upon them. We may recall that Ovid makes no mention of the mistress erasing the tablets when she composes her 'hasty' reply (19: *nec mora*), but simply that he hates to see an empty page (20: *odi, cum late splendida cera vacat*). As we know, the *tabella* was a two-paged document, something that Ovid makes clear in 1.12.27 when he refers to them as *duplices*, a word that intrinsically puns on their two-faced duplicity as well.[13] Therefore, it is plausible that the lover sent her his tablets with one side blank, intending for her to write there – hoping at first for many words, but then hoping only for '*veni*'. The lover would have been placing an entire text at Venus' shrine, one that included not only the wanted response ('*veni*'), but the well-crafted letter that coaxed from Corinna such an answer. It is therefore the lover's text, and Ovid's poetry, that is the worthy offering to a god; the common wooden tablets have been transformed to a persuasive text worthy of preservation. Ovid pays his writing the ultimate compliment as he depicts the overeager hopes of his *amator*.

The placement of Ovid's own name, *Naso*, within the inscription merits further comment. Although Ovid and his *amator* can be seen as two separate entities that exist outside and inside the poems respectively, the use of *Naso* in the inscription suggests a conflation of these identities since both depend on the tablets, on the text, for their personal success and glory. Elizabeth Meyer's article about the significance of the *tabella* in Roman literature (Meyer 2001), discusses Propertius 3.23 in which the lover has lost his tablets and tortures himself thinking about the various responses that Cynthia might have sent him on their waxen pages. He calls the tablets *doctae* (1) and *fideles* (9), and sorely laments their loss, despite the fact that they were of little monetary value, being made of cheap wax on common boxwood (8: *vulgari buxo sordida cera fuit*). To get them back he sends his slave to mount another tablet on a column in a public location asking for them to be returned to his Esquiline address (24: *et dominum Esquiliis scribe habitare tuum*). The message is representative of a category of inscriptions that defy precise labelling: those thousands of notices placed by groups or individuals on the public 'message boards' of Roman cities and towns.

Meyer's idea of the *tabella* as a sidekick-facilitator of the *amator*, and its messages as representations of the persons who write them, is constructive here.[14] Without his tablets, the lover in Propertius 3.23 cannot know his lover's thoughts and desires. The loss leaves him desperate to reconnect with Cynthia in the medium that best represents him – his written words on his favourite tablets.[15] As for Ovid's lover in *Am.* 1.11, with his tablets as yet unsent, or on their way to his mistress, he can only hope that the answer he gets will be what he desires. Even with a slave-girl working for him, the lover pins his hopes on the power of his words and the medium of his text. The phrase *fidas sibi Naso ministras* that he dedicates to his tutelary goddess explicitly links the process of writing to the shared identity of the poet and the lover – both of them aiming to impress their audience. The placement of Ovid's *cognomen* within an inscription finds intriguing correspondence with another poem in the *Amores*.

SERVATA NASO CORINNA

Amores 2.13 and 2.14 operate together to consider the implications of abortion.[16] In the first poem we find the *amator* in a profound state of anxiety because his beloved Corinna is near death (2: *in dubio vitae*); she has self-induced an abortion by unknown means (1: *dum labefactat onus gravidi temeraria ventris*) and without his knowledge (3: *clam me*). After deciding that fear overrides his anger (4: *sed cadit ira metu*), he prays to

Egyptian deities for several lines before returning to his own anxiety in lines 15-16: *huc adhibe vultus et in una parce duobus: / nam vitam dominae tu dabis, illa mihi*, 'spare her please, for you will give life to my mistress, and she will give life to me'. That last phrase, the dramatic mid-point of the poem, establishes a radical interdependence between the life of Corinna and the life of the *amator*. Certainly the *amator* does depend on her: Corinna is the object of his love and the justification for his literary existence; she gives him purpose and a place among erotic elegists. The lover's anxiety in the poem is not purely an altruistic concern for the health and happiness of a woman – rather it is a reflection of his own concern that he will lose his position as lover in an elegiac world.

He addresses Ilithyia, the goddess of childbirth and the protector of parturient mothers, and vows that if she grants favour to his prayers, he will make an offering (24: *ipse feram ante tuos munera vota pedes*), and he will inscribe these words, 2.14.25: *adiciam titulum SERVATA NASO CORINNA*, 'Naso – for Corinna saved'. As Mary-Kay Gamel has demonstrated, the inscription establishes an interdependence between the lover and his mistress. Gamel highlights the placement of Naso nestled between the words *SERVATA* and *CORINNA*, and explains the significance of the dependency: '[there is an implicit] comparison between the *amator* and the foetus ... ; the inscription can be read with the *amator* inside Corinna like the foetus and similarly dependent on her' (Gamel 1989, 192).

Indeed, the arrangement of words is compelling, for by placing his own name within the inscription Ovid also represents his own poetic interest in the wellbeing of the elegiac mistress and thereby his work. Every elegiac *puella* or mistress is, for the most part, a useful fiction; modern Classical scholarship has been precise in establishing this,[17] and Corinna's fictionality has indeed been the easiest to establish.[18] It is the fictional mistress who truly inhabits the elegiac world; she is the antagonist in many and various scenarios that meet the criteria of the elegiac *topos*, and it is through her interaction with the lover in the poems that the reader judges the skill of the poet and determines his fame.

As mentioned in Chapter 2, Propertius juxtaposes his own name with his *puella*, Cynthia at 2.34.93-4: *Cynthia *quin etiam* versu laudata Properti, hos inter si me ponere Fama volet*, 'surely renowned Cynthia will live in the songs of Propertius, if Fame will see fit to place me among these eminent poets.' The placement of Cynthia and Propertius on opposite sides of the verse emphasize their link to each other. The genitive form of Propertius' name draws attention not to the man himself, but to his works. It is in and through his renowned (*laudata*) mistress that much of his fame resides, so long as Cynthia resides and lives in the poetic world he has created. It is true that Corinna does not hold the same power in Ovid's poetry as Cynthia did in that of Propertius, but she plays a very large part in the first and second books of the *Amores* in establishing a necessary link between Ovid's elegies and their precedents (namely Tibullus and Propertius).[19] Corinna is necessary within the *Amores* to place Ovid's *Amores* within a recognizable *genre*. The revolutionary nature of Ovid's elegiac talent would eventually, as Jim McKeown notes, 'push Corinna still further from the limelight' (McKeown 1987, 22). Indeed, Ovid diminishes her role dramatically and still remains in the elegiac mode, always reinventing the *genre*; but having once made Corinna his *domina*, albeit as late as the fifth poem of his collection, her name is forever linked with his own.[20] Thus, the drama that surrounds Corinna's necessary survival in 2.13 can also represent the need of the poet to preserve Corinna, and thereby the literary world he has created that includes her.

Gamel's interpretation is that the theme of abortion in poems 2.13 and 2.14 allows the lover to express his insecurities about the lack of power he has over his female partner in the game of love: 'In this reading, the *amator*'s commands, prayers and promises, his attempts to keep the focus on himself, reflect not confidence but insecurity, anxiety, awareness of his lack of power. He has no control over the powerful female he invokes' (Gamel 1989, 193). Additionally, I suggest, the abortion theme and the strategically formulated inscription in 2.13 serve to express the poet's insecurities and anxieties about the lasting presence of his poetry in an atmosphere that grows increasingly antithetical to the independence of the elegiac voice. Just as the lover expresses concern *within* the poem about the increasing dangers concomitant to destroying biological foetuses, Ovid, I suggest, expresses concern *outside* the poem about the dangers to the literary foetus, the poetry that is the 'child' of its author. Indeed, at *Tristia* 1.1.114 Ovid even calls the offending books of the *Ars Amatoria* parricides (*Oedipodas facito Telegonosque voces*), referring of course to Oedipus who killed his father Laertes, and to Telegonus, the son of Ulysses who killed him according to some versions of the ancient tale. Like children, poems have the capacity to do their 'father' both harm and benefit. Yet the context of this comment suggests that it is the atmosphere in which Ovid's works have arisen that condemns him, rather than the works themselves, as he points out painstakingly in his long *apologia* in *Tristia* 2.

Although the precise dating of Ovid's *Amores*, particularly the second edition, is no easy task, dates as late as 7 BC have been put forward, leaving ample room for reaction within the collection to Augustan legislation regarding adultery and marriage, the first part of which was issued in 18 BC.[21] After all, legislation that threatened the lover's status had already resonated deeply in Propertius' poems, completed nearly a decade earlier than Ovid's first edition. For example, Propertius speaks plainly of a law that briefly threatened to divide his lover from Cynthia, 2.7.1-3: *gavisa es[t] certe sublatam, Cynthia, legem, / qua quondam edicta flemus uterque diu, / ni nos divideret*, 'surely you rejoiced, Cynthia, that the law was repealed which, when it was passed, set us both to long bouts of weeping that it would separate us.' That particular law in question is not the Augustan marital legislation of 18 BC, but a law imposing taxes on bachelors in 32 BC to raise money for the ensuing naval battle at Actium, repealed in 28.[22] Yet Propertius may refer to the Julian laws on adultery in his final poem, Cornelia's eulogy, when he has her explain (4.11.41-2): *me neque censurae legem mollisse neque ulla / labe mea nostros erubuisse focos*, 'I never did injury to censorial dictates, nor did I ever make my ancestral fires blush because of any wrongdoing of mine.' If this poem was written, as most scholars believe, in 16 BC, then these 'censorial dictates' may refer to the laws Augustus authored as tribune of the plebs in 18 BC, mentioned in *Res Gestae* 6: *ut curator legum et morum summa potestate solus crearer*.[23] As we all assume, it was precisely Augustus' views on the character of Ovid's *Ars Amatoria* that resulted in his exile in AD 8. Therefore the anxiety of the lover fretting over societal conditions that drive young women to injure themselves and their offspring can also be seen, I suggest, as a poet's concern over what his society is doing to the (pro)creative effort of poets like himself whose works require experimentation and freedom of the artistic voice. Thus Ovid associates his name's survival with the safety of Corinna, and thereby the safety of his poetic world.

There is further evidence of this suggestion in poem 2.14. The lover, still upset at Corinna for having induced an abortion, lists many mothers of heroes who, had they been as reckless as she, would have erased the heroic deeds and achievements their offspring could perform: Thetis, mother of Achilles; Ilia, mother of Romulus; and Venus, mother of Aeneas (2.14.9-18):

si mos antiquis placuisset matribus idem,
  gens hominum vitio deperitura fuit,
quique iterum iaceret generis primordia nostri
  in vacuo lapides orbe, parandus erat.
quis Priami fregisset opes, si numen aquarum
  iusta recusasset pondera ferre Thetis?
Ilia si tumido geminos in ventre necasset,
  casurus dominae conditor Urbis erat;
si Venus Aenean gravida temerasset in alvo,
  Caesaribus tellus orba futura fuit.

If mothers of old had chosen the same practice, the race of men would long ago have perished because of their shortsightedness, and those conceived to provide the beginnings of our race would lie, repeatedly, as stones in an empty earth. Who would have shattered the riches of Priam, if right-minded Thetis had thought it right to alleviate the weight of her womb? And Rhea Silvia, if she had slain the twins in her ponderous belly, would have cut to the quick the very founder of our mistress Rome; and if Venus had defiled the heaviness in her womb, the lands would miss their Caesars.

Gamel examines this poem also, and poses the possibility that such a list dares the reader to imagine a world where such destructive and brutal personalities had not existed: '[would] the world have been so much worse off without them and their violent accomplishments?' (Gamel 1989, 198). Gamel's insight is defensible (although one must always consider whether a Roman would see 'violence' in the same negative light as we moderns do), but given what we know about the tendency for Ovid to focus so much attention on the fruit of his labours, his *fama*, this analysis demands further consideration.

Ovid's list includes the great heroes of Greek and Roman epic, and therefore also considers the narratives constructed around these noble heroes: the *Iliad*, the *Annales* of Ennius and Virgil's *Aeneid*, among others. Not only are the heroes' lives in danger, but so are their stories. With such abortive, destructive powers as that which Corinna has applied, what narratives would be left to write? The attack on poetic subjects suggests an attack on poetry, and if heroes like Achilles and Romulus could not have survived such erasures, how will Ovid's *amator* fare? The dependency of the lover on Corinna, as shown in 2.13, is reflective of the poet's dependency on a dominant, cultural *ethos* that determines the viability of poetic expression. If the censorious force of Augustus' moral reforms is applied without distinction, too rashly, and all poetic subjects are deemed inappropriate, then all poets – even Homer and Virgil – become suspect.

This is precisely Ovid's assessment when he writes defensively in *Tristia* 2 about the intrinsic problem with deeming poetry the equivalent of personal beliefs and private behaviour. Criticism of his *Ars Amatoria*, he admits, is justified *per se* (2.241-2: *illa quidem fateor frontis non esse severae / scripta, nec a tanto principe digna legi*), but should not extend to punishment of the author; otherwise, what poet would be safe from penalty? He lists a plethora of works, most notably among them the *Iliad*, the *Odyssey*, the *Annales* and the *Aeneid*, whose themes enter also into erotic and adulterous territory (*Trist.* 2.371-80, 423-4 and 533-6):

> Ilias ipsa quid est aliud, nisi adultera, de qua
>   inter amatorem pugna virumque fuit?
> quid prius est illi flamma Briseidos, utque
>   fecerit iratos rapta puella duces?
> aut quid Odyssea est, nisi femina propter amorem,
>   dum vir abest, multis una petita procis?
> quis, nisi Maeonides, Venerem Martemque ligatos
>   narrat in obsceno corpora prensa toro?
> unde nisi indicio magni sciremus Homeri
>   hospitis igne duas incaluisse deas?
> ...
> utque suo Martem cecinit gravis Ennius ore,
>   Ennius ingenio maximus, arte rudis:
> ...

> et tamen ille tuae felix Aeneidos auctor
> contulit in Tyrios arma virumque toros,
> nec legitur pars ulla magis de corpore toto,
> quam non legitimo foedere iunctus amor.

> What else is the *Iliad* except a tale of adultery and a fight between a lover and a husband? More than that, what about the passion for Briseis, a war-captive that caused a war between allied commanders? Or what is the *Odyssey* except the hot pursuit of a woman by many suitors while her husband is away? Who except the Lydian bard tells us about Venus and Mars in a snare, bodies pressed together, in their adulterous bed? How would we know, except by the poem of Homer, that Calypso and Circe burned with passion for their guest Odysseus ... By the same token, earnest Ennius sang in his poem of Mars – poor Ennius, great-hearted in his attempt but in technique, hardly capable ... And yet that blessed author of your *Aeneid* laid out his 'arms and a man' on a Carthaginian couch; no part of the poem is read more frequently than that love forged in illicit intercourse.

Ovid's ironic dialogue with Augustus' censorious dictates, and in reaction to his absurd reductions that follow from too wide an application of such sensitivity to art has greater effect when we see *Amores* 2.14, written two decades beforehand, as a blind prediction of this situation. Ovid's words remind us that the poet must have licence to cross the boundaries of social custom, or else the opportunity to explore the depths of human experience is lost. Poets and writers may take liberties with the truth, but it is better, Ovid implies, to have lying texts (or images) than repressed dreams, silenced voices and fanatical ideologies. *Amores* 2.13 and 14 form a theme of anxiety regarding the safety of any poetic legacy in autocratic times. The poems constitute both a consideration of the unfortunate practice of abortion that must have been well known to urbane Romans, and an expression of anxiety over the fate of poetic freedom and experimentation that lead to artistic legacy. In light of Augustus' unique position as political, cultural and moral arbiter, the anxiety here expressed is not without justification. The placement of the votive inscription in 2.13 establishes a correlation between the danger of losing characters within the poem and the danger of losing poetry itself.

The position of Naso in 2.13, embedded within a safe Corinna and, ultimately, within his poetry preserved, correlates to the position of Naso in 1.11, placed emphatically beside the instruments of his art, the secrets of his success as a lover and a poet. Just like the lover in Ovid's *Amores* who, without Corinna and without the cooperation of his writing tablets, loses his purpose, Ovid, without the fiction of the elegiac world and without the texts that convey his words to the public, loses his voice and his *fama*.

These votive inscriptions, because of the way they evoke permanence in the real world, serve the specific purposes of the *amator* within the poem, but also reflect Ovid's position as a Roman poet reliant on written works and a literary world to serve as his memorial. Interestingly, in each of these cases, Ovid also suggests that women are partners in the completion and preservation of text. Nape is the crucial messenger in 1.11, and Corinna is the one whose life must be saved in 2.13. Corinna's figurative womb in 2.14, which I interpret to mean the cultural crucible in which all literary effort is sustained, suggests a creative process that must include, not exclude, a feminine element: that must harness women's procreative powers to achieve a continuous literary development. The masculine traditions of Rome are antithetical to the aims of the elegiac poet, who seeks to alter, at the very least to mollify, some of the harsher and more rigid aspects of the Roman social structure. Ovid, like his elegiac brethren, infuses a femininity into his literary fiction that also has implications upon his own self-determined paths of career and success. Therefore Ovid's decision to memorialize himself and his poetic characters in relation to the divine sphere by 'posting' these votive inscriptions that include his name – seeking, in effect, divine sanction of his artistry – suggests the strength of Ovid's conviction that he was indeed providing something worthy of preservation.

The spoils of victory

Ovid's manipulation of triumphal imagery provides another intersection of cultural and poetic inter-play. In *Amores* 1.2.19-51 the *amator* conjures a triumph to illustrate the power that Cupid has over him. He points out that he is the *praeda* or booty of Cupid, and that his overwhelming force has chained the poet's hands to the authority of his 'jurisdiction'.[24] Again, in 1.7, the lover chides himself for striking Corinna, making ridiculous his conquest over a helpless girl by imagining the pathetic nature of a single, dishevelled woman in a Roman triumph. Many scholars have contributed to the debate as to what the triumphal imagery is meant to signify. The predominant view is neatly summarized in McKeown's assessment: 'In transferring the triumph to a personal erotic context, whether with Cupid as the *triumphator* or, as in 2.12, claiming a triumph for himself in celebration of his success as a lover, Ovid is using the grandeur of an important Augustan institution to throw into humorous relief the representation of his own *vita ignobilis*. His purpose in doing so is simply to amuse, and his naively irreverent humor should not be considered to be an expression of antipathy to the regime' (McKeown 1989, 33).

Perhaps not total antipathy to the regime, but I must concur with others who wish to see more than 'naively irreverent humor' at work here.[25] The uniqueness and pre-eminence of the honour bestowed in triumphal display make it a significant cultural phenomenon. That Ovid co-opts it for his own sphere of operation suggests an attempt to subvert the culturally iconic display to one that can bear multiple metaphorical associations. Domination, subjugation, pursuit, rivalry and spoils are all as potentially present in the realm of seduction as they are undoubtedly present in the martial sphere.[26] Ovid's use of the triumphal scene in the erotic context suggests that the shackles of the loser (1.2.30: *et nova captiva vincula mente feram*) can be pleasantly endured. Moreover, the chariot of the triumphant general can be seen to represent a hyperbolic manifestation of power. The use of triumphal imagery to advertise the concomitant joys of being dominated is at play with the overt relationship of triumph to Roman hegemony; Ovid suggests that it can be more fun to lose than to win. Ovid's poetic triumphs infuse arbitrariness into a cultural performance of victory, translating an ancient ritual of patriotism into a poetic *topos* precisely at a time when Augustus was attempting to link the triumphal honour very closely to imperial legacy.[27]

I think it unlikely that Ovid pokes fun at the triumphs of Augustus' household *per se*, but I do not think it coincidence that he takes aim at an institution that was becoming increasingly exclusive.[28] If the exclusivity of triumph makes it one more indicator of the loss of personal agency, particularly aristocratic male agency, then Ovid's transformation of the triumph into something ambiguous demotes its significance. Emperors may bastardize the ritual into something conferred upon favourites rather than those who merit it, but poets can bastardize it as well into something parodic, even shameful, as in the case of poor Corinna paraded as a captive enemy in the lover's triumph in *Amores* 1.7. Most importantly, the poet can construe the triumphal procession as he sees fit. As we will see, the use of triumphal inscriptions in the *Ars Amatoria* plays very much on the ambiguous signifiers of the display that Ovid's treatment creates.

Mary Beard aptly identifies the 'complex choreography' of the triumphal procession and the images within it (Beard 2003, 24), and finds that the parade performs 'a whole series of mimetic strategies', written accounts of which 'repeatedly emphasize the modes of representation, the artifice and contrivance which constitute the ritual' (2003, 29). Many features of the procession markedly contribute to an atmosphere of irony and contrast: soldiers chant taunts and jokes at the expense of the triumphant general who appears dressed as a god, probably Jupiter himself;[29] enemy chieftains and soldiers are often displayed in their barbaric finery, savage and fearsome to behold, while there can be no doubt that they are the defeated who face death, depending on the will of the conqueror.[30] Even the very appearance of armed soldiers on the city's streets temporarily defies the ancient laws forbidding armies to enter within the *pomerium*, the sacred boundary of the city, yet we do not hear of the ritual causing concern among anxious lawmakers, or of the presence of so many armed men inspiring street-warfare.[31] Such potentially conflicting aspects leave room for interpretation of what the triumph represents: what it means for the person in the chariot, and for those on the ground.

Peter Holliday discusses the various means at one's disposal to convey meanings of triumphal scenes to the crowds, such as paintings and placards, but notes possible slippage: 'the distribution of codes necessary for the interpretation of triumphal paintings was unequal: some systems could have been known by most of the lower classes, whereas others would be discernible by only the most sophisticated of viewers' (Holliday 1997, 144). Thus inscriptions in triumphal contexts, *tituli*, serve the important purpose of marrying particular images to meanings that are relevant to the conqueror's claims. When text accompanies an image, the act of interpretation, the process of reception, is fixed firmly to distinct parameters of signification.[32] Holliday notes one further complication: 'The efficacy of *tituli*, however, presupposes a literate audience. The educated elite would discern their significance, and literate spectators who read the *tituli* aloud for their company would have been overheard by other viewers within earshot. Some *triumphatores* may have hired special attendants (*apparitores*) or claquers to read the passing inscriptions to the crowds' (1997, 146). Dismissing, to some extent, the problem of literacy, the profit derived from potentially transparent meaning makes the inscription in the triumphal context a useful tool in forming images into a narrative, or providing information that images cannot convey. For example, Julius Caesar's famous three-panelled inscription, '*Veni. Vidi. Vici.*', emphasized the speed and efficiency of his campaign at Pontus, and it clearly demarcated the sphere of responsibility for the victory as belonging to Caesar himself rather than to all Romans – the placards did not read '*Venimus*' or even '*Venistis*'.[33] The consular army as servant to and extension of the public will collapses in those three words under the sway of the all-powerful 'I', a prophetic pre-cursor to the imperial state and the breakdown of the traditional relationship between *senatus populusque Romanus* and the armies of Rome.

When no text is present, the viewer is free to interpret things as he wishes, and to publicly render his own conclusions as to an artwork's significance. There is the expectation that he will decipher, when possible, in accordance with his degree of sophistication and familiarity with the codes, but there is no guarantee that interpretations will approach the intentions of the images. We have no clearer demonstration of this than Ovid's own encouragement to his artful seducer within the *Ars* to liberally interpret whatever he sees in a triumphal parade for the benefit of the woman he is trying to impress (*Ars* 1.219-23, 227-8):[34]

> atque aliqua ex illis cum regum nomina quaeret,
>   quae loca, qui montes quaeve ferantur aquae,
> omnia responde, nec tantum si qua rogabit;
>   et quae nescieris, ut bene nota refer.
> hic est Euphrates, praecinctus harundine frontem;
> ...
> ille vel ille duces, et erunt quae nomina dicas,
>   si poteris, vere, si minus, apta tamen.

> And when some woman from the crowd asks for the names of kings, sites, mountains and rivers that are borne before the crowd, answer regarding everything, not only what she specifically inquires about; and if you are not certain about something, make as if you are: 'this is the Euphrates, girded about the forehead with a reedy crown ... the leaders included that guy and perhaps that guy', – and all that you say will be believed, so make it a true account if you can, but if not, make it good.

The art of interpretation is as much on display in this account as the array of artistic and patriotic images themselves. The poet's encouragement to his seducer to engage in free association serves also as dubious advice about how one learns to *read* the images.[35] Euphrates wears a reedy garland, he suggests in line 223, and in line 224 (not included in the passage above) he hints that the one with long blue hair (*cui coma dependet caerula, Tigris erit*) will be the Tigris River.[36] Ovid confidently asserts that no one will argue with him who boldly provides his interpretation. He even assures his reader that a false interpretation does little or no harm. One may become better, by degrees, at this art of interpreting objects, but the overall interpretive act is what will impress, not necessarily the specific elements of the interpretation provided. As John Clarke points out, 'the elite Romans valued the ability to make fanciful connections between what they saw and what the image could signify. For the elite viewer, the work of art was just a jumping-off point for a virtuoso display of rhetoric and erudition' (Clarke 2003, 10).[37] Triumphal, titular inscriptions close both lessons of the *Ars*; by diagnosing the interpretive openness and seductive potential of the triumphal parade, Ovid suggests in his closing triumphal lines that the seduction achieved in the *Ars* is duplicitous: it is a matter of interpretation. The variable, as I will show, is the one who has been seduced – the only fixed identification is the *praeceptor amoris*, the author and the *magister* in the inscription.

The *Ars* is essentially divided into two 'lessons', one directed to men, consisting of two books, and one directed to women, consisting of a single book. At the end of each lesson, Ovid invents a vague triumphal context in which his pupils (both male and female) can boast of their success over their amatory conquests, made possible, of course, by their adherence to his advice. He asks them to erect an inscription to commemorate the achievement; to the men he writes, 2.742-4:

> vincite muneribus, vicit ut ille, datis.
> sed quicumque meo superarit Amazona ferro,
> inscribat spoliis NASO MAGISTER ERAT.

> Win, like Achilles did, with the arms I have provided. But whosoever defeats the Amazon with my sword, let him inscribe this upon his spoils: NASO WAS MY TEACHER.

and to the women he writes, 3.811-12:

> ut quondam iuvenes, ita nunc, mea turba, puellae
>   inscribant spoliis NASO MAGISTER ERAT.

> Therefore now, as once I instructed the men, let the ladies, my followers, write upon their spoils: NASO WAS MY TEACHER.

The instruction to erect spoils accompanied by an inscription was a duty typically performed by the conquering general at the end of his triumphal procession.[38] It is likely that the inscription that accompanied the spoils, if one existed, would have made its way through the streets of Rome to be seen by the public before being enshrined in the Temple of Jupiter Optimus Maximus atop the Capitoline Hill.[39] Therefore the inscription accompanying the spoils was an important part of the narrative of conquest, identifying the general responsible for the victory, the place of the conflict, the peoples defeated and the legality of the display.[40]

In his commentary, Roy Gibson points out the rhetorical advantage of placing an inscription such as this at the end of the work, to serve as a 'sphragis', a word deriving from the Greek word for 'seal' or 'signet' by which a person lays claim to the authenticity of a document (Gibson 2003, 405).[41] Thus Ovid's magisterial claim to the text receives double reinforcement by way of its triumphal context and its signatory purpose. The triumphal context performs the cultural assumption that the inscription's claim is compelling and indisputable, and it greatly diminishes the possibility of the inscription being interpreted incorrectly. By providing a *titulus* for the display, Ovid commemorates his influence with a phrase that delineates the boundaries of interpretation. '*Naso magister erat*' brings the lessons to their ends: the seduction has been completed, and Ovid has made it possible.

But the question remains – who has been seduced? Alison Sharrock (1994a) has indicated the great degree to which Ovid expertly seduces his reader in the *Ars*. Utilizing aspects of reader-response-theory, Sharrock demonstrates how Ovid reduplicates parts of his poem, cleverly re-directing them into the mouths of different speakers, in order to capture both the 'sophisticated reader' and the 'naïve Reader, the addressee' (1994a, 205). She argues that Ovid creates layers in his poem that attract a variety of readers. In the end, 'the reader is the victim of Ovid's teasing seduction, which draws him further and further into Ovid's power … Specific to the *Ars*, however, is the muted but self-conscious display of authorial seduction, facilitated by the peculiar stance of the didactic poet *vis-à-vis* his audience' (204-5). Building on Sharrock's analysis, I intend to show how the repetition of the triumphal *titulus* at the end of *Ars* 3 is a final joke played upon the principal, male reader.

Ovid's literary adaptation of the triumph appears to undermine the linear, patriotic nature of the victory celebration. Despite the intended narrative and authority of the triumphal procession, at its core, the procession is an act of display that is perceived and interpreted without much guidance. The attempts of triumphing generals to control the way certain images were received indicate the potential multiplicity of the reception. By showing the crowd's reception of a triumph in the *Ars*, and by distorting the triumph's *raison d'etre* in the *Amores*, Ovid reveals the triumph to be an arbitrary array of symbols that can be put to use for a variety of purposes – one of which is to seduce women. Having already emphasized the erotic subtext of triumphal display in the *Amores*, Ovid further pursues the idea in the *Ars* that the interpretive potential of the triumph lends itself well to creating an erotic atmosphere. After all, interpretation is a form of persuasion, and seduction lies within the category of persuasion. Ovid thereby positions the ritual within an amorous context that leads his reader to think not so much about victorious generals, but about desire and seduction. Thus Ovid transforms the triumph into a metaphor for his act of writing.

In the same way that Ovid encourages his artful seducer in the *Ars* (1.219-28) to interpret freely the images that another man has erected in self-benefiting ways, just so has Ovid made use of the didactic genre (its stylistics and tone) to promote his own poetic agenda: his own interpretation of things.[42] The interpreter/seducer in the triumphal scene is akin to Ovid himself, and the engagement of his amorous interpreter in the piracy of other people's images for the purpose of seduction reflects Ovid's role as didactic narrator. When the interpreter of the parade in the *Ars* claims that the figure wearing a reedy garland is the river Euphrates (he could have said the Nile or the Ganges), he has succeeded in beating any rivals to the punch – his interpretation will sit in the mind of his listener as long as no one credibly counters it – an unlikely event in the swirl and excitement of the parade.

Likewise, when Ovid manipulates mythology or explains the behaviours of men and women, as he does consistently in the *Ars*, he places in the reader's mind an interpretation, a way of looking at things that will only be removed by another didactic treatise. The authority of the didactic treatise goes a long way to validate its own claims, and thereby seduce its reader.[43] Perhaps not everyone in ancient Rome believed everything they read, but as we know even today the text holds power. It takes discourse, debate and hard work to distil truth from fiction, and the reader of the *Ars*, once pulled in to the delightful aspects of Ovid's confectionary literature, would have to work awfully hard to argue – especially with nearly 2,330 lines of text! As if Ovid anticipates the danger of losing ground to his didactic predecessors or to those who would attempt to de-construct his pleasure-dome too soon, he inscribes his magisterial authority over the *Ars*. By doing so he stakes his claim as the one who has ultimately, like it or not, seduced the reader to complete the lesson – to read the text. The reader may come to realize that, while he thought he was learning how to become an artist of seduction (if he did), he has actually been seduced to read 'Naso', and to think of him as '*magister*'. What lessons the reader gathers from the poem are beside the point – the reader has been seduced.

But who is the reader? The text that precedes the triumphal inscription at the end of the women's lesson, Book 3, presents a problem. Gibson offers this comment on the closing lines (3.811-12): 'the reversion to military metaphor is rather startling after the emphasis on equality … there is irony too; how can these women who must fake sexual pleasure to please their lovers, and are told not to ask for *munera* after intercourse, be seen as victors inscribing trophies?' (Gibson 2003, 404). Indeed Gibson raises a good point; that the 'equality' that Ovid mentions in a variety of places has a false ring.[44]

Ovid ends Book 2 saying that women will be his concern, not that their concerns will be his own, 745-6: *ecce, rogant tenerae sibi dem praecepta puellae: / vos eritis chartae proxima cura meae,* 'see, the ladies now clamour that I give them instructions: so you shall be the next concern of my treatise'. As John Miller points out (Miller 1993b, 236-7), at the beginning of his third book Ovid compares the men to the victorious Achaeans while he compares the women to the Amazons, and more specifically to doomed Penthesilea (3.1-4):

> Arma dedi Danais in Amazonas; arma supersunt
> quae tibi dem et turmae, Penthesilea, tuae.
> ite in bella pares; vincant, quibus alma Dione
> faverit et toto qui volat orbe puer.

> I have given weapons to the Greeks; let me now give the weapons that remain to you, Penthesilea, and your squadron. Go into battle as equals; let those win whom loving Venus champions, along with her boy who flies everywhere.

Ovid nowhere makes the claim that he will make these ladies triumphant over men, only that he will make them 'equal' (3.3: *ite in bella pares*) or at least not so shamefully mismatched (3.6: *sic etiam vobis vincere turpe, viri*). The next word, after 'equal' in line 3, expresses the wish that women may win (*vincant*), but the use of the optative subjunctive here in juxtaposition with Penthesilea is clearly ironic.[45] Thereby Miller suggests that Ovid's lessons in Book 3, 'seem aimed at an exclusively male audience' (1993b, 240). Gibson likewise observes that Ovid directs the third book to, 'a second unnamed audience. Male readers, prime beneficiaries in any case of much of Ovid's instruction, are the obvious candidates for membership of this latter audience … . Clearly the wider audience of *Ars* 3 is frequently envisaged as a 'male' one' (2003, 36).

Similarly, in the triumphal context of the ending of the first lesson, at the end of Book 2, men are told to erect the spoils they can imagine themselves winning: a fantasy that has its roots in the cultural milieu. Women are instructed to do the same thing, 'because the men were likewise instructed' (3.811), but in doing so, Ovid asks women to perform a difficult fantasy: one in which they dress as men, perform an imagined triumph, and erect spoils and an inscription – none of which were activities inclusive of women in their society. Besides all that, he orders them to give credit to a teacher who has taught them how to be passive and lose the battle. It is all too absurd – unless women are not the intended audience. Ovid's repeated entreaty to his audience to erect victory-displays is further evidence that he still speaks to his male audience. Since the execution of triumphal processions and the commissioning of inscriptions are principally (exclusively) male activities, the closing lines of *Ars* 3 firmly and finally dispel the notion that the text is truly meant to be read by women, or designed to educate them. The martial ending demonstrates that the possibility of women's powers being increased by the exercise was simply an illusion.

In turn, the repetition of the inscriptional *sphragis* at the end of each lesson, *Naso magister erat*, emphasizes the narratorial voice that dominates the poem, while begging the question – has the audience changed at all? Considering that Ovid's didactic treatise is also, let us not forget, an entertaining poem, the use of *magister* is a boast by the author that he has seductively drawn his male reader to the collection's endpoint, beyond the first lesson, the end of the second book of the *Ars* (how can the reader resist such entertaining stuff?). The leadership that Ovid has displayed in guiding his reader to the poem's end has one more intriguing consequence: the male reader has had to 'relate to women', and assume a feminine *persona* to read the third lesson. The transvestitism that Ovid has forced upon his male reader is the final joke of the *Ars*, and one that surely must have been noted by some as early as line 3.6 when he addressed his true readers point-blank as '*viri*'.[46] The martial display of 'spoils' at the end of the third lesson has been posted by 'she-males', men who have just read 811 lines of poetry on how to seduce – each other! Ovid has made his pupils participate in a mental-cross-dressing exercise to consider the behaviours and sexual desires of women.[47] I would not call the third book of the *Ars Amatoria* a feminist text, but I am suggesting that it may be a unique attempt at getting Roman men to think like women (for a change).

Finally, the use of his own name, Naso, is reminiscent of the inscriptions in the *Amores* in which the name representing both the artist and the *amator* plays a double role – expressing both the investment that the lover has in the outcome of events, and the hopes of the author that his own name will be preserved in and through his texts. In the *Ars*, however, 'Naso' is not so easily removed from the author's *persona* as the *amator* of the *Amores*. Naso is the author of the *Ars*, and it is his voice, layered though it may be with humour and irony, that guides the reader through the lessons, making the placement of his name within his texts a bold declaration of responsibility, for which, so it seems, Ovid ultimately paid the price.[48] Augustus' irritation at the *Ars Amatoria* may have been the defensive response of a man preoccupied with re-ordering the moral atmosphere at Rome, but looking back it is clear to the 'sophisticated reader' that the *princeps* did not get or did not appreciate the joke.

PERII NASO POETA

A final inscription brings these issues into focus. In one of the few letters he addresses to his wife from exile, Ovid composes an epitaph for himself that includes his own name in a way that subtly evokes the epitaph of Tibullus discussed in the previous chapter (*Trist.* 3.3.73-6):[49]

HIC EGO QUI IACEO TENERORUM LUSOR AMORUM
  INGENIO PERII NASO POETA MEO,
AT TIBI QUI TRANSIS NE SIT GRAVE QUISQUIS AMASTI
  DICERE NASONIS MOLLITER OSSA CUBENT.

> Here I lie, Naso the poet, deviser of tender loves; I perished for my talent, but you, passer-by, if ever you were in love, may it not be a bother to pray that the bones of Naso rest easy.

Ovid commemorates his literary career, even summoning as readers and well-wishers those who have experienced love and who most enjoyed his works. Tibullus, by contrast, focuses attention on his military career and his obedience and loyalty to his patron Messalla. Ovid's epitaph has perhaps more in common with the epitaphic passages that Propertius creates, in which lovers and Maecenas appear at his graveside and say words to recall the poet's devotion to the life of love and its elegiac expression.[50] Ovid and Propertius develop their authorial *personae* with respect to their literary output, while Tibullus views his literary contribution as an added component to his responsibilities as a citizen and a soldier. But then Ovid and Propertius, as far as we know, chose no other livelihood than poetry. In light of the traditional roles of the Roman elite males, the choice of men like Ovid and Propertius, members of the upper class, to pursue literary careers of this sort is novel and even daring. As we can see, in his epitaph Ovid does not back down; he highlights his love poetry as the gem of his collection. In doing this he positions himself alongside his famous predecessors: Gallus, Propertius and Tibullus; in addition he reminds us of his fame – for there are many who have loved, and Ovid was their teacher.

Moreover, the request and composition of the epitaph reflects the poet's rational desire to control his last public appearance, his lasting depiction. It is curious that Ovid's memorial makes no mention of his other, considerably more serious works.[51] The authority of the epitaph forces us to reconsider the importance or relative significance of Ovid's works, as Peter Green does.[52] The epitaph communicates the poet's hopes: that he has achieved the fame that will inspire remembrance. This is a different voice speaking from that of the epistles: the litany of Ovid's personal sufferings and his pleas for recall recede for a moment as Ovid contemplates the words that may mark his tomb. The authorial voice of the epitaph is compelling, even if the fulfilment of the request, that such verses be erected, cannot be assured. The epitaph is confirmation of the poet's lasting reputation, at the same moment that it cries out for fulfilment. The epitaph bears authority while dressing itself as an orphan hoping for handouts, much like Ovid's book, cautiously making its way to Rome in *Tristia* 1.1.

Conclusion

Ovid's use of his own name within so many of his inscriptional verses, ones that are naturally granted the emphasis that inscriptions typically brought to bear, indicates an authorial eagerness to verbally authenticate the artist's interaction with his work. In the *Amores* Ovid posts his name among votive inscriptions that highlight the dependency of the poet on the safety and the integrity of his medium, the written word. In the *Ars Amatoria* he places his name inside a type of inscription whose rights of display and authorship had become increasingly exclusive. What's more, the repetition of this triumphal line belies his claims that the lesson of the third book is directed at women; the author knows who his readers really are – inquisitive men. In the *Tristia*, Ovid names himself in his last elegiac inscription, his very epitaph, in an attempt to fashion his literary legacy despite the enormous forces conspiring to destroy his life's work. Ovid's inscriptional self-representations, therefore, also imply that there exists a connection between the fate of those works and the fate of the author. More than those of any writer before him, Ovid's literary anxieties become historic realities. The mounting threats against erotic elegy not only destroyed a single author's career, but also brought to an end the genre as a whole. Gallus' suicide and Ovid's exile stand like bookends to showcase the brilliant and risky artistry of the elegiac movement at Rome.

5

The *Heroides* Inscriptions

The previous chapter analysed a number of inscriptions in which the author includes his own name – Naso. Some of these inscriptions suggest literary concerns that pertain to the poetry or to the process of writing in general; but some offer expressions of what we must imagine are the author's thoughts, hopes and anxieties. In this latter role, the inscriptions act very much as real inscriptions do in the wider Roman context. Their frequent placement inside elegiac poems, particularly Ovid's, is a reflection of the precarious position of poetry in the final decades of the last century BC. Indeed it was becoming increasingly evident by Ovid's time that the control of the *princeps* over the culture, the traditions and even the domestic lives of citizens was not about to relax.

A greater number of Ovid's invented inscriptions, however, do not include his name, but typically grant female characters the opportunity to determine inscriptional content. In fact, with the exception of three inscriptions placed by two males (Paris and Acontius in the *Heroides* will be discussed in the second part of this chapter), and of course those inscriptions that 'Naso' offers under his own name, the 'authors' of Ovid's elegiac inscriptions are always women. Women in Rome were not traditionally the subjects of public record or monumental representation, nor did they tend to provide more than a small percentage of funds for the memorials of loved ones. We see some literary or archaeological evidence that men willingly surrendered the act of final memorialization to women, but the overwhelming evidence points to the fact that men memorialized women to qualify further their own status. The existence of burial clubs even among the lowest segments of society seems to point to a desire or requirement that men dedicate memorials for their friends, fellow soldiers and kinsmen.[1] Mary Lefkowitz and Maureen Fant (1992) discuss the extent to which Roman women were the subject of funereal and dedicatory inscriptions, and they demonstrate by the examples they provide that women less often provided the inscriptions themselves.[2] Ovid repeatedly imagines women in the position of leaving indelible marks on the world in which they live, and rendering permanence to the sentiments and the circumstances of their lives. By creating text within the text of their narratives, Ovid allows his women to make a place for themselves within the dramas he creates: he leaves the impression on the reader that these women really lived and that their stories have more than an element of truth.

This chapter examines the inscriptions in the *Heroides*, for this collection of fictional epistles includes a fascinating array: four epitaphs, one dedicatory inscription and three instances of graffiti.[3] The purpose of every epistle in the collection is to give legendary heroines the opportunity to challenge literary precedents with stories of their own. In the process, several of these heroines include inscriptions as ways of cementing their final thoughts to lasting monuments, thereby adding to the illusion that theirs is the final say; the tactic beckons the reader to remember them in their own words.

As we know, Ovid's experimental collection of letters takes great care to call into question various aspects of previous, perhaps more authoritative, literary accounts. Homer's Odysseus gets the third degree from Ovid's Penelope; Virgil's Aeneas gets a roasting by Ovid's Dido. Although these women seem to speak for themselves, they are, like female characters on the Roman stage, 'played' by a man, and these female voices can be seen to marginalize themselves in their own narrative.[4] I argue, however, that Ovid lends the feminine voice an opportunity for 'authority' that no one had previously attempted, and I will not fault it here for not measuring up to modern sensibilities. Ovid himself is happy to point out the innovative aspect of his epistles at *Ars* 3.345-6: *vel tibi composita cantetur epistola voce / ignotum hoc aliis ille novavit opus*, 'or quote my Epistles with a gentle voice: I invented this work, (a sort) untried by others.' Part of his pleasure and pride clearly derives from the novelty of his chosen subject matter, not merely the epistolary format of the whole. According to my interpretation in the previous chapter, Ovid's final lines in the *Ars Amatoria* issue a provocative challenge to his male reader to recognize that he has been knowingly seduced into reading a women's lesson. So too might Ovid reveal a certain pride in the fact that his *Heroides* also require the male reader to read and think like a woman.[5] As my study has demonstrated, the voices that speak through inscriptions often belong to the disadvantaged: the poet aiming to immortalize someone or something (Catullus' brother or Tibullus' sense of duty); Cynthia attempting to immortalize herself in a way that counters the prevailing narrative of her role in Propertius' poetry as a love object; and Cornelia, staving off as long as possible the obliteration of what she configures as a meaningful life. Likewise the majority of the female 'authors' speaking, as it were, through the inscriptions in the *Heroides* are traditionally figures with very little authority in the societies within which they operate; yet in these verses they have the opportunity to craft an argument of reason and emotion and, occasionally, set in stone their final words.

Inscriptional insertions serve as authoritative moments within the text whereby the inscriptions themselves speak with greater clarity and purpose than the surrounding verses. If the epitaph is a marker of permanence upon a sea of shifting historical and cultural circumstances (most dramatically seen in the case of Ovid's epitaph, examined in the previous chapter), then the epitaphs in the *Heroides* similarly appear as signposts to distil, in dramatic fashion, the final thoughts of these despairing heroines. Though their 'authors' focus more on despair, anger and self-destruction, these women are competitively laying claim to their own stories, having their say so to speak, in refutative responses to preceding versions. In the *Heroides* four women compose their own epitaphs: Phyllis (poem 2), Dido (poem 7), Hypermestra (poem 14) and Sappho (poem 15). In the first three cases each woman's epitaph sets the record straight, explaining the circumstances that surround her imminent demise. Sappho's epitaph, by contrast, dedicates her lyre to Apollo, whose temple would be the only suitable resting place for her instrument. These epitaphs are each significant within their individual letters, and within the context of the collection and the literature of the period.[6]

PRAEBUIT CAUSAM MORTIS

Phyllis is a second-generation Ariadne. Demophoön, son of Theseus, is her guest in Thrace; before he re-embarks, he promises her he shall return to make her his queen; he never returns. Phyllis' letter is important for two reasons. It dramatically breaks the reverie left by the languishing Penelope of the first epistle, whose husband strays so long away from home. We know that Penelope will be united with Odysseus, and so her expressions of impatience and despair bear the charm of potential reprieve. Her protests against his wanderlust are the reader's delight, since they offer embellishment and a close-up view to the passions of Penelope that Homer mentions. Phyllis, however, can share with the reader no private delusions – her abandonment is total, her suicide, as she deems it, necessary. Phyllis lets us know what the *Heroides* are really about. Rather than a charming retelling of standard classics, this collection turns out to be an exposé of the wicked ways of men – a table-turning opportunity for the jilted women of antiquity to have their say. The second important aspect of this letter is that Phyllis is reasonably obscure. Thus it becomes clear that the purpose here is not merely to showcase the dastardly deeds men have committed, or to re-write important literary precedents, but to give the more faded phantoms of mythology a chance to sparkle with undiscovered rhetorical potential.

Phyllis composes two *tituli* in her epistle: the first is an inscription she desires to see posted on her former lover's statue in Athens (2.74): *hic est, cuius amans hospita capta dolo est*, 'here is a man whose gracious lover was brought to ruin by his deceit.' The label that Phyllis wishes inscribed reflects her all too human desire to see a wrongdoer publicly humiliated. Yet Demophoön is an heir to the Athenian throne; Phyllis is a Thracian, a member of a people that the Greeks and the Romans considered, in their range of barbarian contacts, among the lowest and least civilized of the human race.[7] Her desire to leave a mark on Demophoön's character is understandable, but her desire to leave it on his statue, on a work of public art, is surprising. Ovid has Phyllis momentarily transcend her limited power as she contemplates the public erection of a marble monument that would make permanent her vengeance and his humiliation. It is an unfulfilled wish, but it illustrates Phyllis' awareness of what matters in Greco-Roman society: reputation and record. Phyllis' wish is a small but important rebellion against the marginal place she holds in the world and in the mind and heart of the man who has abandoned her.

Phyllis closes the epistle with the epitaph she composes for her Thracian tomb (2.147-8):

> PHYLLIDA DEMOPHOÖN LETO DEDIT HOSPES AMANTEM;
> ILLE NECIS CAUSAM PRAEBUIT, IPSA MANUM.

> Demophoön, invited guest, rewarded his loving hostess Phyllis with death;
> he provided the reason for her death, she provided the means.

Her justification for her suicide is a foreshadowing of the more famous suicide that soon follows in Ovid's collection, and even her sentiment finds verbal echoes in Dido's epitaph: (7.195-6):

> PRAEBUIT AENEAS ET CAUSAM MORTIS ET ENSEM;
> IPSA SUA DIDO CONCIDIT USA MANU.

> Aeneas provided the reason and the weapon of death; Dido died, however, by her own hand.

The predicament of these two women finds further repetition in the *Heroides*, and evokes the plight of all those mythological women who hosted and trusted a stranger, only to be disappointed.[8] Ovid's placement of their epitaphs at the ends of their letters artistically and graphically represents those final words that will remain on the tomb, the final expressions of Phyllis and Dido, and their literary monuments.

These two epitaphs are markedly different in the way they designate agency: Phyllis makes Demophoön the subject of *dedit* in the first line of the epitaph, and the subject of *praebuit* in the first half of the second line. She is the object of *dedit* and the final subject of *praebuit*, rendering herself agency only at the end, and only against herself.[9] By contrast, Dido symmetrically renders two agents – Aeneas and herself – in juxtaposed lines that proclaim his blame, and her effectiveness. The combined use of *concidit* and *usa* suggest a process of dying that emphasizes her agency and control over her end. Phyllis provided her hand for the suicide, an impersonal process, while Dido used hers. So Phyllis, in her obscurity, renders what agency she can muster in the liminal situation that she inhabits, while Dido renders agency that befits her legendary and literary renown. In fact, when Ovid mentions Dido's story again in his later *Fasti*, he repeats her epitaph verbatim (3.549-50). The poet quotes the monument as if it really existed; this inclusion in another work offers his version of her story in the *Heroides* a bold stroke of validation.

Furthermore, the claim in each heroine's epitaph, that her hand (*manus*) will provide the stroke of death, merits further comment. The use of *manus* as a term of possession and appropriation, particularly in relation to conjugal arrangements in legal and historical writings of the same period, makes their claim to 'use of their own hands' a bold statement of defiant, albeit self-destructive, autonomy.[10] Yet there is special irony in Dido's use of the word, because as she writes she holds on her lap Aeneas' Trojan sword (7.184: *Troicus ensis*) soon to be stained with her blood. Dido's use of the sword to take her own life suggests virile potency in her self-annihilation. But by taking up the sword of Aeneas, she commits the final act that he all but committed, as Ovid clearly shows in the repeated act of wounding, figuratively and literally (189-90): *nec mea nunc primum feriuntur pectora telo; / ille locus saevi vulnus amoris habet*, 'nor now does this breast feel the bite of the sword for the first time; that spot already bears the wound of a savage love.'

Hypermestra's epitaph in poem 14, by contrast, focuses not on any impending suicide, but on her piety, on her righteous decision to abide by a higher law than the edict of her treacherous father. Her inscription reads as follows, including its introductory line (14.128-30):

> sculptaque sint titulo nostra sepulcra brevi:
> EXUL HYPERMESTRA, PRETIUM PIETATIS INIQUUM
> QUAM MORTEM FRATRI DEPULIT, IPSA TULIT.

> And let my grave be inscribed with this brief epitaph: Hypermestra, an exile, on her own bore the too-high price of righteousness: a death which she diverted from a brother.

She alone, among the fifty daughters of Danaus, spared her new bridegroom Lynceus and now awaits her death in prison, 14.5: *quod manus extimuit iugulo demittere ferrum, / sum rea*, 'because my hand would not slit your throat, I am fighting for my life'. Ovid makes no mention of hands in her epitaph. Nonetheless, her power of agency, or *manus*, makes eight appearances in her epistle, *dextra* appears once, and once she speaks of Lynceus' hand nearly cutting itself on her blade as he rolls over in his sleep. The words used to describe that near accident ironically evoke the words of wounding that the poets use in relation to passionate love, 14.70: *paene manus telo saucia facta tua est*, 'your hand was nearly wounded by my dagger'.[11] The contrasting irony is that Hypermestra's love is displayed in her restraint, not brought to bear through the act of wounding. Moreover, amidst the many men callously wounding the women who love them,

Hypermestra spares Lynceus both the fatal wound she is commanded to offer, and the accidental one he nearly brings upon himself.

Her defiance against the Danaid conspiracy, the staying of her hand, finds pathetic reflection in her later inability to complete her letter, or her epitaph. The poem continues with these two lines that state her desire to write more (131-2):

> scribere plura libet, sed pondere lapsa catenae
> est manus, et vires subtrahit ipse timor.

> It pleases me to write more, but the weight of chains makes my hand falter, and fear itself saps my strength.

Her hand falters as it did once before to her credit, but now resulting in her misery, or at least in the truncation of her memorial. She interrupts her letter and her eulogy, a tactic that tempts the reader to imagine the inscription's continuation were it completed. Yet Hypermestra's inscription leaves her reader with the lasting impression that she was a true heroine, a champion of *pietas* and capable of a manly virtue like Virgil's Aeneas (*Aen.* 1.10: *insignem pietate virum*), and was not, like so many of her 'heroic' sisters, merely a victim of love.[12] Furthermore, according to Helen Nielsen, *pietas* (or its variants, *pius*, *piissimus* and *pientissimus*) in epitaphic inscriptions drew upon normative expectations that a child would support or had already supported his parents in old age, and that the designation of *pietas* still appeared on the tombstones of children who died before they had the opportunity to fulfil that duty (Nielsen 1997, 193-204). Thus Hypermestra's self-designation as one exhibiting *pietas* applies not only to her actions towards Lynceus, but to the relationship she would have had towards her father, were he a just man. Her piety operates despite the ironic circumstances that she will soon die because she disobeyed her father's unjust command.

Sappho's epitaph in poem 15 likewise ushers in all the considerations of authority, choice of self-memorialization, and agency, but adds the aspect of her actual authorial persona.[13] As Linda Kauffman points out, Ovid links the known facts of Sappho's life to the constructed misery that he has her perform (Kauffman 1986, 53). Sappho's love of women and her immortality through her poetry belie her epistolary obsession over an obscure male, and her postured anxiety that she has lost her art and her audience due to her distracted mind. Her epitaph seeks to restore her place among Apollo's ministers, (15.183-4):

> GRATA LYRAM POSUI TIBI, PHOEBE, POETRIA SAPPHO:
> CONVENIT ILLA MIHI, CONVENIT ILLA TIBI.

> I, Sappho, grateful poetess, have placed at your feet, Phoebus, my lyre: it suited us both, me and you.

The reader is well aware that Sappho need not recover her fame – her admirers were many throughout the ages. Kauffman shows that Ovid claims ownership to a direct relationship between himself and Sappho, imbuing his writings with the inherited qualities of her style, most notably music, alternative models for constructing desire, and 'her focus on the moment of parting' (1986, 53-5). Her epitaph, therefore, exposes the subtle deceit in Ovid's construction of Sappho as a heterosexual victim of love, for it makes no mention of Phaon. She does not leave in her memorial any mention of her victimization or abandonment. Instead her epitaph reminds us all of her great poetic achievement, stating quite directly that she and Apollo shared the same instrument. Sappho calls the lyre, or shell (*chelyn*), an endowment shared (*communia munera*) between her and the great god of culture. Reading the epitaph, one realizes that although Sappho uses more words to complain about Phaon, her purpose in 'authoring' this letter is to clarify her lofty position within the pantheon of poets and disciples of Apollo. Kauffman's assessment is quite clearly correct, for Ovid is working through Sappho to his own claim of poetic brilliance. Just as Sappho's epitaph clarifies her true legacy, so too does the true author, lying behind the persona of Sappho, clarify his position as inheritor of that talent.

Yet it is true that not every letter in the *Heroides* contains an epitaph, and, that being so, should we venture to say that the letters without epitaphs are less authoritative, or that their purposes are less clearly stated? Not at all, rather the four epistles that do contain these funerary epitaphs are markedly important in what they represent. In each letter, the 'author' is very close to death, as opposed to most of the remaining women who write at extremes of emotional despair, but are not facing imminent destruction. The four epitaph-providers are clearly leaving their final thoughts in the most dramatic fashion: they cement their lives to words. Also, Ovid places each woman within the collection in counterpoint to some other figure or version of herself. Phyllis (2), as mentioned, serves to disrupt the tender expressions of fidelity and marital bonds seen in Penelope's letter (1), and furthermore she prepares us for Dido (7) yet to come. Dido is arguably the most important suicide in Roman literature thanks to Virgil. Her anticipated monument in Ovid is counterpoint to her Virgilian disintegration on her wretched pyre. Hypermestra (14) has spared her bridegroom Lynceus' life in contrast to Deianira (9) who has submitted her lover Hercules to a horrible and painful end, having sent him a poison cloak that burns off his flesh. Deianira (9) is intent on suicide in her letter, but no doubt the fact that she caused her husband's excruciating death keeps her from immortalizing herself in epitaphic form as Hypermestra does, whose *pietas* is her immortal attribute. Also, Hypermestra's letter momentarily diverts the collection from the dominant theme of victimization, in that her story is one of female defiance, agency and piety. Sappho's epitaph (15), although not an expression of blame against a lover, still indicates the author's need to validate her agency and creative ability. We are better off assigning Sappho's letter and her inscriptional desires as communicative of her creator's admiration and aspirations than making sense of the epitaph within the context of the intended suicide.

The only other suicide worthy of an inscription, but who leaves none, is poor Canace (poem 11). Forced to kill herself by her father Aeolus after his discovery of her incestuous affair with her brother Macareus, Canace's story is made even more pathetic by her lack of a monument. A tomb is mentioned, however, although it is merely an urn that she prays will contain both her bones and those of their murdered child – recently snatched away by Aeolus and destroyed (11.121-4):

> tu tamen, o frustra miserae sperate sorori,
>   sparsa, precor, nati collige membra tui,
> et refer ad matrem socioque inpone sepulcro,
>   urnaque nos habeat quamlibet arta duos!

> It did your miserable sister no good to hope for you – still, I pray that you will gather up the mangled pieces of your child and inter them with his mother's bones; oh please, let the same, shared urn hold us both.

Canace's urgent concern that her baby's bones rest with hers for eternity, perhaps, counts for more than any inscription in stone. Canace is cut off before she has the opportunity to accomplish anything, save the birth of her son. Canace's ephemerality and her humble wish for an urn reflect her child's brief life. Moreover, it is impossible to resist the temptation to compare her grave with the humble urn that holds the bones of Tibullus in *Am.* 3.9. The silenced voice of the dead poet in Ovid's tribute authors no epitaph for himself, nor receives any, save a prayer with the formulaic tone of an epitaph.[14] The injustice of Tibullus' too-soon demise may have inspired Ovid's treatment of miserable Canace.

The epitaphic impulse, repeated four times in the *Heroides*, reveals a recurring desire for permanent self-identification. Certainly desire is the chief motivation and structural theme in the epistles, but in the epitaphs desire for the beloved plays a secondary role to the women's desires to get their story straight, and to preserve it in a medium that was often unavailable to women, although there certainly were exceptions.[15] These fictional characters, however, do not wait for commemoration; on their own they condense and transform their poetic pleas into lasting, petrified forms of expression. The role of petrification and all its philosophical implications need not be examined here, but Ovid's penchant for transforming bodies to stone in his epic finds important reflection in these heroic verses where a few otherwise wasted words are granted the permanence of inscribed preservation.

In her examination of the *Heroides*, Kauffman notices the inscriptional form of self-representation, and asserts that 'the act of inscribing is an act of absolute isolation, for the beloved's indifference renders all threats, all strategies, all persuasive ploys futile' (1986, 58). I argue, moreover, that the inscription is the memorial marker that lifts the poem off the page and establishes its 'inscribed' couplets in a different place within the reader's imagination. The imagined tomb the reader constructs to hold the inscription lends finality and permanence to the words it bears. The inscribed words leap off the page, whether or not they are asserting themselves as the final decision of their moody authors. The inscriptions serve to marry the fictional world the heroines inhabit to the physical Roman world in which, at every plaza, crossroads and marketplace, inscriptions inform, direct, edify and inspire. The inscriptions are far from isolated acts; rather they provide the link between these remote and often obscure women to the hope of eternal commemoration.

Patricia Rosenmeyer offers a helpful observation regarding the shared sentiments and expressions of Ovid's exile poetry and the *Heroides* (Rosenmeyer 1997, 51):

> Epistolary technique always problematises the boundaries between fiction and reality. Whether the writer claims to write in his own voice or that of a mythical figure, the moment he puts words to paper he invents a self, a life, a set of feelings. Based on a process of selection and self-censorship, the letter is a construction, not a reflection of reality. The similarities between the many voices of Ovid's exile, both his heroines' and his own, originate in their generic affiliation. The voices of Ovid's heroines survive the cataclysmic events in the poet's own life to flourish again in a context that is both different and at the same time hauntingly familiar.

The 'haunting familiarity' between the heroines' experiences of abandonment and isolation and what we know of Ovid's exile leads us directly to Ovid's frequent use of inscriptions as similarly structured, rhetorical pieces that meant to defy their fictional spaces. The problematic nature of fictional personae, differing circumstances and generic differences, I suggest, find temporary resolution in these fixed commemorative moments whose form and function extend beyond the story into the daily lives of readers.

To different ends: men's inscriptions

The use of text by one person to effect a change in another or to motivate a response early captivated the imagination of the ancient Greeks. One of the earlier stories in the chain of events that leads to the age of men, and the legends of heroes rather than the myths of gods, is that of Eris throwing a golden apple among the divine guests at the marriage of Peleus and Thetis on which was written, 'for the fairest'. As we know, the apple spurred an argument among the great goddesses Hera, Athena and Aphrodite regarding who should have the gift. This in turn led to the judgment of Paris, the rape of Helen and the Trojan War. The later byproduct of that quasi-mythical conflict was the first narrative poem in western civilization: Homer's *Iliad*. Eris' mischief with words is nearly as significant as Pandora's curiosity, for the written word has the power to pique the imagination, incite rebellion, and move even the hardest heart to love.

A lover's use of written words to win the heart of his beloved, although occurring often in mythological and historical accounts, did not take poetic form until the Hellenistic poets began poeticizing the catalogues of stories handed down from oral tradition.[16] Callimachus, the court-poet and librarian of Alexandria in the third century BC, tells the story of Acontius and Cydippe in the third book of his elegiac *Aitia*, a series of stories that are linked together by an over-arching theme. Acontius is a frustrated young lover who inscribes an oath upon an apple and makes sure his beloved Cydippe finds and reads the apple aloud. When she reads the words: 'By Artemis, I will marry Acontius', she binds herself unwittingly to the young man and later must fulfil her obligation.[17] A still extant fragment of the poem survives in which Acontius addresses a grove of trees and demands that they bear the inscription, 'Cydippe is beautiful'.[18] The epigraphic habit of Callimachus' young lover is the model for the Roman elegiac custom of having lovers use such inscribed texts in seduction: Virgil's Gallus in *Ecl.* 10; Propertius' *amator* in 1.18; and Ovid's Paris in the *Heroides*. In three complementary instances, male lovers use inscriptions in the *Heroides* to different ends – not to commemorate their final sentiments *in extremis*, but to control women. Paris leaves an inscribed declaration of his love for Oenone in *Heroides* 5, and he scribbles his love for Helen in wine upon a table in one of the double letters, *Heroides* 17. Acontius inscribes his thanks for Cydippe's safety on a golden apple that he dedicates to Venus in another of the double epistles, *Heroides* 20.

The inscriptions 'authored' by these men clearly reflect the power of masculinity to control the events of a love affair; there are no suicide notes among their graffiti. Paris' inscriptions effect changes in his lovers: Oenone's letter reveals a preoccupation with the words Paris has left behind, and when Helen recalls his amorous graffito in her letter to him, her initial resolve to reject him begins to wither. Acontius promises a votive inscription to thank Artemis once Cydippe has officially become his bride. The Acontius who appears in this letter promotes a comparison with the impetuous boy in Callimachus. All these inscriptions in the *Heroides* serve to highlight the intertextual universe in which Ovid creates these re-tellings.

Paris' seductive texts

The face that first inspires Paris to declare his love is not one that launched a thousand ships, but the face of a Phrygian nymph named Oenone.[19] It was she who aided Paris' survival during the rugged, rustic years of his youth. Cast out by his mother after a fateful prophecy concerning the newborn prince and the destruction of the city, Paris spent his childhood in the company of shepherds. In *Heroides* 5, Oenone is arrogantly remorseful that she, the daughter of the river-god Cebren, once stooped to marry a lowly shepherd, his royal lineage not yet revealed (she even calls him 'slave' in line 12: *servus eras; servo nubere nympha tuli*). The back-story continues: after his identity became known, he maintained his relationship with Oenone, but soon after his re-installation in Priam's household his father sent him on his fateful journey to Mycenae. Standing on a cliff, in anticipation of his return from overseas, Oenone spied Helen in Paris' embrace and realized she had lost him forever: 5.68 and 70: *femineas vidi corde tremente genas ... haerebat gremio turpis amica tuo*, 'I saw with trembling heart a woman's countenance, ... a shameless mistress clung to your bosom'.

Early in her complaint she points forlornly to the trees upon which he once inscribed her name, and she goes on to relate the inscription on a single tree which, so she thought, had cemented his allegiance (*Her.* 5.21-30):

> incisae servant a te mea nomina fagi
>   et legor OENONE falce notata tua,[20]
> et quantum trunci, tantum mea nomina crescunt.
>   crescite et in titulos surgite recta meos!
> popule, vive, precor, quae consita margine ripae
>   hoc in rugoso cortice carmen habes:
> CUM PARIS OENONE POTERIT SPIRARE RELICTA
>   AD FONTEM XANTHI VERSA RECURRET AQUA.
> Xanthe, retro propera, versaeque recurrite lymphae:
>   sustinet Oenonen deseruisse Paris.

The incised beech-trees preserve my name gouged by your hunting-knife; I am read, 'OENONE'. As much as the trunk has grown, so has my name increased in size – expand and rise upwards along with my inscription! Poplar-tree, live on, I pray, planted on the bank of the stream, and bearing this verse in your wrinkled bark: 'When Paris shall have taken breath with his Oenone forgotten, the Xanthus will flow backwards to its source.'[21] Oh Xanthus, now is the time to turn back to your source! Paris breathes on, and has deserted Oenone.[22]

Her exhortation to the trees in line 25, that they should continue to grow and feature her inscribed name, reveals the irony in her situation. We would perhaps expect her to hate these trees, to wish them burned to the ground. But instead she encourages their growth and derives some pride or pleasure in the view they afford her of Paris' faithless handiwork. Howard Jacobson offers this interpretation: 'the inscription symbolizes their love. Ovid is clearly imitating Vergil ... , but with very different results. It is not the love which is mirrored in the tree, but Oenone's ego .... Paris' inscription is emblematic, as far as she is concerned, of her glory' (Jacobson 1974, 182).[23] Despite some other unnecessary comments about her character ('a true puritan', ... 'rustic, naïve, foolish, optimistic, and, by and large, blind'), Jacobson provides a crucial argument (1974, 189):[24]

> [Oenone] re-creates, indeed, resurrects Paris' forgotten past in which she occupies a crucial place, and struggles to keep it – and herself – alive. We are witness to the efforts of one of history's lesser figures to keep herself from being written out of history's textbook. But, of course, neither the bark of the tree nor the heroine's own memory can achieve this end; ironically, however, and significantly, this letter, this poem, this work of art accomplishes precisely that.

Although the elegiac woman is rarely provided the opportunity to express her own thoughts, inside the literary world in which she exists there is a pleasure she derives from being written about. The poets frequently imagine that the women they feature appreciate the perpetuity and fame that their works bestow. Yet even the poets are willing to admit to the glittering façade, for in Propertius 4.7 Cynthia dramatically confronts her author regarding his persistent representation of her. Oenone too is tragically depicted as a woman who both hates and loves what is written. Although the inscriptions remind her of her loss, they preserve her name; obscure as she is, Paris' humble homage to her is the only one she may expect.

There is striking consistency in the characterization of Paris in Oenone's letter and in the double-epistle *Her.* 16-17, a written exchange between Paris and Helen occurring only moments before their fateful decision to leave together for Troy.[25] In his letter to Helen, Paris makes the case that she should follow him to Troy. He particularly points out the wealth of his father, his position among his people and the life of luxury and ease that she would enjoy as princess of Troy. Helen responds to Paris with initial protest against his audacity. Like Oenone, Helen makes a point of providing her pedigree: she is the daughter of a god and a queen; she is the product of Greek civilization whereas he lives in a barbarous land (64: *at certe barbara terra tua est*). She goes on to rebuke him for his obvious attempts to seduce her at the banquet hall while her husband sits close by: she tells us that he gazes at her, sighs at her, drinks from the same part of the cup where she has drunk, and makes signs with his hands and eyebrows. Then she relates one final attempt he has made to seduce her, and her tone in the letter changes immediately afterwards, *Her.* 17.87-92:

> orbe quoque in mensae legi sub nomine nostro
>   quod deducta mero littera fecit, AMO,
> credere me tamen hoc oculo renuente negavi;
>   ei mihi, iam didici sic ego posse loqui!
> his ego blanditiis, si peccatura fuissem,
>   flecterer, his poterant pectora nostra capi.

> I also did read upon the surface of the table, written in wine, 'I LOVE HELEN'; of course I denied with my downcast eyes that I believed you: ah me, now I have learned to speak as you do! If I could have given in, I would be bent and my heart could be captured by flatteries such as these.

Helen goes on at once to address his beauty and how it does not affect her, but she protests too much; her unabashed declaration that his rare beauty would inspire many a woman to love reveals her now evident struggle (17.93-100):

> est quoque, confiteor, facies tibi rara, potestque
>   velle sub amplexus ire puella tuos.
> altera sed potius felix sine crimine fiat
>   quam cadat externo noster amore pudor.
> disce meo exemplo formosis posse carere:
>   est virtus placitis abstinuisse bonis.
> quam multos credis iuvenes optare quod optas?
>   qui sapiant oculos an Paris unus habes?

> You have, I confess, an exquisite face, and surely it is capable of drawing in a girl to your embraces. But let it be another lucky girl without restraints rather than my matronly honour that falls to a foreign love. Learn by my example that it is possible to live without beautiful things: that there is virtue in abstaining from delightful pleasures. Do you understand that many young men have chosen as you: or do you, Paris, alone have eyes that see clearly?

This forms the turning point in Helen's argument. The blandishments that he uses to seduce Helen all operate upon her vanity, but the vision of her name written upon the table is the final stroke. Her protests have become subtle praises of the Trojan prince, and her earlier discussion of her virtue has given way to charmed recognition of her beauty's power in lines 123-8:

> non est tanta mihi fiducia corporis ut me
>   maxima teste dea dona fuisse putem.
> contenta est oculis hominum mea forma probari;
>   laudatrix Venus est invidiosa mihi.

sed nihil infirmo, faveo quoque laudibus istis:
nam mea vox quare quod cupit esse neget?

> My confidence in my physical beauty is not so great that I would think myself the greatest gift by a goddess' standard. I am content that my beauty finds favour in the eyes of men; the praise of Venus brings upon me the evil eye. But I dispute nothing, I am also favourable to your praise: for how can my words deny that which they desire to be so?

Finally, just as Oenone's ego emerges when she thinks of her trees inscribed with her name, Helen begins to regret the circumstances that make her ineligible for a love such as his – she is practically on her way to Troy.

Paris' habit of inscribing his love, therefore, is a key component of his seduction: it assures him a special place in the minds of these women; reading is more permanent than seeing gestures or hearing words. The words that Paris has left permanently for Oenone and ephemerally for Helen become pivotal manifestations of his desire. In fact, the nature of Paris' inscriptions demonstrates an ironic, reverse correspondence to his affections. His permanent etchings in tree-bark for Oenone remain eternally to remind her of his betrayal, while his impermanent wine-scrawl on a tabletop begins an affair that will be sung in poetry and art for ages to come. The 'monuments' for Oenone are testament to the fact that words in stone provide no guarantee of human behaviour, but the permanent capability of text at least ensures that the memory of human actions may never fade entirely. Oenone's desire for Paris transfers also to the preservation of the texts that confirm her past and her former place in Paris' heart. Ovid's innovation upon Paris' exploits significantly consists of this capability to seduce with written words, a technique all too familiar to the reader of Ovid's elegiac corpus. As we know, it is within the domain of the elegiac poet to craft a seductive text that ensnares not only the intended object of desire, but the reader as well.

Ovid's Acontius: all grown up?

As mentioned above, Ovid owes the motif of lovers writing on trees to Callimachus' account of Acontius' love for Cydippe.[26] Perhaps in homage to his admired predecessor Ovid devotes one of the three sets of double-epistles to an exchange between Cydippe and Acontius. Interestingly, he does not include the apple-inscription that traps the unsuspecting girl, or the inscriptions the boy carves on tree-trunks. Rather Ovid describes the offering that Acontius promises to render to Artemis once Cydippe will consent to be his bride. The offering will be a golden image of an apple inscribed with these words (20.239-40):

EFFIGIE POMI TESTATUR ACONTIUS HUIUS
QUAE FUERINT IN EO SCRIPTA FUISSE RATA.

Acontius bears witness, by this effigy of the apple, that what words were written upon it have come to pass.

This episode comes long after Cydippe has spoken the oath, and even after she has already suffered several illnesses brought on by impending marriages that would break her spoken pledge to Artemis (and thereby Acontius). Acontius' letter boasts his success and bids Cydippe consummate the marriage that she was tricked into making. By engaging the narrative at this point, Ovid avoids delivering the same situations that Callimachus has already provided, and, by way of the votive inscription, he allows Acontius to continue his epigraphic habits. The apple-effigy represents a more mature and responsible manifestation of the young man's desire to make words work for him. It brings closure to the story as well, for the offering is given in thanks for what the gods have validated. In obtaining Cydippe, Acontius need no longer carve deceptive messages, for now he leaves proper inscriptions to the goddess. Ovid thereby de-emphasizes Acontius' status as the first elegiac lover to carve names on trees. In his place, Ovid has given emphasis to Paris as a scribbler, thereby allowing this better known, epic character the opportunity to usurp this erotic mastery of text.

Ovid's Acontius even speaks admiringly of Paris for taking action to acquire Helen (20.47-50):

si non proficient artes, veniemus ad arma,
inque tui cupido rapta ferere sinu.
non sum qui soleam Paridis reprehendere factum
nec quemquam qui, vir posset ut esse, fuit.

If art will not accomplish my aims, then I will take up arms, and you will be seized and carried off in my desirous embrace. I am not one to deem reprehensible the deed of Paris, nor anyone who acted as a man in order to be a husband.

Ovid's Acontius, by referring to Paris in this fashion, seems uninformed of the accounts of Paris' actions in the recent *Heroides*. Acontius fails to discern the new Ovidian Paris who, to achieve his seductions, has adapted the very skill that brought Acontius success.

Where might Paris' skills originate? As we know, Ovid is the self-proclaimed *praeceptor amoris*, as he reiterates and declares at the end of the second and third books of his *Ars Amatoria* (2.744 and 3.812: NASO MAGISTER ERAT). As the teacher of love, Ovid makes himself, or more accurately his text, the mediating force between his readers and the realization of their desires. Text not only teaches seduction, it achieves seduction as well, as we see in the *Ars* and the *Amores* where it is made clear that literacy is an important tool in the art of seduction.[27] Ovid has cleverly made Paris reflect his own role as both the *magister amoris* and the writer who uses words to seduce not merely the women within his works, but the reader as well. Ovid has capitalized on the well-known seductive powers of Paris to make in him a model for the elegiac lover despite his place in the epic genre. Paris has the great reputation of lover in epic poetry – Ovid, in his *Heroides*, has transformed him into an elegiac lover and poet who goes about scribbling on trees and tables to achieve his seductions. Paris, Ovid slyly suggests, is much like his creator.

Lest I be accused of over-reading these epigraphic passages in Paris' narratives, Brian Breed (2006) has made several significant observations regarding the placement of inscriptions in Virgil's pastoral *Eclogues*. Concluding his chapter on *Eclogues* 3, 5 and 7, he writes: ' "inscription" is a central metaphor for Virgil's pastoral. It signifies, for instance, that despite its mimetic and spoken surface, pastoral is impossible without writing, its means of relating to its authorizing tradition' (2006, 64). The incorporation of textuality within the poem illustrates that, despite the allusions to and borrowings from previous pastoral texts, Virgil's new pastoral poetry will establish itself as a precedent for later writers, a text for future readers, and will exert its 'freedom from the constraints that chronology places on the spoken word' (2006, 73). Ovid's transformation of Paris into a Callimachean, elegiac figure is likewise a response to the Greek literary tradition. Ovid's Paris is a reconstituted elegiac hero who behaves much like the elegiac lover of Roman invention. Though Ovid never claims, like Propertius, to be a 'Roman Callimachus', he demonstrates that he is, all the same. This new, 'Acontian' Paris has the literary tradition on his side – his familiarity to the reader is assured – but his traditional powers of seduction have gained the power of text from the very teacher who encourages all lovers to engage in writing to achieve their aims. Moreover, the new Acontius who admires Paris' heroic confidence has graduated beyond the role of trickster who uses text to deceive and entrap Cydippe. In *Her*. 20 he manipulates text in a bold new way that asserts the fulfilment of his desire and the approval of the gods. Acontius too has assumed the role of a successful and sophisticated *amator*.

Conclusion

The *Heroides* is the most epigraphically-minded text written by en elegist, or any other Roman poet. The penchant for inscriptions that Ovid manifests in this collection demonstrates the rhetorical utility of the poetic inscription as a means by which the personal tone of a poem, particularly these epistolary poems, approaches realism. The inscriptions are hypertext links between the fictions of the poem and the Roman world in which those striving for permanence attach their names, their careers and their final words to tombstones and other monuments.

The women's inscriptions arrange the circumstances of recent events into a narrative that grants each author some dignity amidst the relative powerlessness of her situation. Phyllis and Dido most notably succumb to the narrative of victimization, for they develop a memorial that focuses on the male perpetrator's accomplishments.[28] Dido and Phyllis, by focusing their memorials on the wickedness of the men they loved, negate the effectiveness of their parting, final words that might have imparted some aspect of their innocence. Hypermestra and Sappho defy that narrative of victimization by leaving inscriptions that omit any mention of the men that create their condition. Instead they write for themselves in the way that men do – casting light upon their respective accomplishments: respectively *pietas* and *poiesis*. All the epitaphs, however, call to attention a feminine desire for self-determined representation. In manipulating inscriptional text, these women seek a path of recognition and self-expression typically reserved for or utilized by men.

The inscriptions by Paris and Acontius achieve quite different ends than the women's inscriptions: they are strategic and manipulative, and they aid in creating advantageous circumstances for themselves and their author. Ovid styles Paris and Acontius as lovers who use text to seduce their feminine readers. The successful *amator* of Ovid's *Amores* and his *Ars Amatoria* is one who likewise manipulates and interprets textual media to fulfil his amorous intentions. Ovid thereby draws these two significant men of legend, one made famous in epic, one made famous in Callimachean elegy, into the world of his own Roman elegiac community where seduction is an objective concomitant to acquiring an admiring and devoted readership.

All these inscriptions reflect an acknowledgement that gender significantly determines the manner in which communication of thoughts and desires is achieved. These epigraphic moments in epistolary text are indicative of the unfair realities that exist in a world where self-representation is crucial and yet difficult to achieve.

6

Ovid's Epic Inscriptions

In this final chapter on Ovid I will analyse three inscriptions that appear in his epic, the *Metamorphoses*.[1] Although the metre has changed, the functions of the inscriptions continue to operate as they have done within their elegiac contexts: they serve the function of commemoration and thematic exposition in ways similar to their elegiac counterparts. This is not surprising since many scholars have established that there is common ground between Ovid's epic and his elegiac poems. Joseph Farrell explains: 'where cross-references and narrative doublets used to be taken as illustrations of the differences between epic and elegiac genres, critics are now more apt to find evidence of a more complex relationship that explores the boundaries of genre and even questions the meaning of the concept' (Farrell 2003, 402).[2] Ovid's epic inscriptions match the typical categories of inscriptions, and they inevitably evoke the true Roman experience of erecting them and reading them.[3]

Stephen Wheeler, in the midst of a fuller analysis of writing and textuality in the *Metamorphoses*, offers a helpful analysis of the inscriptions (Wheeler 1999, 55): 'Inscriptions differ from [other types of writing in the narrative] in that they are intended to be permanent ... . The majority of the inscriptions in the *Metamorphoses* are associated with death; hence the desire to commemorate the dead eternally through the permanence of writing.' He goes on to address aspects of feminine representation in the inscriptions (1999, 57): 'it should be evident that this form of communication is introduced in special circumstances that deviate from the norm. More often than not, the act of writing is associated with women, the loss of speech, and memorializing the dead.'

I intend to build on Wheeler's assessment by looking at other purposes these inscriptions achieve besides commemoration of the dead. Iphis' inscription (in *Met.* 9) is votive, not funereal, and although there have been previous interpretations of her story, none have treated the inscription as a key part of the narrative. Her inscription is a bold and provocative declaration of her transformation into a man, and a means by which s/he claims the power achieved by her new form. Phaëthon's and Caieta's inscriptions do memorialize the dead, but in significantly different ways that reflect gender inequalities inherent in modes of commemoration. Caieta's inscription, furthermore, is clearly a response to Virgil's Caieta inscription, and is thereby Ovid's attempt to stake out his own narrative territory in the shadow of Virgil's prior literary brilliance.

HIC SITUS EST PHAËTHON

The failure of Phaëthon (in *Met.* 1.750-2.366) to drive his father's sun-chariot correctly across the vault of heaven is, like the fall of Icarus, one of the great ancient stories that admonishes youthful hubris and warns against indulging childish whims. Phaëthon's unsuccessful attempt to keep the magnificent team of Phoebus on its course allows the intense heat of the sun to scorch many lands; great Earth herself implores Jupiter to strike down the incompetent charioteer. He does so, and the unfortunate boy, killed by Jupiter's bolt, falls to earth in Italy, far from his homeland of Ethiopia. The naiads of Hesperia recover the burnt boy's body and bury him before his mother and sisters have discovered him; they create the following inscription for his tomb (2.327-8):

> HIC SITUS EST PHAËTHON CURRUS AURIGA PATERNI
> QUEM SI NON TENUIT MAGNIS TAMEN EXCIDIT AUSIS.

> Here lies Phaëthon, driver of his father's chariot – a task he performed not well, but with great daring.

After a worldwide search, the boy's mother and sisters, Clymene and the Heliades (no sister is individually named), find his tomb and mourn inconsolably for many days. What the women find is not a body but a monument and a text, and Clymene even pours her tears over the inscription and holds it to her exposed breast.[4] Ovid explicitly refers to the boy's name in the marble as the object of her maternal devotions, 338-9: *nomenque in marmore lectum / perfudit*, 'and she drenched the name she had read in the marble with her tears.' The monument becomes more than merely a petrified form of expression, but a petrified version of the boy himself. The text bears the responsibility of evoking *in corpore* the reality of the boy she has lost.

This association of the body with his monument is certainly in keeping with the human desire to replace the lost physicality of a dead loved one by means of touching a tombstone, embracing a coffin, and other such manifestations of loss and grief. Yet Ovid emphasizes the obsessive nature of the laments of Phaëthon's mother and sisters. He calls their laments 'vain duties in the face of death' (340-1: *inania morti munera*) to connote their inability to bring him back to life, and to suggest that the inscription the Hesperian naiads created for Phaëthon bears more significance than the tears his mother and sisters shed at the completed tomb. The nameless naiads, instead of Clymene and her daughters, have granted Phaëthon a lasting monument. Having read a text that they could not author themselves, these women succumb to an obsessive desire to continue the process of reading and re-reading the text, mourning not only their loss, but their lost opportunity for choosing their brother's memorial. The sisters' unfulfilled desire to mourn properly for their brother leads to their own pathetic demise when they transform into a grove of trees. Their transformation to rooted vegetation may symbolically refer to a stubborn unwillingness to take the epitaph at its word, or to an unwillingness to accept a text written by someone else. Again, as kin to the dead boy, it should have been their words that graced his tomb.[5] Ironically, as they lose their human-ness and their memory, the epitaph before them maintains its authority over the events: only by its words will future generations mark his passing.

This scenario recalls Oenone in the *Heroides*, for she too reads and re-reads her problematic monument that on the one hand promises to commemorate her, yet reminds her constantly of her heartbreaking loss. In addition, these lines evoke the Catullan expression of grief for a lost brother wherein the poet's house becomes a tomb (68b.94: *tecum una tota est nostra sepulta domus*), and the poet grieves that his brother's bones rest not with the tombs of his ancestors but in a foreign land (68b.97-8: *quem nunc tam longe non inter nota sepulcra / nec prope cognatos compositum cineres*).[6] Phaëthon's sisters never leave the spot of his burial – as Catullus says of himself, their house too has become a tomb.

After their transformation into trees, the sisters' tears become sap that flows and hardens. Their amber tears then drop down into a nearby river, destined one day to be prized jewellery for Roman brides. This last Ovidian flourish may allude to the continuous association of women's lives to the experience of loss and unfulfilment.[7] The amber-bride reference may also suggest that women willingly and knowingly take on the ornaments of sadness and inability to determine their self-expression when they enter the institution of marriage. It is certainly true that much of Ovid's previous literature was aimed at illustrating what benefits could potentially derive from free and idealistic love without the trappings of marital ownership, even if he was primarily demonstrating what men, rather than women, had to gain from it.

Structurally Phaëthon's epitaph serves a purpose as well, bringing to completion a string of narratives where two fathers (Peneus and Inachus) and one mother (Clymene) mourn their lost children.[8] The inscription that the naiads create and the sisters mourn remains a grim and poignant reminder of the association between legacy and memorial – children provide a measure of eternity, but the text is more permanent. One message here appears to be that as long as a woman's grief is separate from or is denied a textual representation, it bears little significance. As we have seen, in many of Ovid's works the poet features women who express their desires to lament the dead, even themselves, in their own words, particularly in the *Heroides*. What really matters most is a lasting monument – weeping women are transitory and ultimately mute. As the next epic inscription demonstrates, perhaps the only way for a woman to slip the bonds of impotence and silence is to become a man.

QUAE FEMINA VOVERAT IPHIS

In *Met.* 9.666-797, a man of Crete tells his wife that if the child she carries is a girl, they must give her up because of their limited means. After delivering a daughter, the mother hides the fact from her husband and dresses her like a boy, and, as a result, the couple raises Iphis (a unisex name that the father unwittingly bestows) as a son.[9] When the time comes for the 'boy's' betrothal, however, the obvious problem arises that Iphis' secret will be discovered on her wedding night. Coincidentally, young Iphis has taken quite a fancy to Ianthe, the young lady to whom she is betrothed. Iphis and her mother visit the temple of Isis and pray for help; the goddess delivers. As mother and daughter leave the temple, Iphis transforms into a man before her mother's eyes. In their joy, they leave an inscribed offering, (9.786-94):

> mater abit templo. sequitur comes Iphis euntem,
> quam solita est, maiore gradu; nec candor in ore
> permanent et vires augentur et acrior ipse est
> vultus et incomptis brevior mensura capillis,
> plusque vigoris adest habuit quam femina. nam quae
> femina nuper eras, puer es. date munera templis,
> nec timida gaudete fide. dant munera templis,
> addunt et titulum; titulus breve carmen habebat:
> DONA PUER SOLVIT QUAE FEMINA VOVERAT IPHIS.

> As the mother leaves the temple, her companion Iphis follows, but with larger steps than she was accustomed; her face is not as pale, her strength has increased, her face is more angular, and she sports a short hairdo in place of her unadorned locks, and there is more vigour in her stride than she usually possessed. Indeed – you who were a maid, are now a man. Give offerings at the temple and rejoice faithfully and openly. They dedicate offerings at Isis' temple, and they add an inscription, consisting of a brief verse: 'The young man Iphis has dedicated the gifts which he once had sworn as a girl.'

This episode has received attention with particular regard to how we should receive Ovid's tale with respect to its homosexual aspects. Diane Pintabone (2002), on the one hand, believes that Ovid provides a balanced, non-judgmental representation of same-sex love, and that the marriage at the end exists merely to place Iphis' love for Ianthe in an appropriate societal context, while Ovid shows sympathy for the love itself, formed when both are women. John Makowski (1996), on the other hand, believes that Ovid firmly comes down on the side of heterosexual union, denigrating the homosexual attraction that is represented here: the narrative of Orpheus that surrounds the Iphis tale, he asserts, associates Iphis' love with the impugned pederasty of Orpheus.

These two scholarly treatments provide well-developed arguments for their positions, but Pintabone provides the most convincing assessment of the story itself. If the tale is taken aside from the Orphic context, its own narrative provides many instances where the reader views Iphis' struggle, understands her dilemma, and sympathizes with her plight. Even the loathing that Iphis demonstrates for her own position, Pintabone shows, is not reflected in Ovid's surrounding narrative.[10] The love that she has for Ianthe develops without manipulation or exploitation, without any outside agent, like Cupid, driving Iphis from within. As Pintabone shows, moreover, the love that Iphis has for Ianthe makes her wish that either she or Ianthe become male so that their marriage might take place. Marriage is on her mind, not lust, and commitment is her aim, not merely sexual union. Pintabone makes the intriguing claim that Iphis' transformation comes about, by contrast to many other non-traditional loves, because she maintains the demeanour and gentle spirit of a woman (Pintabone 2002, 276). Among many significant insights, Pintabone points out that, despite her desire for Ianthe, she does not force herself upon her, she does not seek the means to become a woman with manly assets (using a dildo or other sexual accoutrements), nor does she inform Ianthe that she is a woman – a move that would force Ianthe either to reject her or to choose her and thereby choose the socially awkward practice of tribadism. Iphis simply loves, and in doing so remains within her nature. Isis, therefore, rewards Iphis with a transformation so that she and Ianthe can be together in the socially acceptable way that will please them both.

In light of Pintabone's analysis, the inscription that appears at the end of the story becomes a further validation of Iphis' love, despite the non-traditional nature of its same-sex derivation. As stated earlier, the votive inscription is an opportunity for those without the means for public commemoration of their own achievements to publicly celebrate the blessings received from, as they see it, divine helpers. The inscription is notably a public event, and Ovid emphasizes this aspect in his narratorial remarks. In lines 9.791-2 he encourages Iphis and his mother to leave an inscription and rejoice (*date, gaudete*) in their blameless faith (*nec timida fide*) in the gods. In fact the wording of the inscription (794: *DONA PUER SOLVIT QUAE FEMINA VOVERAT IPHIS*) cleverly and boldly illustrates the transition that has occurred.

It is noticeable in the inscription that Iphis and his mother have not shied away from proclaiming the precise nature of their gift from the goddess. Besides the obvious mention of *puer* and *femina* to denote that a single person has experienced two genders, the structure of the inscription places emphasis on the feminine nature of the resulting person who is

Iphis. *Quae* appears at the centre of the line (the fourth of seven words), and immediately after the principal caesura, and is therefore in a metrically dominant position. *Quae* is, of course, both the feminine (singular or plural) and the neuter (plural) form of the relative pronoun. By itself, it can express more than one gender. In the grammatical structure of the line, the antecedent of *quae* is most likely the gifts that have been offered (*dona*), making it the object of *voverat* ('the gifts *which* Iphis as a woman had offered'). Alternatively, however, within this unique, gender-switching context, *quae* could be operating with *femina*, which appears within the relative clause making it the subject of *voverat* ('*who* as a woman had vowed [the gifts]'). It would be highly irregular to understand *puer* as the antecedent of *quae*, and yet the transformation from *femina* to *puer* can allow the pronoun to exist relative to both. I am not denying the grammatical evidence that makes *dona* the suitable antecedent of *quae*, but certainly Ovid has shown in numerous places his capacity for playing with the possible meanings of words, particularly with respect to pronouns.[11]

Therefore *quae*, with its own concomitant ambiguity, conjoins the opposing entities of masculine and feminine that lie unresolved in the juxtaposition of *puer* and *femina*. The unisex name Iphis, in emphatic last position, finishes the line as signifier of both the male and female identities present in the new boy. Pintabone's assertion that Iphis transforms into a man, but keeps a woman's heart, is very much in keeping with the spirit of the inscription that Ovid imagines. The public nature of the inscription, furthermore, emphasizes the fact that the new man has nothing to cause him shame. The love that Iphis feels is proper and good, and now, thanks to Isis, it is made possible. As a woman, Iphis' love for Ianthe, though genuine, could not have been freely enjoyed without the transformation. Iphis the man needs fear no reprisals for his intentions have always been honourable. From the optimistic tone of the narrator's encouragement to leave a memorial of the transformation, we gather that Iphis and her mother had no cause to fear that others, mortal or divine, would condemn their ordeal and resolution.

Given that Ovid does indeed validate the love between Iphis and Ianthe in the end of his story, it is important to ask the question – did Ovid merely include this story to show a demonstrable difference between the love that Iphis has for Ianthe and the love that Orpheus and others (like Myrrha and Byblis) misdirect towards inappropriate partners in the stories that surround it? To begin to answer this question requires a look at another recent argument put forward about the story of Iphis. Shilpa Raval, in the course of her analysis, examines 'the notion of the coherently gendered self' in Ovid's epic (Raval 2000, 170). She shows that Ovid emphasizes the dependency of social institutions such as marriage on the binary opposition of 'man' and 'woman'. When the frailties of such binaries are exposed, as in the case of Iphis' desire to marry Ianthe, only divine intervention (Isis) can restore gender-appropriate designations to the situation so that marriage can occur. As Raval rightly points out, this story in which Iphis poses as male throughout her youth is the only case of female-to-male transvestitism among many tales of male-to-female transvestitism in his works. She reasonably explains the reason for the appearance of so many male-to-female crossings in the epic (Vertumnus, Hercules, Jupiter, Achilles, Sol) as 'vehicles for "playing the other", meant to articulate insecurities (both on the part of the poet and his male readers) about the precarious nature of masculinity, particularly during the Augustan period' (2000, 170). When Raval comes to her conclusions about this singular incident of female-to-male transformation in the story of Iphis, however, she offers this interpretation: 'Ovid could be explicit in his message about the ways in which heterosexual marriage with its reproductive imperatives demands an easily identifiable differentiation between male and female. The emphasis on social institutions and practices in the tale of Iphis, as well as the (literally) transformative power of her gender performance, undermined the notion of a coherently gendered self and denaturalized the binary opposition of "man" and "woman" ' (2000, 170).

Thus, according to Raval, Ovid's male-to-female transvestitism explores the problematic nature of manhood in a society where political agency has been diminished – where all men become feminized relative to the emperor's masculine identity. When a woman dresses and acts like a man, and eventually becomes a man, Raval suggests that Ovid poses the problematic relationship between desire and marriage – the self and society. Raval's point is well taken, but there is another aspect of the argument to be discussed. If male-to-female transvestitism is meant to reflect a lack of political agency, then perhaps this woman's adoption of male behaviours and her eventual transformation into a man reflects a new class of empowerment whereby figures not traditionally associated with power come to possess it.[12]

As shown above, the inscription lends valuable aid to the argument that the love Iphis has for Ianthe, even as a woman, was acceptable provided it was not acted upon until she became a man. Once Iphis becomes a man, he has the power not only to marry Ianthe, but to leave a bold inscription proclaiming his status. As I demonstrated in my analysis of the funerary inscriptions erected within the *Heroides*, when a woman leaves an epitaph, she may undermine her attempt at self-expression by focusing her text on the perpetrator who has brought her to her untimely end. It is the rare case that a woman commemorates herself as a man would do. When Iphis leaves his inscription, he fearlessly embraces his dualistic nature. He does not flinch from reporting that he was a woman, nor does he doubt that he has become, truly, a *puer*.

Raval rightly shows that Ovid chooses not to focus on the private, genital change that Iphis undergoes, preferring rather to demonstrate the outward appearances that display his masculinity: 'the physical change from girl to boy puts forth the idea of mutable sexual characteristics and of a body secondary to performance ... Ovid describes the change (from girl to boy) through the cultural signifiers of masculinity ... : shorter hair, greater physical strength, sharper facial features' (2000, 163-4). What feminine characteristics lie inside his heart become evident in his inscription, but Iphis looks and feels, every inch, a man. The radical nature of this transformation is shown not merely in the consummation of a love initially conceived in a homosexual context, but in the fact that Iphis obtains, with the sanction of the gods and the narrator, the status that protects him within society. Unlike Orpheus, who must wander like a vagrant looking for a place where he can proclaim his sexual desire in peace, free from the crowd of maenads that eventually tears him to pieces, Iphis gets to remain in her hometown, among her friends and family.

If we seek to find Ovid posing an answer to the problem of power-emasculation arising in Roman society, we may find it in the story of Iphis. In that story, Ovid points us to the optimistic possibility that what has been lost may once again be found. The aristocratic, male elite may have lost its inherent right to self-determination, but just as nature abhors a vacuum – the power vacuum will be short-lived. Someone will surely step into the breach, and those to whom power has been denied for centuries, may well find it within their grasp. That an Egyptian goddess bestows upon Iphis this newfound potency suggests that the new elite of society may well be from foreign lands, or from layers of society that appear currently incapable of power. It is certainly true that the cult of Isis was becoming ever more popular among Roman women, partially because within that cult a woman could attain the order of priestess.[13] The idea of women acquiring power long denied them in the Republican political context may have catalysed many who read this story to consider the fluidity of power structures in the new Imperial age, and the forces that would establish the new hierarchy.[14]

Interestingly, the reverse position has been illustrated in another story from Ovid's epic: in the tale of Pygmalion (10.243-97), an artist's desire for an ivory statue of a woman that he has created leads Venus to animate the statue and make her his companion. Many have convincingly interpreted the transformation of the ivory-girl to a woman of flesh and bone (who is immediately taken to the artist's bed) as the consummate exemplification of the male gaze reifying masculine desire, and as reflective of the elegiac impulse towards what Alison Sharrock aptly dubs 'womanufacture'.[15] In part, because Pygmalion desires what he sees, the woman is created. I do not wish to laboriously retell the whole story, or recount all the theoretical implications unfolded within the scholarship, but if an inanimate thing becoming a woman elucidates Roman attitudes about masculine privilege and feminine subordination to male desires, then surely the story of Iphis offers some counterpoint to that. Despite what nature originally granted, Iphis is allowed to behave as a man to the fullest extent in his society because he has fully become one.

In the Roman context we are reminded of the process of Romanization that was especially operational under the imperial system – whereby race and origins mattered less than knowledge of Roman customs, law and methods of organization. Indeed, only a century later, Tacitus expresses characteristic, aristocratic disdain for the political scene in which former slaves rise to levels of power just below the imperial throne.[16] The important common denominator between the process of Romanization and the transformation of Iphis is the extent of its fulfilment. Romanized citizens are not pretenders, transvestites, if you will, parading as Romans for the benefit of generals and visiting statesmen. Evidence has led some to conclude that Romanized peoples adopted Roman culture nearly wholesale, and viewed its concomitant benefits as well worth the sacrifice of formerly fractious tribal traditions and allegiances.[17] Yet it can never be credibly asserted that Romanized peoples shed their Gallic, African or Celtic identities.[18] As we know, the adaptation of Roman culture to fit the various systems of values and social praxis is primarily responsible for the emergence of strongly differing cultural (nearly national) entities after the Middle Ages – Rome's empire created universal ties, but in no way made its peoples uniform. The transformation of Iphis from disempowered woman to empowered man, with a difference, allegorically predicts, I suggest, the inevitable paradigm-shift of the power-structure in Imperial Rome where it becomes possible for non-elites to merit political potency.[19]

HIC PIETATIS ALUMNUS

The third and final inscription in Ovid's epic appears in *Met.* 14. Aeneas leaves an epitaph to mark the cremation and burial site of his nurse, Caieta. Aeneas and his men land on shore, a place *nondum nutricis habentia nomen* (14.157); they meet Macareus, a former companion of Ulysses (not the same Macareus as in *Her.* 11), who then launches into several hundred lines of storytelling. His verbose narrative recounts the fate of mournful Canens who dies by weeping herself into thin air (432: *inque leves paulatim evanuit auras*). The tale is a reiteration of the aspects of so many Ovidian tales in which women meet their end in acts of grief; it is a fair warning against obsessive lamentation. When Macareus finishes his monologue, the urn carrying Caieta's ashes is granted an inscribed tomb (that suitably makes no mention of lamentation), and, immediately afterwards Aeneas' band sets sail and heads for Latium (14.443-4):

> HIC ME CAIETAM NOTAE PIETATIS ALUMNUS
> EREPTAM ARGOLICO QUO DEBUIT IGNE CREMAVIT.

Here do I, Caieta, lie; my charge, a man of distinguished piety, did properly cremate me after helping me evade an Argive pyre.

Although Aeneas, the *alumnus notae pietatis*, does not mention his own name in the inscription, he nevertheless summarizes his nurse's existence in terms of his own accomplishments. The only words that denote Caieta herself are her name and her role as *nutrix*. If we compare this representation of Caieta, written by a man, to the self-representations of the women of the *Heroides*, a pattern emerges. When Ovid's created woman succumbs to the narrative of victimization, she develops a memorial that focuses on the male perpetrator's accomplishments. When Ovid's woman defies that narrative of victimization, she leaves a memorial that reveals her self, and even erases any mention of the man that creates her condition (as seen in the inscriptions of Hypermestra and Sappho).

When a man writes an inscription for a woman, as in the case of Aeneas for Caieta, he frames her narrative in light of his own accomplishments or her role in his life. This is also shown in the way the Hesperian naiads write for Phaëthon, or in the way that Ovid asks his wife to write his own inscription: they avoid the language of victimization and prefer to mention accomplishments, even those that are scarcely accomplishments at all, as in the case of Phaëthon's disastrous attempt to drive his father's team. By creating so many portraits of feminine suffering, Ovid has offered insight into the hopeless irony of the woman's condition: unless lament and complaint are codified or textualized, they count for little. Yet, the difficulty for a woman to achieve the appropriate means of memorializing her accomplishments and her feelings place her in the precarious state of utter dependency and victimization.

This leads us to another aspect of Caieta's inscription: namely that it evokes so strongly the Virgilian narrative. In the *Aeneid* the hero speaks words over Caieta's tomb that evoke an epitaph (7.1-4):

> Tu quoque litoribus nostris, Aeneia nutrix,
> aeternam moriens famam, Caieta, dedisti;
> et nunc servat honos sedem tuus, ossaque nomen
> Hesperia in magna, si qua est ea gloria, signat.

> In your death, Caieta, nurse of Aeneas, you have granted lasting fame to these (eponymous) shores; even now your excellence preserves your final resting place, and whatever its claims to glory, great Hesperia bears your name to mark your burial.

Here Aeneas' words focus on his preoccupation with the land where he and his companions are destined to reside. To him, Italy is still strange and unknown, and his careful qualification (*si qua est ea gloria*) suggests a hesitation from assuming too much about the future glory he will attain there. Nevertheless, as Barchiesi (1979) and Kyriakidis (1998) have suggested, these inscriptional words serve to highlight the involvement of

Aeneas in the land he is destined to win. There is confidence in his assignment of Caieta's name to the surrounding shoreline.

Aeneas' inscription for Caieta in the *Metamorphoses* more firmly associates the hero with the act of marking the landscapes he has discovered with evidence of his emerging identity as founder of the Latin race, and Aeneas is more aware of his literary reputation as 'duty-bound' (*notae pietatis alumnus*). In many ways the inscription faithfully reports the story of Aeneas as told by Virgil: markedly alluding to the tenth line of the *Aeneid* (*insignem pietate virum*), and to Aeneas' various labours at Troy and the sack of the city that Virgil describes in Books 2 and 3 of his epic (*ereptam Argolico igne*). By pointing the reader to the *Aeneid*, the epitaph conveys the significance of Virgil's accomplishment and Ovid's desire to achieve the kind of immortality where a brief allusion can instantly raise before the reader the spectre of a writer's creative genius. Caieta's epitaph also isolates the considerable differences between Virgil's narrative and Ovid's, but to Ovid's benefit. Were he merely to parrot the events that Virgil had already masterfully narrated, his effort would automatically be diminished. Ovid emphasizes his innovations, however, on the already traditional narrative of Aeneas' journey. The epitaph validates Virgil's authority while it directs the reader to notice Ovid's wonderfully elaborate structure of stories built upon the foundation of his predecessor's approved text.

Conclusions

Like Phyllis and Dido in the *Heroides*, the Heliades in Ovid's epic represent the women of the past – those who utilize text (whether they write it or read it) merely to ossify their grief and fossilize their dependence on men. The Heliades treat the tombstone of their brother as an idol that they worship, and their obsessive lamentations trap them into immobility and stagnation. Iphis, however, is a woman transformed; as a man he uses text to assume the power long denied him. Caieta's lesson is this: serving a man all her life achieved her nothing but the promotion of her ward. The epitaph Aeneas leaves for her demonstrates, in light of the other inscriptions, how easily men will insert themselves into the narratives of women's lives. To change this, women must act, use the text to their advantage, and persist in creating their own narratives and by achieving such deeds that will result, as for Virgil's Caieta, in the commemoration of their *honos*. Iphis' inscription expresses pleasure in the fact that feminine desire has been matched by the capability for execution. I believe that Ovid suggests by her inscription that power is transmutable, and as one group adopts, and improves upon, and shares in that power, it may find itself in the position to usurp power altogether. Although Iphis' transformation bears the characteristics of *deus ex machina*, it is also confirmation that what lives in the hearts of those who long to be free of the restraints of cultural normalcy may find themselves in the opportunity to operate within, and not outside their own society.

What do the last three chapters say about Ovid? His inscriptions are inheritors of a long-standing relationship between elegy and epigraphic self-representation. Ovid follows Catullus, Propertius and Tibullus in using the epigraphic text (evoked or explicit) to identify poetic and personal anxieties. His particular penchant for naming himself in his inscriptions is a literary continuation of Tibullus' self-identification as a client of his commander and patron Messalla. However Ovid shows no allegiance to any Roman institutions *per se*, only to his poetic persona – one that faces a threat, and must be preserved against prevailing circumstances. When Ovid boldly asserts mastery over his reader in the closing lines of his lessons in the *Ars Amatoria* (*NASO MAGISTER ERAT*) he perhaps inadvertently issues a challenge to Augustus' attempt to control marital and sexual behaviours.

His inscriptions also continue the Propertian experiment of granting the power of inscriptional 'voice' to women – non-traditional tenants of authority and self-determination. The heroines who leave inscriptions in Ovid's epistles display differing degrees of self-validation – some continue to play the victim, while others find the words of self-commemoration that focus more on their gifts and virtues. As Ovid suggests by way of Iphis' inscription, it may very well be new and yet unheard voices that determine the direction of Rome's future.

Ovid's epitaph from exile is a literal 'last word' on the elegiac act of commemoration, for with these words, *INGENIO PERII NASO POETA MEO*, Ovid explains what is clearly at stake under imperial rule. By claiming that he, an artist, died because of his poetic talent, he points to the fact that political and artistic freedom were undergoing permanent change, change which would soon silence the independent voices of the elegiac movement.

Conclusion

The Romans inherited epic and elegiac metres from the Greeks, and it was through the artistry of Ennius that we trace the dawn of a Roman poetic age. Ennius, a native Italian, a cultural Greek, and a Roman by circumstance, embodied the rich, cross-cultural milieu of the third century BC that fostered the creation of Greco-Roman poetry. The willingness of Romans to receive the imported, Greek metrical form indicates that they were already familiar with a poetics of their own. Ennius was not necessarily introducing culture to the Romans, but a new method of articulating their own poetic traditions and tendencies.

The earliest Roman inscriptions demonstrate that poetry was a part of its religious and domestic life. The probably indigenous, Saturnian, verse-form held a prominent position as the metre of choice in honouring the dead at the height of the Republican period. The Cornelius Scipios, whose status among the Romans approached heroic proportions, honoured their dead by gracing their tombs with Saturnian verses that paid homage to their virtues and achievements. They did this even when the new, elegiac metre had shown itself capable of application to honorary epigram in the reverent verses that Ennius composed: verses that reflect the Roman preoccupation with memorial and eulogy, and a Roman predilection for poetry that serves the pragmatic function of remembering historic deeds.

This in turn reflected Roman character. In his popular and insightful narrative of the late Republic, Tom Holland reminds us that the Romans used the word *honestas* to express both moral excellence and reputation (Holland 2003, 5): 'the approval of the entire city was the ultimate, the only, test of worth. This was why, whenever resentful citizens took to the streets, it would be to demand access to yet more honours and glory.' The representative political structure at Rome, the involvement of citizens in governance and the army, and a conservative desire to maintain the status quo until reform was deemed absolutely necessary all formed significant parts of the unique political and cultural conditions of Rome. The resulting cooperation of self-determination and civic duty created a eulogistic literary culture, one witnessed most significantly on the grander monuments of Rome's great citizens during the Republican period.

Even after elegiac inscriptions began to appear on the tombs of Rome's best men, some elected to preserve the older, more traditional means of funerary monument. The lists of political achievements so vital to Roman self-representation could be more easily accommodated within the somewhat lax and long-measured Saturnian verse; elegy required brevity and precise syllabic arrangement. Once the elegy took hold, however, it became an important metre in the poetic narratives of the dead, expressing more nimbly the last words of the deceased, a family's grief, or a society's gratitude. To make up for the lost flexibility of the archaic form, elegiac inscriptions were often accompanied by long, un-metrical strings of words or abbreviations to present the lists of offices and titles that defined a man: his duty to the state and his success among his peers. By usurping the role of the Saturnian and persistently appearing on the tombstones of Rome's leading citizens, elegy assumed the responsibility of documentation. Its fluid, poetic expressions, conceived under the influence of Hellenistic epigram, were an aesthetic complement to the formulaic but essential identifiers of service to Rome, the marks of a life well lived. Hellenistic elegy may have entered Rome a light and frivolous thing – a deposit of fleeting sentiments – but under Roman influence the metre found itself burdened with the responsibility of speaking true things, identifying patriotic deeds and great men, and representing a life marked by politics and war.

My study has shown that this associative aspect of record and personal representation continued to exist within the elegiac metre even as it was being applied to less morbid tasks. The emergence of elegy as a narrative, poetic form in the seven decades before the death of Augustus featured a focus on eroticism and Hellenistic refinements – that cannot be denied; Roman poets had carefully honed the elegiac craft to match their Greek predecessors both thematically and rhetorically. Nevertheless, this study considers another important theme in elegy, one unjustly relegated to the concept of grief (although grief is a great part of it), but one that likewise shaped the vast range of physical remains of Rome's recorded legacy: namely a desire for permanence – the will to designate certain things for preservation. The Roman elegists fashioned this metre to bear a heavy load: eroticism, rhetorical ingenuity, the depth of human expression, and graphic moments of documentation. As I have shown, Roman elegy occasionally flaunts its kinship to the epigraphic impulse to commemorate prizes won, honours achieved, love attained and those persons and things that have been lost in reality, but that still live within the text.

The intended purpose of this study is to provide fuller vision of the epigraphic passages of Latin elegy, these texts within texts, as more than remnants of the epigrammatic, epigraphic (or even epitaphic) aspects of the elegiac genre, and more than primitive impositions upon a graceful, Hellenistic poetic form. This study has shown that in a steady and diachronic fashion, Roman elegy, even in its Catullan infancy, has always accommodated these epigraphic expressions not as mere intrusions, but as thematic partners to the inherited, Hellenistic material. Catullus' grief for a lost brother in his first elegy (poem 65) indicates that the metre need not be freed from the here and now, the personal and the subjective. The desire of Catullus, implied in poem 65 and blatantly expressed in poem 68, to bury his brother among the tombs of his ancestors is not so much an intrusion upon the elegiac text: it is an acknowledgement that his elegiac craft is pulled in two directions between the duty-bound task of eulogizing the dead and the challenge of composing in Latin the artistically ingenious aspects of many centuries of elegiac *poiesis*. The allusions to eulogistic epigraphy in Catullus 65 and 68 are ultimately expressions of identity, and they establish the literary interdependence of *Romanitas* and Greek erudition that would become the hallmark of the elegiac movement.

In the fully formed elegies of the great masters – Propertius, Tibullus and Ovid – the embedded, poetic inscription is a significant elegiac *topos* as seen by its frequent inclusion in Augustan elegy. So imitative of the countless inscriptions that meet the eye of the city-dweller, it constitutes a means by which the Roman reader might form an understanding of the world of a poem. It creates an intersection between the fiction of the poetic characters and the experiences of the readers who occasionally post such sentiments of their own. The ability to manipulate words in a public context – not to mention the notable ability to read (and then interpret!) what is written – held the respect of the ancients. The poetic inscription is therefore a mimetic signifier of the process of preservation and commemoration that was such a vital part of Roman cultural identity. The Augustan elegists capitalize greatly on the Roman penchant for codification, self-representation and publicity that is so grandly on display during the Republican period. By usurping this process of commemoration within their poems, they attempt to harness Republican-style approbation for their literary and slightly humbler achievements.

Yet as these poets composed their elegies, the Roman world was undergoing a radical upheaval of its political system whereby the traditional notions of service to state were becoming re-oriented towards service to the *princeps* and the imperial family. Some viewed the new political system as a degradation of the self-determination that had long been so essential to Roman character. It is around this time, in the early half of the first century AD, that elite families choose less and less to commemorate their dead in the grandiose fashion of their Republican ancestors. The summaries of great lives devoted to civic service could never surpass the narratives of achievement on the monuments of emperors and members of their families. Meanwhile the increasing wealth among members of the lower classes allowed any who could afford a monument to publicly tout the virtues of good bookkeeping, bread baking, gladiator training and midwifery. Of course the increasing opportunities for self-representation newly granted to so many may also be called advantageous and a sign of progress. Yet, for the generations still enamoured with the institutions and class structures of the Republic, Rome changed unalterably and for the worse.

Trimalchio's epitaph in the *Cena Trimalchionis* can be seen as a boundary marker of sorts between the elegiac attempts to manipulate epigraphic language and context for the purpose of lending authority to the text, and the later scepticism among the Roman elite regarding inscriptions as reliable modes of representation. When Trimalchio composes his epitaph,[1] he uses words and phrases once attributed to involved citizens in the Roman Republic (*pius* and *fortis*), yet his career is marked not by a summary of offices of statesmanship, but by slavery, a network of associations with the craftsmen of Rome and the accumulation of Croesus-like wealth.[2] Added to this, Trimalchio boasts of never having consulted a philosophic idea. This is perhaps a jab at the philosopher Seneca – a contemporary of the author Petronius and fellow-member of the Neronian court – but it is also an ironic allusion to the deterioration of Rome's intellectual community vis-à-vis its inclusionary and widening structure. It might also imply that Rome has always featured men of action rather than men extensively involved in philosophical matters. Petronius' Trimalchio is in some ways not so unlike the self-made and powerful men of Rome who lived a century earlier – yet Trimalchio represents the new, debased, and ignoble *novus homo*. His presence makes notable the gaps where great men like Cicero, Caesar, Pompey, the Scipios and the Catos once existed – men whose aims were to guide and improve the Republic for future generations. Trimalchio's monument is a sad commentary on the future of Rome's civic participant, and was no doubt galling to those who continued to hope for a return to Rome's Republican institutions.

I have argued that the inscription in poetry is an indicator of the confidence that Romans held in the integrity of text. Given the multitude of inscriptions that hyperbolized the emperor's deeds in the Imperial period, the traditional Roman reverence for public text that had existed among the elite began to diminish. Moreover, the debasement of the inscriptional text by virtue of its widespread appeal among the lower classes caused even literary inscriptions, so prevalent in previous elegiac poetry, to lose their lustre, and this may explain the dearth of poetic inscriptions in later poetry.[3] The future applications of the metre reflect this cynical atmosphere, most notable indeed in the provocative and sarcastic expressions of Martial's epigrams.[4] Augustan elegy, by contrast, subsisted and prospered on the inter-play between the nobility of traditional careers and dilettantism, between conservative mores and libertinism, and between the growing anticipation of a new and peaceful Rome and the increasing anxiety that Rome was never going to be the same – between past and present. Elegies by Propertius, Tibullus and Ovid did not suit the new age of conformity to an imperial regime. The former, subtle ambiguities between what people did and what they were supposed to do, that had been so intriguingly discussed and examined in the elegiac poems, dissipated under the stern gaze of an emperor's will (or whim).

The death of Ovid, alone in humiliating exile, marks the end of the elegiac movement. It was a movement motivated by the challenge of improving upon the poetic precedents of the Hellenistic age. In the process of improving the elegiac form, the poets infused their works with indigenous, cultural qualities that heightened their audience's identification with their literary products, and one of these qualities was the manner of epigraphic commemoration in the middle and late Republic. Its eventual association with the elegiac poetic form had significant influence on the poetics of the elegiac movement. The Augustan elegists feature funereal, dedicatory and even whimsical inscriptions within their works to emphasize the link between literate activity and their literary worlds, and between those poetic worlds and the real world at Rome. Poetic inscriptions serve to reify the fleeting concerns of poetic *personae*, and they suggest that what happens in a poem might truly be reflective of a wider cultural reality. This study has shown that the inscriptions that grace these poets' monuments of words provide one more window into the complex interrelations between Latin poetics and Roman culture, and into the hopes and anxieties of their authors. In a desire for literary achievement, the Augustan elegists granted their verses the power of textual permanence.

Notes

Introduction

1. These phrases come from MacMullen 1982 and Mann 1985 respectively.

2. Sandys 1927, 2, identifies three important areas in which inscriptions aid our understanding of the Classical world: (1) the history and chronological development of the Roman name; (2) the *cursus honorum*; and (3) the names and titles of the Roman emperors, and of members of the imperial family. See also Corbier 1974 on the many civic, societal and cultural aspects of the Roman world that can be gleaned from inscriptions.

3. Cooley 2000, 2: 'inscriptions are not objective records of past history, but subjective monuments generated by individuals whose motivation is to present a particular image of themselves.' MacMullen 1982, 246: 'In the exercise of the habit, people counted on their world still continuing in existence for a long time to come so as to make neatly permanent memorials worthwhile; and they still felt themselves members of a special civilization, proud (or obliged) to behave as such.'

4. Breed 2006, 4, makes a similar defence in his analysis of voice and text in Virgil's pastoral poetry by suggesting that such poetic complexity is more than 'preciosity, merely an affectation'.

5. See Copley's 1956 study, for example, on the origins and evolution of the elegiac paraclausithyron.

6. On my use of the phrase, 'elegiac movement', see Cairns 1979, 229: '[Roman patrons] wanted to be part of a movement which was consciously emulating and surpassing ... the greatest achievements of the five centuries of Greek literature.' I will offer a few remarks about Horace and Virgil, but as I discuss in Ch. 1, previous scholarship has already given direct attention to these authors. In addition, I believe that one cannot treat Ovid's epic as entirely exclusive from his elegiac work, and therefore I consider inscriptional passages in the *Metamorphoses* as being within my analytical purview.

7. Admittedly, the notion of genre is something that is always being tested in Augustan poetry, especially in Ovid. See Conte 1992, 120, on the slippage between artistry and the rubrics of genre: 'Every new text, as it unfolds, justifies its own relation with the system of literary genres, which it simultaneously takes as norm and evades.' See also Farrell 2003, 392, who points out the historical contexts that accompanied the most fervent attempts to identify miscegenation and impurities in ancient generic categories (e.g. nineteenth-century attitudes towards ethnicity). Farrell, 396, suggests we challenge Platonic and Aristotelian categories of genre by weighing these rubrics against the cross-pollinated texts of numerous poets throughout the centuries: 'generation after generation found the idea of genre as essence or recipe to be the perfect foil for a poetics that was more concerned with teasing indeterminacy than with purity of any kind.'

8. One anonymous reader justifiably pointed out that this assessment may be problematic in the cases of inscriptions that do not constitute whole verses or distichs – that the incompleteness of the inscription is part of a deliberate strategy to make them non-separable from their context. I allow that this is possible, but I am also counting on lines that lead up to such incomplete verses to play a part in announcing the inscribed text, such as in the case of Paris' graffito for Helen in *Heroides* 17.88 (the single word, AMO). The following words serve aptly to emphasize the coming inscription 87-8: *orbe quoque in mensae legi sub nomine nostro / quod deducta mero littera fecit* AMO. The details of placement suggested here render the inscription's reception a physical dimension.

9. Janan 2001, 156, provides an example of how this poem might have seemed to her male audience: 'Her chastity, like Verginia's, figures the integrity of the body politic. Propertius represents feminine sexuality as guarantor and model of Rome's national coherence and integrity ... Woman thus becomes the guarantor of the Laws' consistency: successful control over her sexuality attests the Law's effectiveness and the coherence of the body politic underwritten by the Law.'

10. On this topic there are numerous discussions including those found in almost all commentaries on the Roman elegiac poets; for a distilled discussion of posing the poetic career as a substitute for traditional Roman careers see especially Farrell 2002, 37-44, and 2004.

11. Cairns 1979, 228-9.

12. See Laird 1993, 18-19, for a summary of the various approaches, and their concomitant problems. See also Fowler 1991 on the significance of focalization, loosely described as point of view, in any narrative presentation of objects.

13. *Iliad* 18.478-617; *Aeneid* 8.625-731 and 1.456-94.

14. See Fowler, 1991 and 1996, on the problems of the term, but note especially his comforting conclusion (1996, 74): 'The variety of points of view that we construct in art and about art is not some shameful consequence of the Fall that we need to overcome but the point of the phenomenon ... What matters is not the medium ... but the metadiscourse about it, the stories we tell.'

15. See Sandys 1927, 3-19 on the various references to and quotations of Latin inscriptions in authors such as Livy, Suetonius, Cicero and Polybius. Sandys, 19, concludes: 'inscriptions are alluded to in about 50 passages, and are actually quoted in about 30 others.'

16. Admittedly, Hellenistic literary developments in the modes of representation and description can account for a closer association between an ekphrastic passage and narrative structure; see Christiane Reitz' entry on 'Ekphrasis' in Cancik and Schneider, eds, 2002, 875-6: 'from the Hellenistic period, we witness an increase in the desire to turn the ekphrasis in to the focal point of the plot, and to employ it for greater emphasis of its statements. The representation is presented directly or indirectly, that is, conveyed through a fictitious recipient, in realistic special conceptions or as an illusion.' Nonetheless, poetic inscriptions do not provide enough explicit artistic viewpoints to be held in the same category as objects in which descriptive narrative is clearly at work.

17. *Daniel* 5:5-9; 24-8.

18. In Ovidian inscriptions, for example, *Am.* 2.6.60: *lapis exiguus*; *Met.* 14.441-2: *urna ... marmorea*; *Fasti* 3.547: *tumulique in marmore*; *Trist.* 3.3.72: *grandibus in tituli marmore caede notis*.

19. In fact, this reticence to explicitly describe context may be related to the general failure of inscriptions on monuments to comment on or explicate any images they accompany. It requires the work of one widely experienced with the Roman images to understand what they signify; see Hope 2000. On the problematic nature of the relationship of images to text, see Z. Newby and R. Leader-Newby, eds, *Art and Inscription in the Ancient World* (Cambridge, 2006).

20. Halliwell 2002, 16, adds this rebuff to New Critical approaches: 'the mimeticist tradition stands as a cumulative repudiation of anxieties over the so-called affective fallacy: if representational artworks are communicative acts, as mimetic theories consistently hold, then it cannot be fallacious to understand and evaluate them partly on the basis of the emotional effects that they produce on their audiences.'

21. Sörbom 1966, 28, addresses this important problem regarding the nature of representational art by pointing to a speech of Dolon in Euripides' *Rhesus* (lines 208ff.). Dolon claims he will mimic the wolf's four-footed gait in order to confuse the enemies. Sörbom concludes (29): 'The *mimema* is produced to exhibit something by means of characteristic or characterizing similarities and the exhibition should be of such a kind that the beholder of the *mimema* takes the *mimema* for its "model".'

22. On the term 'heterocosm', see Halliwell 2002, 4, n. 10; he attributes the term to A.G. Baumgarten, *Meditationes Philosophicae de Nonnullis ad Poema Pertinentibus* (Halle,1735).

23. See Koortbojian 2005 on the mimetic and figurative aspects of viewing images and text on tombs.

24. E.g. Plin. *Ep.* 5.6 on his house at Tuscany at the foot of the Apennines.

25. See Pierre Du Prey, *The Villas of Pliny from Antiquity to Posterity* (Chicago, 1994), for architectural conjectures based on Pliny's narrative. See also Andrew M. Riggsby, 'Pliny in Space (and Time)', *Arethusa* 36 (2003) 167-86, on the variety of mitigating factors that come into play when we perceive Pliny's villas through his eyes.

26. See Griffin 1986, passim, on the presence of Roman life in Roman poetry. See also Cairns 1979, 229, 'The work of any great artist must represent, symbolize or incorporate the overall concerns of the age in which he lives.' Note also Edward Said, *The World, the Text and the Critic* (Cambridge, MA, 1983), 4: 'even when they appear to deny it, nevertheless [literary texts] are a part of the social world, human life, and of course the historical moments in which they are located and interpreted.'

27. Compare Ovid's descriptions of Tomis at *Trist.* 3.10 with Virgil's descriptions of the Scythians at *Georgics* 3.349-83. Cf. also Horace at *Carm.* 3.8.18 and Prop. 4.3.9 on pointed reference to these Pontic tribes as barbarian others. Cf. also Herodotus on a particularly savage habit of the Getic tribes (4.94.1-3). A splendid example to illustrate his view of the backward nature of the Pontic coast appears at *Pont.* 3.8.17-20 where Ovid writes to his friend Maximus that the only gift he can find to send him is a quiver of arrows. See Williams 1994, 17, on the modes of description: 'Transferred to a Roman context, the thesis identified the climactic conditions of central Italy as the norm by which all other areas were to be judged;' and on uses of previous literary works, 20: 'The skillful blending of such disparate reminiscences is a display of sophisticated artistry wholly at odds with the nature of the subject-matter. The tone of Ovid's poetic diction here exhibits an ambivalence which it owes to the fundamental incoherence of the source material.'

28. Ovid mentions his waning poetic abilities at *Trist.* 3.10.1-5, and laments his transformation to a Getic poet (writing in a foreign tongue) at *Pont.* 4.13.17-23. See Nagle 1980, 165: 'One fundamental assumption underlies Ovid's assessment of the quality of his exilic poetry, namely, that there is a direct causal relationship between condition in exile and the contents, style, and mood of the poetry written there, such that these elegies are monotonous, melancholy, and inferior to his earlier work.'

29. See also Williams 1994, 54: 'In the exile poetry Ovid does more than pay lip-service to the *topos* of self-depreciation. Far from employing the theme as an occasional ornament which literary precedent obliges him to use, he makes it fundamental to his Tomitan persona by adapting the *recusatio* motif of the poet's enfeebled *vires* and *ingenium* to represent a much more radical, personally damaging and seemingly irreversible decline in poetic creativity.'

30. On the notion of the text as a weaving of 'heard' narratives, see Scheid 1996, 127: 'the voice of the reader is in some sense transferred into the graphic sphere, which in turn raises its voice: ... [the reader] hears the "voice" of the writing in front of him in his head, as if the letters had a voice, as if the book were a talking subject.'

31. Wheeler 1999, 40: 'The fiction of viva-voce performance in the *Metamorphoses* turns out to be a critical point of difference from his elegiac poetry in which he experiments with different forms of textuality.'

32. Here is the text of the poem 'This is Just to Say' (in the original the three stanzas appear in a single, vertical, almost serpentine column):

I have eaten	and which	Forgive me
the plums	you were probably	they were delicious
that were in	saving	so sweet
the icebox	for breakfast	and so cold

By William Carlos Williams in *The Collected Poems of William Carlos Williams, Volume I, 1909-1939*, reprinted edition, A.W. Litz and C. MacGowan, eds (New York, 1991); permission to reproduce this poem was received from New Directions Publishing Corporation.

33. See Bolter and Grusin 1999, 12, on the power of new media, particularly hypertext; they point to illuminations in medieval manuscripts as layered media, whereby their 'large initial capital letters may be elaborately decorated, but they still constitute part of the text itself, and we are challenged to appreciate the integration of text and image'. My point in providing this study is that poetic inscriptions are also a sort of hypertext, an integration not so much of text and image, but of text, cultural topography and literary experience.

34. Neither does this study treat the development of epigrammatic and inscriptional overlap in the Greek world, for some definitive and significant studies in this area have already appeared; see in particular the series *Hellenistica Groningana* (Leuven), particularly the following three volumes: Rossi 2001; Harder, Regtuit and Wakker, eds, 2002; and Bruss 2005. I also have elected to exclude some elegiac works: Tibullus' second book of elegies, Propertius' third book of elegies, and Ovid's *Fasti* and the *Remedia Amoris* get very little or no mention in this study.

1. Elegy and the Inscription

1. *Carm.* 4.14.1-6: *Quae cura patrum quaeve Quiritium / plenis honorum muneribus tuas, / Auguste, virtutes in aevum / per titulos memoresque fastus / aeternet, o, qua sol habitabilis / illustrat oras, maxime principum.*

2. See Susini 1973, 23-4, on the value and quality of marble as a surface for incision (especially the so-called 'V-section trench') in the early principate, and also p. 29 on the relatively infrequent practice of painting letters in inscriptions. Conversely, some marbles were purposely chosen to minimize the visibility of certain inscriptions: Susini 1988, 119, comments on the fact that veined marbles were sometimes used in dedications to later emperors to confound and disguise 'sneers of protest'.

3. Woolf 1996, 22: 'At the end of the last century BC – roughly co-incident, then, with the transition to autocracy, the Roman cultural revolution, and the formative period of provincial cultures throughout the Empire – an epigraphic boom occurred, in Italy and in every province of the Empire.'

4. See Sparrow 1969 on the catalogues of inscriptions that begin to emerge in the sixteenth century.

5. E.g. A. Amante, *La poesia sepolcrale latine* (Palermo, 1912); C. Bonner, 'Some Phases of Religious Feeling in Later Paganism', *Harvard Theological Review* 30 (1937): 119-40; C. Buresch, 'Consolationum a Graecis Romanibusque Scriptarum Historia Critica', *Leipziger Studien zur classischen Philologie* 9 (1886); P. Harrington, 'Conceptions of Death and Immortality in Roman Sepulchral Inscriptions', *PAPA* 30 (1899): 28-31; and M.I. Rostovtzeff, 'The Mentality of the Hellenistic World and the After-Life', *Harvard Divinity School Bulletin* (1938): 5-25.

6. See also Susini 1988, 121: 'The *respublica* – whether it was urban or municipal – took possession of and displayed its own dead as tokens of the respective historical memories; the community employed its dead for its own historiography ... In this, the Romans laid the foundations of part of the modern sense of existence.' At the dawn of the twenty-first century there are many exciting new studies on the inscriptional legacy of the ancient Romans, such as the successive volumes on the Vindolanda tablets edited by Alan K. Bowman and J. David Thomas (*The Vindolanda Writing-Tablets: Tabulae Vindolandenses*, vol.1: London, 1983; vol. 2: London, 1994; and vol. 3: London, 2003); see also Valerie Hope's studies (2000 and 2001) of inscriptions chosen by various social groups, particularly members of the Roman military; see also the collection of essays on epigraphy in Roman Italy edited by Alison Cooley (2000).

7. This number creates a small percentage of the more than 300,000 inscriptions that are known; see Keppie 1991, 9.

8. Lissberger 1934 identifies many cases in which epigraphers or their patrons borrowed verbatim from the Augustan poets.

9. This provides some challenge to the conclusions of Bruno Lier 1902, a study of Latin verse inscriptions that makes little note of endemic sources of Roman expression, and attributes far greater influence to Greek epigram and early Greek inscriptional practice in determining the tone and content of Roman inscriptions. Yet Lier's conclusions have drawn criticism; see Lattimore 1942, 18-19, for the problems and arguments.

10. E.g. Stein 1931, 10, refers to the dedicatory inscription that accompanied an image of Minerva offered by Cicero at the Temple of Jupiter that appears identically in both Dio (38.17.5) and Plutarch (*Cic*. 31.6).

11. E.g. Stein 1931, 11, refers to Suetonius' (*Calig*. 8.1) criticism of Pliny the Elder (probably in the *Bella Germana*) for taking Ambitarvium in Germany as the birthplace of Gaius because an altar there bears the inscription, *ob Agrippinae puerperium*. Suetonius explains that *puerperium* can also refer to the birth of a daughter, and Agrippina was known to have delivered at least two daughters in the province.

12. E.g. Stein 1931, 18 and 33, shows that Tacitus (*Ann*. 11.24) reports the speech of Claudius on the *ius honorum* of the Gauls true to the original content, but 'in seiner eigenen Stilausprägung'.

13. See Stein 1931, 72, for lists of examples.

14. Stein 1931, 77: 'Immer wieder zeigt es sich, daß von epigraphischen Studien bei den Römern keine Rede sein kann, und selbst die Aufnahme von Inschriftterten [sic] zum Zweck urkundlicher Beglaubigung gehört doch eigentlich nur zu den Ausnahmen.' See also loc. cit., 76, on the authors who prove most reliant on inscriptions (and who also tend to report them accurately): 'so finden wir unter den Autoren, die am häufigsten und am genauesten Inschriften mitteilen, Cicero, Cassius Dio, Livius, den älteren Plinius, Suetonius, auch Appian und Plutarch, bezeichnenderweise nicht Tacitus.'

15. Stein 1931, 78: 'Es ist übrigens interessant, daâ bei dem geringen Interesse für echte Inschriften die gefälschten oder fiktiven doch eine gewisse Bedeutung in der antiken Literatur erlangen.'

16. Stein 1931, 78, points out that the Romans were not unfamiliar with attempts to pass off inscriptions as evidence of fact where none existed, as in the case of Mark Antony's posting bronze tablets stipulating the provisions allegedly left by Julius Caesar in his will, a document that Antony had tampered with considerably (Dio 44.53.2-4).

17. Stein 1931, 58, also notes the parody effected in epitaphs created by Seneca (*Epist.* 89.7) and Martial (9.15) – contexts in which all aspects are, indeed, parodic.

18. Stein 1931, 58: 'Nur einem poetischen Zweck will Ovid *Am.* 2.13.25 f. genügen mit der Angabe einer Phantasieinscrift und nicht anders steht es mit seinen Versen *Heroid.* 14.126 ff.'

19. See Lissberger's useful appendices that offer all the citations of Roman poetry found in epitaphs available to him in the early twentieth century.

20. Lissberger 1934, 156-9. His table of regional adherences to poetic diction shows that African Romans comprise nearly the largest population of verse-borrowers, second only to Rome, with Upper Italy and Pompeii nearly tying for third place. In as remote a place as Britannia, Lissberger finds three evocations of the elegiac poets among inscriptions discovered there.

21. Kenney 1973, 119, calls Ovid's Latin a 'poetic *koine*, a stylistic instrument which was freely manageable by writers of lesser genius'.

22. See Harris 1989, 222-8, on the confluence of three significant factors in the first centuries BC and AD: an increasing desire for inscribed tombs, the growing interest in using text already written by others, and the expanded opportunities for poetic fame.

23. See the first appendix of Lissberger 1934, 157-9, in which whole lines or couplets are borrowed verbatim from specific poems.

24. Yardley 1996, 271, shows how even non-elegiac poets use the motif, as in Horace's *Carm.* 3.26, a dedication rather than an epitaph, and in Alcaic metre.

25. Yardley 1996, 273: 'Because graves were located along the roads, Romans, at least those who traveled (elegiac poets included), were exposed to funerary *topoi* to a much greater extent than we moderns ... That being so, one should not be surprised to fine the *topoi* and the language of epitaph in those places in elegy where the poets are discussing death, as they often do.'

26. Cf. Wheeler 1915, 163: 'Elegy and epigram run a closely connected course in almost every period of their history. In addition to the metrical form ... the two genera so often overlap in content, in tone, and even in treatment, that no discussion of one genus is complete without frequent reference to the other; indeed it is often difficult and sometimes impossible to classify a given poem as an elegy or an epigram.'

27. *Aen.* 5.870-1: '*o nimium caelo et pelago confise sereno, / nudus in ignota, Palinure, iacebis harena.*' Although the metre of the *Aeneid* is obviously in hexameters, Barchiesi 1979, 7, calls the second hexameter line of the passage an imitator of the pentameter line of the typical elegiac epigram – a phenomenon he aptly dubs a 'disguised epigram'.

28. *Aen.* 7.1-4: *Tu quoque litoribus nostris, Aeneia nutrix, / aeternam moriens famam, Caieta, dedisti; / et nunc servat honos sedem tuus, ossaque nomen / Hesperia in magna, si qua est ea gloria, signat.*

29. Barchiesi 1979, 10-11.

30. Kyriakidis 1998, 83: 'The poet's intention is to make himself emphatically noticed not only in this initial episode of Book 7 but in the whole passage that follows and is concluded with the delayed invocation and proem (7.37-45); for there too, the poet repeatedly presents himself in the narrative. Once his presence is established, then the allusion to his poetic programme can be more easily conceived.' See also my p. 139f. on purposes achieved by Ovid's insertion of Caieta's inscription within his epic (14.443-4).

31. Dinter 2005, 155, shows that the *Iliad* provides crucial information about Iphition, the first man Achilles slays after re-entering the war: his 'name, patronym, epithet, genealogy and homeland, and manner of dying – all that a good epitaph would give to the reader to make the death meaningful to those outside the circle of family and friends'. Further on, 156, he shows that the purpose of the 'epitaphic gesture' serves to boost the *kleos* of Achilles since it is of course important that his first kill be a man of import and that his 'deed has ramifications far beyond the battlefield. A whole chain of social life is ended by the prowess of the victor.'

32. Dinter 2005 cites and studies many examples of the various types: sepulchral examples are *Aen.* 3.45-6, 3.709-11, 4.561-8, 5.870-1, 6.164-7 and 7.1-4; the dedicatory examples are *Aen.* 3.288 and 11.768-81; and by 'metapoetic' he means 2.784-9 – ultimately another sepulchral text, but one that responds antithetically to Andromache's epitaphic lines in the *Iliad* (6.459-61). See Dinter 2005, 164 and n. 64, on Aeneas' dedication at 3.288 and its possible response to Augustus' vast memorial after the battle of Actium in the same location.

33. E.g. Galinsky 1975 and 1996, Leach 1988 and 1997, and Fantham 1997.

34. Respectively: Prop. 4.3.71; Ovid *Am.* 2.13.25; Ovid *Ars* 2.744; and Prop. 2.14.26.

35. The dedicatory inscription at *Aeneid* 3.288 is the only one quoted as it appears on the monument.

36. The two earliest extant and unproblematic examples are from the tomb of the Scipios: *CIL* 1.2.7 (*CLE* 7) and *CIL* 1.2.9 (*CLE* 6). The song of the Arval Brotherhood (*CIL* 1.2.2; *CLE* 1), although inscribed as early as the sixth century BC, originated as an oral song: see Freeman 1998, 80-1, and Cole 1969, 12.

37. In *CIL*, Buecheler, Lommatzsch and Engström, I could find no Saturnian inscriptions later than the age of Cicero, e.g. *CLE* 12 (*CIL* 10.5282), *CLE* 13 (*CIL* 1.2.1203 and 1204) and *CLE* 14 (*CIL* 1.2.1206).

38. Cole 1969, 47, cites (and takes issue with) Pasquali's argument (in *Preistoria della poesia Latina*) 'that the Saturnian used by Livius [in his translation of Homer's *Odyssey*] was ultimately derived from Greek metres introduced to Rome at a much earlier date, during that period of extensive contact with and borrowing from the Hellenic East and South which ... can be dated, on archaeological evidence, to the 6th or 5th centuries BC'. Later Cole (58) asserts: 'it seems that the regular alternation of longer and shorter cola is subsequent to the composition of the Arval hymn, and so an indigenous Roman development, whatever we assume the ultimate origin of the cola themselves to be.' Freeman 1998, 86, observes similarities between Saturnian metre and qualities found in other indigenous Italic metres in South Picene and Faliscan, but concludes cautiously: 'Certainly, the influence of Greek poetry was felt throughout Italy from early Republican times and in some minor ways influenced Saturnian style and rhythm, but there is no need to see Saturnian as deriving primarily from Greek prototypes when the native elements of the verse were present at Rome from the beginning.' See also Parsons 1999, n. 17: '[The ancient] grammarians' testimony on Latin accentuation often misleadingly imports features of Greek prosody ... [S]uch pedantic fantasies do not constitute useful linguistic evidence.' Elsewhere, Parsons (135) calls Saturnian metre, 'an old-fashioned Italic relic' that diminished as 'Greek poetry was quickly becoming the canon against which all Roman poetic production would be measured'. In addition, Cole 1969, 66-72, has shown that the Saturnian's frequent use of heptasyllabic cola cannot be found in Greek poetics, but shows intriguing similarity to Old Irish verse, and this suggests an indigenous evolution of Indo-European poetic forms rather than direct borrowing from Greece; see also Freeman 1998, 82-6. On Old Irish poetics, see Calvert Watkins, 'Indo-European Metrics and Archaic Irish Verse', *Celtica* (1963): 194-249.

39. Parsons 1999, 134: 'Our literary testimony of Latin begins at a time when production of Saturnians is practically at an end, and when the Plautine system of accentuation is in use. This linguistic innovation broke the hierarchical compatibility between the Saturnian meter and Latin prosody.'

40. The two oldest Scipionic inscriptions are cited above, n. 36, and three more are the following: *CIL* 1.2.10; 1.2.11; and 1.2.14 (*CLE* 8-10). The citations of the other inscriptions are as follows: for Mummius, *CIL* 1.541 (*CLE* 3); for the Vertuleii, *CIL* 1.1175 (*CLE* 4); for Caecilius, uncle of Atticus, *CIL* 1.1006 (*CLE* 11); and for Eurysaces and his wife, *CIL* 1.2.1203, 1204 (a repeat of 1203) and 1206. I should point out that Cole 1969, 12-16, does not include the inscriptions from the Eurysaces monument as clear examples of Saturnian verse; he excludes all but 125 lines of Saturnian verse for his study (28 come from inscriptions). Also, see Petersen 2004, 237-8, on the possibility that *CIL* 1.2.1206 (Astitia's epitaph) does not belong with Eurysaces' monument. See also Goldberg 2006, 442: 'At the very least, these counter-Ennian tendencies suggest that his eclipse of the old aesthetic was neither complete nor immediate.'

41. At *Tusc.* 1.7.13 Cicero mentions the Scipionic tombs as examples of many aristocratic monuments visible to visitors and passers-by: *An tu egressus porta Capena, cum Calatini, Scipionum, Serviliorum, Metellorum sepulcra vides, miseros putas illos?* A couple of generations later, Livy mentions statues of the Scipios at the same location (38.56).

42. See Coarelli 1988 for detailed site maps and descriptions of the monuments and inscriptions. See also Claridge 1998, 328-31, for a description of the site and the location of its holdings.

43. Two inscriptions honouring female members of the family also remain, consisting merely of their names: *CIL* 1.2.16: [P]aulla Cornelia Cn. f. Hispalli, and *CIL* 6.1392: Cornelia / Gaetulici f. / Gaetulica.

44. Coarelli 1988, 16-17: The lengthy verse inscription that includes his name appears on the outward-facing long side of the sarcophagus, and the man's name (*CIL* 1.2.6: [L. Corneli]o(s) Cn. f. Scipio) appears painted on the lid of the sarcophagus. See Tanner 1961, 216-20, for a more detailed study of the Saturnian metre of these *elogia*.

45. Freeman 1998, 69, points out that this inversion of the expected word order (Lucius Cornelius) is indicative of the attempt to make this line fit into verse-structure (lest one be tempted to take these lines as mere prose).

46. Coarelli 1988, 19: The lengthy verse inscription appears on the outward-facing long side of the sarcophagus, and on the lid of the sarcophagus is painted the man's name and his key offices (*CIL* 1.2.8: L. Cornelio(s) L. f. Scipio / *aidiles, cosol, cesor*). Ernout 1957, 14, reconstructs the inscription with '*Romai*' rather than '*Romane*', thus the translation would be: 'Most men at Rome know that this one man was the best of good men.'

47. The Greek influence seen in the older man's epitaph led Mommsen (and most later scholars) to conclude that it was composed after the death of his son to match the quality of the younger man's inscription; see also Courtney 1995, 217. On the Hellenic ideals expressed in lines 2-3, see Wolff 2000, 60, and Purdie 1935, 59. Cf. *AP* 16.2.3: κάλλιστον μὲν ἰδεῖν, ἀθλεῖν δ' οὐ χείρονα μορφῆς (fifth-century BC inscription for the athlete Theognetos). Coarelli 1988, 19, notes the similarity in wording between the younger Barbatus' inscription and the words Cicero uses to honour a contemporary of Barbatus, A. Atilius Calatinus, at *Fin.* 2.116: '*hunc unum plurimae consentiunt gentes / populi primarium fuisse virum*.' Tanner 1961, 216, believes both inscriptions to be written no earlier than 200 BC.

48. *CIL* 1.1006 (*CLE* 11): *Hoc est factum monumentum Maarco Caicilio. / hospes, gratum est quom apud meas restitistei seedes: / bene rem geras et valeas, dormias sine qura.*

49. The practice of making the dead speak from their monuments is well attested in archaic Greek inscriptions dating to the fifth century BC; see Kurke 1993, 147-9.

50. According to Coarelli 1988, 20, some doubt has been cast upon the identification of the person named. Also, the inscription appears on the side of a sarcophagus but no painted inscription appears on the lid to corroborate the inscription.

51. Cf. also *CIL* 1.2.11 (*CLE* 9) for L. Cornelius Scipio, son of Cnaeus.

52. Courtney 1995, 226: 'the deceased is directly addressed, which emphasizes, though in restrained fashion, the pathos of his early death.'

53. Coarelli 1988, 24, explains that this is the only complete Republican inscription recovered from a later addition to the tomb complex, opened between 150 and 130 BC. Tanner 1961, 222, suggests 120 BC as the date of this inscription.

54. His name and list of titles is part of the same inscription. It appears in larger and more widely spaced letters as a *titulus* above the distichs of the poetic inscription: *Cn. Cornelius Cn. f. Scipio Hispanus / pr(aetor), aid(ilis) cur(ulis), q(uaestor), tr(ibunus) mil(itum) (bis), (decem)vir sl(itibus) iudik(andis), / (decem)vir sacr(is) fac(iundis).*

55. In fact, archaic Greek elegies reflect a similar adherence to state-sponsored achievements such as military victory; Luck 1969, 40: 'From its very beginning, the archaic elegy serves a practical purpose ... [It] is hortatory in character; it needs an audience on whose imagination it wants to act.'

56. Cf. Courtney 1995, 229, on *CIL* 1.2.15 (*CLE* 958) (a late second-century elegiac inscription): 'Ennius' influence has now driven the Saturnian from the field.'

57. Claridge 1998, 330: 'The Cornelii Scipiones were unusual (and rather pretentious) not only in choosing to have their tomb rock-cut in the Etruscan manner but also in preferring inhumation in stone sarcophagi when most of their contemporaries practised cremation.'

58. Hexameter inscriptions appear before elegiac ones; see *CIL* 1.297 (*CLE* 361) for Protogenes, a slave and a mime. Buecheler dates this inscription to the time of Ennius.

59. Wolff 2000, 57: 'Ensuite l'usage – souvent approximatif – du vers ... semble s'etre rapidement répandu dans les milieux – notamment affranchise – imprégnés de culture grecque, sous l'influence de la florissante épigramme funeraire grecque et parce que la poésie grandit ce dont elle traite.' See also the useful summary of the development of epigram in Hellenistic culture in Bruss 2005, 1-13.

60. Luck 1969, 47: 'The history of elegiac poetry at Rome begins with Ennius.' See Miller 1993, 280-1, on Ennius' Hellenistic influences and his resonance in the Augustan, elegiac poets.

61. Courtney 1993, 39; see also Conte 1994b, 77.

62. Courtney loc. cit.: the epigram was quoted in two parts by two separate sources: Cic. *Leg.* 2.57 (*hic est ille situs*) and Sen. *Ep.* 108.33 (*reliqua*); the two were joined by Turnebus (1552-7) on *Leg.* Cf. *CLE* 368: *hic est illa sita ... / cui pro meriteis ab coniuge gratia relatast.*

63. On the sense of *opis* (not necessarily help, but any kind of action), see Courtney loc. cit.

64. Courtney 1993, 40-1: the epigram was quoted in two parts by two separate sources: Cic. *Tusc.* 5.49 (the first couplet) and Sen. *Ep.* 108.34 (the second couplet); the two were joined by J.J. Scaliger [*Catalecta* (1572)].

65. On the sense of a lost line or couplet that completes the expression 'from East to West', see Courtney, loc. cit., and Skutsch 1985, 289, n. 15.

66. Courtney 1993, 43: the epigram is quoted in Cic. *Tusc.* 1.34 and 117, and in *Sen.* 73.

67. On the possibly Sapphic origins of the sentiment expressed here, and the significance of *volitare* over other possible words for 'flying', see Klaus Lennartz, 'Fliegen oder Flattern? Zum Epitaph des Ennius', *Philologus* 143.1 (1999): 181-2.

68. Courtney 1993, 43: the epigram was transmitted in Cic. *Tusc.* 1.34. Courtney, loc. cit., explains that although this epigram has been attributed to Ennius as an autobiographical inscription for the poet's own bust or statue, it cannot be attributed to him with any certainty, and it is probably from Varro's *De Poetis*. Courtney, loc. cit., also discusses the unlikely pairing of the inscription with a statue, although it is mentioned in two sources (Cic. *Arch.* 22 and Livy 38.56.4): 'the references speak about it with considerable reserve, which they would not have shown if the statue had been identified with an inscription.' This epigram should probably not be joined with the more certain autobiographical epitaph (V 17-18), though it appears this way in H.W. Garrod (*The Oxford Book of Latin Verse*, 1912) and in some other translations.

69. In a discussion on the chronology of Rome's great orators, Cicero laments the loss of convivial verses that were sung at banquets in honour of great men; Cic. *Brutus* 75: *atque utinam exstarent illa carmina, quae multis saeculis ante suam aetatem in epulis esse cantitata a singulis convivis de clarorum virorum laudibus in Originibus scriptum reliquit Cato*. On the evidence regarding these *carmina convivalia* and their significance to Roman cultural history, see Zorzetti 1990.

70. Propertius' Cornelia says at 4.11.101-2: *moribus et caelum patuit: sim digna merendo*. See Ch. 2 for further discussion.

71. The actual epitaph for Scipio Africanus is not attested in material or literary evidence, and Courtney (see n. 68) does not find convincing evidence that Ennius' epitaph appeared with his bust.

72. Yardley 1996, 268, suggests that the poets of the age drew on or alluded to Greek sepulchral tradition as well as the other forms of Greek elegy.

73. Lommatzsch on *CIL* 1.2.9 (*CLE* 6) states that Eduard Woelfflin (*Dichter der Scipionenelogien*, Munich, 1892: 188-219) suggested that Ennius or Pacuvius wrote these epitaphs, 'though this cannot be proven'.

74. See Gutzwiller 1998, 47-8: In Greece, elegiac verses became literary material towards the end of the fifth century (after they had served epigraphic purposes) when 'written documents came to be valued for their contents as well as for their symbolic meaning'. See Gutzwiller (loc. cit.) also on an important reference in Thucydides (1.132) that may demonstrate the point at which the function and form of the verses begin to diverge.

75. Wolff 2000, 114: 'En même temps c'est reprendre l'ideé, exprimeé entre autres dans l'Antiquité par une réplique d'Alexandre devant le tombeau d'Achille, que le grand homme a besoin d'un grand poète pour survivre dans la mémoire des hommes.' Commemorations of other poets show this same tendency; see Courtney 1993, 47-50, on three funerary epigrams for poets: one for Naevius, one for Plautus, and one for Pacuvius which was probably a true inscription. See also Bruss 2005, 13, with regard to poets in Greece: 'at some point late in the fourth century or early in the third, the manumission of the epigram ... from its role of service to the monument had come so far as to free it to an independent life on the page ... The freedom from stone led to an explosion in the use of the epigram by talented poets.'

76. Cato apud Gellius 11.2.5: *Equos carius quam coquos emebant. Poeticae artis honos non erat. Si quis in ea re studebat aut sese ad convivia adplicabat, 'crassator' vocabatur* (= *Carmen de Moribus* fr. 2, Jordan 1860, 83). See Gruen 1992, 72, on the term '*crassator*' or '*grassator*'; on this issue see also Zorzetti 1990, 293-4.

77. Gel. 11.2.6: *Nam vita humana prope uti ferrum est. Si exerceas, conteritur; si non exerceas, tamen robigo interficit. Item homines exercendo videmus conteri; si nihil exerceas, inertia atque torpedo plus detrimenti facit quam exercitio* (= *Carmen de Moribus* fr. 3, Jordan 1860, 83).

78. Cic. *Tusc.* 1.3: *in qua obiecit ut probrum M. Nobiliori, quod is in provinciam poetas duxisset. Duxerat autem consul ille in Aetoliam, ut scimus, Ennium.*

79. Zorzetti 1990, 294-5, finds friction arising not from Roman attitudes against poetry in general, but from 'a sympotic culture still hostile towards the *technitai*, a culture which was still able to use these principles against Hellenistic professionalism, and with a heavy tone of moral censure, as late as the end of the second century'.

80. See Lyne 1980, 12-18, on the *demi-monde* and the difficulty of 'whole love' at Rome; Galinsky 1996, 270, on elegy's dialogue with Augustan and other political themes; Habinek 1998, 103-4, on the new potential for economic and social power through literary production; and Fredrick 1997, 179, on the self-definition of the Roman male elite in an age in which Republican institutions had crumbled.

81. Hutton 1935, 11-12, points out two epigrams that gained currency through Cicero: *AP* 7.249 (*Tusc.* 1.101) and *AP* 7.325 (*Tusc.* 5.101).

82. Cic. *Pro Arch.* 3.6.

83. On Catulus' poetry see Gutzwiller 1998, 238. Gellius 19.9.14 quotes six lines of an elegy by Catulus within the context of defending Latin capability for matching Greek lyricists in erotic verse. In the same passage, Gellius quotes two other Roman elegists, Valerius Aedituus and Porcius Licinus. See Luck 1969, 47, on their influence and later reception.

84. Easterling and Kenney 1989, 80-1.

85. Buecheler counts (from all periods) more than 640 elegiac inscriptions, the poetic form of choice second in frequency only to hexameter, seen in over 700 inscriptions.

86. On Lucilius see Gruen 1992, 272-317.

87. Habinek 1998, 54: '[T]he instances of *existimatio* and related terms in early classical Latin also help us to understand why Latin literature, despite its similarities in its preclassical phase to Greek, did not remain rooted in the sympotic environment as long as Greek literature did. … [T]he praise or blame of a Roman aristocrat has ramifications chiefly for his status within the larger community and with respect to potential rivals for the approval of that community, rivals who hail from other sectors of the aristocracy or from elsewhere in society altogether.'

88. Iser 1978 does not anywhere point specifically to the use of texts featured within texts, as in the case of the quoted inscription, but he does refer to the use of quotations, indirect speech and words highlighted in italics which authors use to focus the reader's attention on the changed perspective, or on an emphasis that word-order itself would not make clear.

89. On the notion of the hyperlink as a concept that far pre-dates the current age and the internet, see Bolter and Grusin, 1999.

90. See p. 97f. below.

91. I do not make it a priority to provide lists of words, phrases or abbreviations characteristic of the various epigraphic types; readers unfamiliar with the stylistic tendencies of inscriptions are certainly encouraged to read one of the many excellent guides to inscriptions that serve that purpose, e.g. Lindsay 1897, Egbert 1923, Sandys 1927, Gordon 1983 and Keppie 1991.

92. See also Varner 2004, especially 2: 'The term *damnatio memoriae*, literally the damnation or condemnation of memory, is modern, but it accurately reflects the Romans' preoccupation with the concepts of memory and fame. The Latin term *memoria* has much broader repercussions than its English cognate, memory, and encompasses the notions of an individual's fame and greater reputation. The belief that a deceased individual enjoyed an afterlife through the perpetuation of his memory or by being remembered is at the core of Roman cultural identity and is amply witnessed by the innumerable surviving works of funerary art and architecture created for all classes of the society, throughout the empire.'

93. See also Woolf 1996, 38: 'It is difficult to see what might have so swiftly derailed such a widely and long-established cultural practice. The military and political crises of the Empire began too late to be relevant, and were not generalized until the 260s: it is difficult, in any case, to see what impact they might have had on private acts of devotion, commemoration and self-advertisement.'

94. See Mouritsen 2005, 50-2, on the group of burials belonging to the Lucretii Valentes found at Scafati in the *ager Pompeianus*. The stele that marks the grave of the family's most prominent member (and one of Pompeii's leading men), displays only his name. Mouritsen, 52, comments: 'Such epigraphic modesty in a funerary context is not unique … but the enclosure itself and its location are remarkable, demonstrating … the complete withdrawal from funerary competition by a leading Pompeian family.'

95. See Mouritsen 1988 on the large amounts of source material proving that the epigraphic habit was alive and well in the political sphere, particularly at Pompeii.

96. Cf. Woolf 1996, 25: 'Monuments, if they lasted long enough and were prominent enough, would preserve the fame of the commemorated, acting like mnemonics to trigger memories and perhaps speech.'

97. Lattimore 1942, 341, may overstate the case, calling Roman poetic expressions, 'completely dictated from the Greek'.

98. Lattimore 1942, 59. There is uncertainty as to how close to divinity these spirits came; see Beard, North and Price 1998 vol. 1, 31. See also Beard et al. 1998 vol. 2, 236: 'epitaphs quite commonly express the expectation that death is the end for the individual human existence. The thought is even familiar enough to have a shorthand form of its own inscribed on numerous tombstones: nf f ns nc (*non fui, fui, non sum, non curo*).'

99. See also Lattimore 1942, 342, where he concludes: 'from the evidence of the epitaphs, the belief of the ancients, both Greek and Roman, in immortality, was not widespread, nor clear, nor very strong.'

100. Purdie 1935, 56-9, cites in particular the epitaphs of the Scipios that extend from the early third century to the late second century BC.

101. On the pre-Roman Greek tendency to praise military achievements, see Lattimore 1942, 237-40.

102. See also Hope 2000, 158-9, and Ian Morris, *Death Ritual and Social Structure in Classical Antiquity* (Cambridge: 1992).

103. See Nisbet and Rudd 2004, 368, on the reference to *monumentum* in previous writers as works of literature (e.g. Cicero *Off.* 1.156). See also Hor. *Carm.* 2.20.21-4 where Horace dismisses any desire for a tomb when he dies, since his words will make him immortal (23-4: *compesce clamorem ac sepulcri / mitte supervacuos honores*). See Nisbet and Hubbard 1978, 336: though the editors take great pains to demonstrate the many Hellenistic models that Horace could have been emulating in this passage, they admit that there is something strikingly Ennian and Roman in his application of the claim of immortality to himself rather than to other poets or to loved ones.

104. Horace uses epitaphic language, but no true epitaphs; what is relevant to my study will receive treatment passim. Virgil includes quotations from and references to epitaphs and votive dedications in his *Aeneid* and the *Eclogues*. See the above discussion on Virgil's epic inscriptions; on the pastoral inscriptions, see Breed 2006. As stated earlier my focus is on the elegists.

105. 'Lygdamus' also creates an epitaph at [Tibullus] 3.2.29-30.

106. I have chosen to use the term 'votive' inscription in order to refer to dedicatory inscriptions that are specifically dedicated to a divinity. Other types of dedicatory inscriptions will fall under the category of *tituli*.

107. On the construction of an audience in the act of correspondence see Ong 1977, 56-7.

108. In addition to the elegists, Horace writes one votive inscription in *Carm.* 1.5.13-16, and mentions a votive tablet in *Sat.* 2.1.33.

109. This inscription serves a double purpose, both being dedicated to Apollo and serving as Sappho's epitaph.

110. See Rex Wallace, Michael Shamgochian and James Patterson, eds, *Etruscan Texts Project*, http://etp.classics.umass.edu, for examples of sixth-century religious inscriptions.

111. Dio Cassius 63.26.4: ἐπιγράψας αὐτῷ ὅ τι Σαβίνῃ αὐτὸ θεᾷ Ἀφροδίτῃ αἱ γυναῖκες ἐποίησαν. Of course Nero was not known for honesty: according to Cassius, he had actually stolen the money from the women to whom he gave this credit. I thank Jean M. Turfa for suggesting this example.

112. Caracalla, after the death of his father Septimius Severus, had his brother and co-regent murdered and his name removed from the arch's architrave. Claridge 1998, 75, provides a concise summary of the deletion and what was inscribed over it. Note that the practice is quite old: Livy 6.20.14 mentions an erased *praenomen* in 384 BC.

113. Zanker 1989, 211: 'Beneath each statue was a brief *titulus* giving the name and *cursus honorum* of the honorand, as well as a longer *elogium* recounting his greatest services to the state ... These portrait galleries thus offered a revised version of history suited to the purposes of Augustan Rome, conveyed equally in image and text.'

114. Pliny *NH* 22.6.13.

115. Zanker 1989, 213.

116. See p. 103f. below.

117. See Corbier 1987, 36 on the variety of surfaces that 'bear witness to the capacity for writing.'

118. Franklin 1991, 80; his study analyses form also: painted graffiti (*pictae*) and inscribed graffiti (*graphio exaratae*).

119. Franklin 1991, 87: on the walls of Pompeii, the first line of the *Aeneid* was found written by three separate hands.

120. For an example of sentiments found repeatedly at Pompeii and that therefore must have acquired the appreciation of their readers, see Franklin 1991, 82, on *CIL* 4.2487: *admiror te paries non c(e)cidisse (ruinis) / qui tot scriptorum taedia sustineas*, and *CIL* 4.8114: *venimus huc cupidi, multo magis ire cupimus / ut liceat nostros visere, Roma, Lares.*

121. See Ch. 5 below.

122. E.g. McKeown 1987, 321, on *Am.* 1.11.27-8: 'quotation of dedicatory (and sepulchral) inscriptions is common in Augustan poetry, and particularly in elegy, which employs the most usual metre for inscriptions'; Putnam 1973, 82, on Tibullus 1.3.54: 'epitaphs made occasional appearances at more gloomy moments of elegy'; and Richardson 1977, 254, on Prop. 2.14.26-8: 'the *carmen*, a metrical inscription to explain the dedication, is a common addition but not essential.'

2. Epitaphic Revelations in Catullus and Propertius

1. See a brief summary of some of the more vigorous efforts in Allen 1962, 113-14.

2. On the identity of Cynthia, see the biographies of Propertius in Butler and Barber 1933, Camps 1961, Sullivan 1976, Richardson 1977 and Hodge and Buttimore 1977. See particularly Sullivan 1976, 76-7, who discusses reasons for avoiding the issue of biography or degrees of reality in Propertius' love affair. For example, Butler and Barber attempt to piece together the chronology of poems within Book 2 in accordance with the presumed trajectory of the relationship with Cynthia. See Hubbard 1974, vii, for a thoughtful justification of dismissing such issues.

3. This notion of the elegiac mistress as a prop or cipher is simple summary of a variety of ingenious interpretations and analyses of the woman in the poetic text; for more on the elegiac mistress and what she represents, see an excellent summary and a virtual manifesto of the modern idea in Wyke 2002, ch. 1.

4. Cf. Janan 2001, 45: 'as if historical event *x* "explained" the presence of detail *y* in the poems'.

5. See Severy 2003, 7-22, on specific aspects of the Roman family in the late Republic and the significance of traditions and remembrance.

6. Cf. Prop. 2.13.19 where the poet explicitly asks that his funeral not include a procession of ancestor-masks. See also Flower 1996, 2-11, and especially 91-127; see also Severy 2003, 19. The best ancient sources are Polybius 6.53-4 on the significance of Roman funerals in advertising a person's legacy, and Sallust *Jug.* 4.5-6 on the power of ancestor-masks.

7. See Janan 2001, 45-7, on the relationship between the fractured characterizations in Propertius' Gallus poems (1.5, 10, 13 and 20) and the displacement of position brought about by these land acquisitions.

8. See Harris 1971, ch. 8.

9. The people Catiline found most eager to join his revolution lived in Etruria (Sall. *B.C.* 28.4), a fertile region that had absorbed many of these land seizures, and the same region that would soon absorb the savagery of conflict with Octavian's forces at Perusia. Perusia and its significance to Propertius will receive more comment later in this chapter.

10. See also Hickson 1991.

11. Eck 1984, 140-1.

12. Eck 1984, 143.

13. Eck 1984, 131; and Dio 53.23.5.

14. Eck 1984, 151: 'One may well postulate a formulation of the new inscription according to the pattern of the texts beneath the statues of the *viri antiqui*.' Eck also points out that Augustus ordained that recipients of the *ornamenta triumphalia* also appear in this forum.

15. This right (*ius trium liberorum*) was passed as part of the Julian law (*lex Julia de maritandis ordinibus*) in 18 BC; see Severy 2003, 53-4. Note also the granting of this right to Livia on the occasion of the death of Drusus, despite her having borne only two children (Dio 55.2.5). On the power and significance of memory in Republican times, see Gowing 2005, 1-15 and passim.

16. See Nicolet 1984, 97-8, on the limitations also placed on freedmen to rise into the ranks of propertied classes. Nicolet, 100, also points out that some sons of freedmen did achieve the rank of military tribune, one chiefly associated with the equestrian order.

17. See also D'Ambra 2002, 223.

18. Mouritsen 2005, 44 and 52.

19. Copley 1956, 70: 'The lament of the *exclusus amator* is in [the elegists'] eyes the first, the chief, and the most characteristic manifestation and symptom of love, and as such it becomes the vehicle for the expression of the totality of love, as they understood and depicted it.'

20. *Ad Fam.* 4.5.6 (by Servius Sulpicius Rufus, 45 BC): *fac aliquando intellegamus adversam quoque te aeque ferre posse neque id maius quam debeat tibi onus videri, ne ex omnibus virtutibus haec una tibi videatur deesse*, 'be sure to show us that you are able to bear misfortune with an even keel, and that this burden is no heavier than it ought to be, so that you do not show yourself lacking in this important virtue (of Stoic forbearance).'

21. As Fuller 2003, 398, explains, the elegists acknowledged the preoccupation with grief in their poems: '[T]he elegists regularly brood on death, labeling their genre a poetry of lament. Of course what they normally lament is not anyone's death, but the fact that they are themselves living out their lives as slaves to love. But because the two notions of "love" and "death" share in the idea of "lament", they are treated as if they were perfectly compatible, even equivalent, constituents of the genre.'

22. For an intriguing and somewhat controversial analysis of a fractured persona, see Janan 2001, 33-52, on the Gallus poems of Propertius.

23. It is also true that many other non-elegiac poets came from outside Rome, such as Virgil and Horace. Indeed there are surely reflections of 'things lost' in these authors' poems as well, particularly Virgil's *Eclogues*; see Breed 2006, 1-6. But as we know Virgil and Horace selected metres untainted by associations with grief and erotic desire.

24. It has not been proven that the volume was ever formally called *Cynthia*, though 2.24.2 (*et tua sit toto Cynthia lecta foro*) does suggest it. According to Butler and Barber 1933, xxxiv, there is no evidence in the literary or manuscript tradition to support any initial title. There is also no evidence that the work was called by the Greek title *Monobiblos* before it is so attested in Martial (14.189). The first word of the first poem may have served as a popular label at the time of publication until *Monobiblos* became a useful reference to the first book when later books were issued.

25. See Richardson 1977, 6, on the conjectures regarding his namesake and family ties.

26. Cairns 1979, 227, sees likewise how Catullus shaped the elegiac collection as well: 'once Catullus had shown how myth could be subordinated within a long subjective elegy, the need for an elegy book to be a single united poem had passed. Each small subjective elegy could introduce itself.'

27. 2.34.91-2: *et modo formosa quam multa Lycoride Gallus / mortuus inferna vulnera lavit aqua*: 'and how many wounds has Gallus, dead because of lovely Lycoris, washed recently in the waters of the underworld.'

28. The works of contemporaneous and slightly later Latin poets give us some clue as to the nature of his elegies; see Luck 1969, 51-4. Virgil's tenth *Eclogue* features Gallus as the mournful victim of lost love, and Servius' commentary on line 46 of the poem mentions that many lines were direct quotations of Gallus' poetry, though he does not specify; see Clausen 1994, ad loc. On the recently discovered fragments of Gallus' elegies, see Anderson, Parsons and Nisbet, 1979.

29. See Butler and Barber 1933, lii-lix, on the possible sources of Catullus' longer elegies (66-8) and the nature of their influence on later Roman elegy; see also lv: 'as far as the Alexandrians are concerned the debt of Roman elegists was confined in the main to Narrative Elegy, Elegiac Epigram, and Lyric Paegnion.'

30. See Copley 1956, 49, on the *diffamatio* and the relationship between Catullus' poem and the role of the door in Plautus' Curculio in which it issues a perceptible response to the drama. See also 51-2 on the three articulations of the paraclausithyron: the conventional, literary form, the form that incorporates the theme of adultery (the *diffamatio*), and the type that incorporates the setting within the brothel (the *lupanar*). On Catullus 67, see also Butler and Barber 1933, lviii; Merrill 1893, ad loc.: Quinn 1973, 368-9. See also Skinner 2003, 44-50, for an intriguing interpretation of the poem that drives further the wedge that separates Catullus from Callimachean goals (50: 'his stance as leading proponent of a Callimachean aesthetic is deftly skewered'). For examples of later 'closed door' (or *exclusus amator*) poems, see e.g. Propertius 1.16 and Ovid *Am.* 2.1.25-6, 2.2.2 and 3.4. Note also Copley 1956, 121-4, for an elegant argument on the resulting 'top-heavy' evolution of the paraclausithyron because of the Roman infusion of other elements to the Greek form.

31. On the unity of 68a-b, some scholars have found structural schematics that support the idea of a single poem (e.g. Wheeler 1915 and Quinn 1973); Skinner 2003, 143, calls it sensibly, 'a poetic diptych'. Merrill 1893, ad loc., believes that 'the weight of evidence seems to lie in favor of absolute division of vv. 1-40 from 41-160'.

32. This capacity for composition while declaring its impossibility is of course a rhetorical strategy that finds frequent repetition in Ovid's exile poetry. The separation from Rome and his barbaric surroundings, he explains, has made his poetry inferior and sluggish. Yet some of his best descriptive and narrative moments are found in these 'inferior' poems; see Nagle 1980.

33. See Skinner 2003, 4-5, for summary of significant arguments brought to the discussion of *recusatio* by other scholars, most notably Gregson Davis (*Polyhymnia: The Rhetoric of Horatian Lyric Discourse*, Berkeley, 1991).

34. Poem 116 is a short (eight-line) epigram that rebukes a former friend named Gellius who has apparently rejected Catullus' consistent efforts to apply himself to Callimachean themes (*carmina Battiadae*). Specifically, Skinner 2003, 21, points to 'archaisms and prosodic anomalies' in 116: e.g. 'line 3 is the only entirely spondaic hexameter in Latin poetry after Ennius'.

35. Wheeler 1915, 168: 'One cannot help surmising that the real reason for the meager elegiac production of Catullus is that such elegies were something new in Greco-Roman literature; that he was feeling his way towards a new type of elegy – a type for which he had no exact Greek models.'

36. The reason for his older brother's trip to the Troad was probably that he was a part of a Roman delegation under the auspices of Julius Caesar, a friend of Catullus' father; see Merrill 1893, xiv-xv. In poem 11 the young poet expresses the possibility that he himself will receive a commission to serve in Caesar's army.

37. Cf. *CIL* 1.2.1211= *CLE* 52; see Quinn 1973 on Catullus 4.

38. Cf. *Aen.* 2.557-8: *regnatorem Asiae. iacet ingens litore truncus, / avulsumque umeris caput et sine nomine corpus.* Cf. also Ovid's exile fears in *Tristia* 3.3 that his Roman soul will wander among Sarmatian shades (62-3: *spiritus … / inter Sarmaticas Romana vagabitur umbras*).

39. See Lattimore 1942, 204, nn. 246 and 251, for thirty-one examples.

40. *Mea vita* appears in reference to Lesbia twice, at 45.13 and 109.1. Note also that Cicero uses the comparative phrase sparingly as well. In the midst of the drama of the first oration against Catiline he calls the Republic dearer than his life (*In Cat.* 1.26); yet in letters to his family he does not use this construction, but refers to his wife as *mea vita* once (*Ad Fam.* 14.2.5).

41. See Thomas 1998, 216, on the 'biographically plausible core' of poem 68.

42. As does 65.11-12: *semper amabo / semper maesta tua carmina morte canam*; with these words Catullus promises the inseparability of the two themes of suffering and longing. Indeed the omission of *te* with *amabo* may seem metrically necessary, but the result of the omission is an ambiguity of the object of that love. Catullus suggests that he will always love his brother, but also that he will use love (for whomever) as the medium by which he dissipates his suffering.

43. However Wheeler 1915, 163, makes the point that attempts of later elegists to follow some of the metrical patterns of Callimachus more closely than Catullus resulted in an unfortunate 'law of the distich'.

44. Prop. 1.7.24: 'you lie dead, great poet of our passion.'

45. On Calvus, whom Propertius lists among other erotic poets at 2.34.89, see Butler and Barber 1933, 262 (ad loc.): Calvus wrote an elegy to honour his dead wife Quintilia and may have written other love-poems; cf. Ovid *Trist.* 2.431-2: *par fuit exigui similisque licentia Calvi, / detexit variis qui sua furta modis.*

46. Veyne 1988, 52: 'Our poets describe a lifestyle rather than their lives, … they are not so impassioned with Delia or Cynthia that they are unable to devote whole poems to literary polemics, patriotic homage or gallant dissertations. Literary friendships and patrons are not forgotten either.'

47. Luck 1969, 43: 'No one will deny that Plautus and Terence were read by the Augustans; but the reputation of the *poeta doctus* was founded on a much more extensive reading which included the Greek epic, the tragic and lyric poets, and the works of the great Alexandrians. On the book-shelf of Propertius, the editions of the comic playwrights surely occupied only a small space next to the editions of Homer, Euripides and Callimachus.' On comedic aspects in Tibullus, for example, see Maltby 2002, 68 and 152 (on 1.2).

48. Fuller 2003, 397, 'Elegy was … a hybrid genre if ever there was one'; and ibid. 396: '[G]eneration after generation [of Roman poets] found the idea of genre as essence or recipe to be the perfect foil for a poetics that was more concerned with teasing indeterminacy than with purity of any kind.'

49. DeBrohun 2003, 2: 'In every aspect of [Propertius'] life ... the poetic, the personal, and the political are represented as inextricably joined, in a manner that consistently dissociates the Propertian *ego* from any active role either as proper Roman citizen or as a poet who can write properly about Rome.'

50. See Richardson 1977, 194, on the generic or thematic types that each of the three poems imitates (17: sea poetry and *propempticon*, 18: bucolic poetry, and 19: death).

51. E.g. (ad loc.): Butler and Barber 1933, Postgate 1962 and Richardson 1977.

52. See Janan 2001, 43-4, for a helpful summary of a previous argument by Oliensis (1997), and her own argument (44): 'Once Cynthia bisects the relation between Gallus and Propertius, the seemingly unambiguous quilting point "Lover" renders neither man whole, but rather troubles their discrete identities ... Elegy 1.20 finally assimilates the amorous Gallus to an image (Hylas) that makes him a new Narcissus, a mythological figure who inextricably confuses the role of Lover and Beloved; but Propertius raises this confusion to the second power when the entity that offers Gallus an image of himself is Propertius (Propertius' poetry) and, like Hylas, when he reaches out to grasp what fascinates him, finds himself absorbed instead.'

53. Gallus died by his own hand in 27 BC, roughly a year or two after the publication of Propertius' first book of poems.

54. Cf. Janan 2001, 45: '[poem 1.20] may be seen as Propertius' critique of how the desire for wholeness malfunctions in the realm of *amor*'; Janan goes on to say that the final two poems, 'focus on the corollary realm, the realm of the political and of *Roma*'. As explained earlier in this chapter, Gallus was driven to commit suicide in 27/6 BC because while serving Augustus as prefect in Egypt he boasted too widely of his own achievements and angered the *princeps* (see also Edward Courtney, 'Cornelius Gallus', *Oxford Classical Dictionary*, 3rd edition, Oxford, 1996: 394-5).

55. Gowing 2005, 18: 'Octavian ... quickly sought to assert control over memory. It was no accident that one of [Octavian's] first independent and official acts in 36 BC, with Lepidus out of the way and Antony in the East, was the destruction of documents pertaining to the actions of the triumvirs.'

56. E.g. Butler and Barber 1933, ad loc.: 'the appeal is addressed to a fellow-soldier and may have been intended for inscription.'

57. See Janan 2001, 36-41, who supports taking the many 'Galli' throughout the *Monobiblos* as manifestations of the elegiac poet Cornelius Gallus. Regarding disagreements over the meaning and wording of line 6 (Fedeli offers: *ne soror acta tuis sentiat e lacrimis*), I agree with Butler and Barber and Camps, contra Postgate and Richardson, that it makes little sense for this Gallus to ask that his betrothed not learn of his death. Hodge and Buttimore 1977, 212-13, offer an interesting compromise: that Gallus wants her to learn his fate, but not merely from lamentation.

58. See Dio 48 and Appian *B.C.* 36 on the details of this conflict. Apparently the Perusines were starved into surrender by Octavian's siege tactics (huge ramparts erected to block the gates of the city) and every captured knight and senator was put to the sword, while the rank and file were spared. The lead instigators, Lucius Antony and Fulvia, brother and wife of Antony the *triumvir*, were allowed to escape. Lucius died soon afterwards and Fulvia returned to Greece to her husband and children.

59. Stahl 1985, 109-10: 'The fine point of course is that Propertius does not make any allusion to the name of the man who, assuming the authority of the judge (App. 5.48), ordered the killings, but points only to the graves of the victims. Whoever would wish to denounce the poet would himself have to name the name first. But who would like to name the name in 29 B.C.?' See also Sullivan 1976, 57: 'Propertius developed other personal and more ironic ways of expressing his dissent. Firstly, he has an insistent way of referring adversely to incidents in the Civil War that Augustus would have, presumably, far rather forgotten.' Sullivan 1976, 58-60, provides more evidence of Propertius' dissent. See also Griffin 1984, 206: 'The First Book of Propertius shows no acquaintance either with Octavian or with Maecenas. The poet has friends rather than patrons, and writes about the life of love. The one incidental allusion to Octavian is far from friendly.'

60. Propertius 2.1.72: 'I will be a brief name on a narrow marble slab.'

61. Richardson 1977, 217.

62. In poem 4.1 Propertius leaves clues that suggest he was the son of a nobleman, most notably in line 131 where he mentions that he once wore a *bulla* around his neck, a charm worn by children of the elite.

63. Richardson 1977, ad loc.: 'Here P. shifts his grounds slightly; he really wants Maecenas to attend his funeral, of course, not simply happen by his grave on a casual outing. The *favilla* is usually the glowing ash and always the fresh ash; cf. e.g. Virgil *Aen.* 6.2.27; Horace *Carm.* 2.6.22-4; and Tibullus 3.2.10.'

64. For example, Virgil, *Aen.* 8.626-731, ekphrastically configures the shield of Aeneas with the centre depicting the Battle of Actium and the procession of foreign kings before triumphant Augustus; he includes no depiction of other civil wars. See Gurval 1995, 10-13, for a summary of poetic and political treatments that emphasize this one battle over all others; see also 247 on the results of this emphasis: 'Former triumphs and ignoble conflicts in civil war are recast in powerfully new ideological and symbolic terms, and memories of a not too distant past are reconstituted to affirm a more illustrious image of conqueror and ruler.'

65. Richardson 1977, 244: 'the poem is, in effect, an epitaph, in form and brevity suitable for an inscription on a tombstone, but omits her name.'

66. On the alternative possibility for *verba*, *verna*, see Goold 1990.

67. See Lattimore 1942, 293-99. See Tylawski 2001 on *laudationes* granted to women, and Flower 2002 on homage granted to women in important families.

68. Butler and Barber 1933, xxiii.

69. See Welch 2005, 10, on Cynthia: 'is she a flesh-and-blood lover? a metaphor for poetry? grist for the poet's mill? Or is she a means for the poet to describe and negotiate his selfhood to the third parties who are his addressees? In all cases, the dominance of the first-person voice indicates that the poetry is focused more on Propertius than on Cynthia, and on his reaction to her, whoever or whatever she is. Cynthia is the presence around which Propertian elegy organizes the questions of the self: she is the focal point for elegy's personal themes.'

70. On the various suggestions for emendation of 93 (*vivet*, etc. for *etiam*), see the app. crit. of Fedeli 1984, ad loc.

71. On the controversy of the poem's division (typically shown as 13a and 13b in editions), see Wilkinson 1966, 141-4, whose assessment that the unity of the poem lies in 'a train of mental association' has influenced many to find unity in the two parts.

72. On the problem of *tres ... libelli* and its implications on Propertius' poetic output at the time of publication of this poem, see Butler and Barber 1933, xxviii, who argue (to those who believe that to make 'three books', our Book 2 must consist of two books) that Propertius might well have expected himself to write another volume before his death. I would add that nowhere in the poem does Propertius suggest his time of death is near; in fact his devotion to a single love becomes more poignant if he means it to extend many years hence.

73. I hasten to mention that Tibullus' first book of elegies pre-dates Propertius' second book, thereby adding here the element of response to the inscriptions in Tibullus 1.3 and 1.9. I postpone further discussion of the nature of this response to Ch. 3.

74. On the contrast between this desire for monument and his desire to lie in an unmarked grave at 3.16.29-30, see Richardson 1977: 'The idea seems to be that he does not want to be buried right along the highway, where every passer-by would read the funerary inscription ... and the tomb might well become well known in an unfortunate way. Elsewhere (2.13.37-8; 3.1.35-8) P. hopes that his tomb will become famous and the centre of a cult, but there he imagines himself a heroized poet, not the victim of tragedy.'

75. See Eur. *Hec.* 518 and Ovid *Met.* 13.448 on references to the sacrifice of Polyxena. Regarding an inscription on the tomb of Achilles, we know from ancient historical accounts that a tomb believed to belong to Achilles existed in the fourth century BC, for Alexander the Great visited it (Plutarch *Alexander* 15.8); but no mention of an inscription occurs in the accounts. Conjecture remains that a burial mound near Troy (the Besik tepe) may have been considered the tomb of Achilles in ancient times.

76. Cf. Heyworth 1992, 56: 'He does not demand immediate suicide ... but hopes that she die, if at all, at a ripe old age. Yet the instruction remains: Cynthia is to die on Propertius' tomb, as Polyxena on that of Achilles.'

77. Cf. Richardson 1977, 248: 'once he is dead, there will be no more poems.'

78. Prop. 4.7.83: 'Here write me a proper poem posted on a column.'

79. See especially Janan 2001 and DeBrohun 2003.

80. See Janan 2001, 85-9; see also Gutzwiller 1985.

81. See Janan 2001, chs 3-7, and passim, for insightful interpretations of these poems and the 'consistent duplicity' (103) of Book 4.

82. Book 1 also ended without mention of Cynthia; its two final poems formed an epitaph-like homage to the poet's home region in a rare moment of autobiographical authenticity.

83. Butler and Barber 1933 suggest that the people Propertius refers to with these pseudonyms, Arethusa and Lycotas, may be the ones mentioned in poem 3.12, Aelia Galla and Postumus. Butler and Barber also suggest that Jupiter Redux is the god to whom Arethusa dedicates her gift, but this is inferred from a passage in Ovid, *Her.* 13.50: *et sua det Reduci vir meus arma Iovi*, where the context is Greek, and there Laodamia says nothing of a gate as the site of her dedication.

84. See particularly Breed 2004 for relevant arguments and for additional nuance to her characterization in the poem, 54: 'she is rather a specifically textual product represented in a way that surpasses both art and reality in its ability to attract and amaze.'

85. Fedeli 1984 supports *Neuricus* at 4.3.8, referring to a tribe near the Danube and akin to the Getes, to emend previous suggestions, *Sericus* (the Chinese) being the most popular and the one I maintained in my list above.

86. Janan 2001, 56-7, compares the list to Catullus 11 and finds correlation between military expansion and Lesbia's (and thereby Lycotas') 'expansion of sexual possibilities. The desire for conquest ... unites both sexual and political spheres.'

87. See Wyke 1987b.

88. Cf. Janan 2001, 68: 'Arethusa sketches a melancholy picture of the citizenry's dispersion: all the world may see Lycotas in the flesh, but husband and wife can only exchange letters.'

89. Propertius erects another votive inscription in his second book when he jubilantly promises to thank Venus for keeping Cynthia by his side one night though other men came knocking on her door (2.14.27-8): *HAS PONO ANTE TUAS TIBI, DIVA, PROPERTIUS AEDIS / EXUVIAS, TOTA NOCTE RECEPTUS AMANS*, 'To you before your temple, goddess, Propertius gives you these gifts, because he was received for a lover's duty all night long.' In this inscription, the lover expresses gratitude for a night of love, emphasizing only his achievement and his relationship to Venus, saying nothing of the woman he loves. By contrast, Arethusa's inscription expresses gratitude for the salvation of her beloved; Arethusa expresses an explicit dependence on her husband's return, and demonstrates her humbler, more domestic concerns (72: *SALVO GRATA PUELLA VIRO*).

90. E.g. 2.6.41-2: *nos uxor numquam, numquam deducet amica: / semper amica mihi, semper et uxor eris* (never shall wife or mistress part us – never; always will you be my dearest, my wife); 2.7.9-10: *aut ego transirem tua limina clausa maritus, / respiciens udis prodita luminibus*, 'or [because of that now repealed law] I, a husband, might have passed by your closed doors glancing with shining eyes at the place I'd forsaken.'

91. See Janan 2001, 108, on Cynthia's plight in 4.7: '[Cynthia's complaints] refer to material relations larger, grimmer, more complex than the elegiac Symbolic can accommodate ... A literary signifying system fetters Cynthia and her poetic sisters as much as the economic system of Rome enslaves their demimondaine counterparts.'

92. I will focus on the significance of the inscription here, for previous scholarship has already treated the nature and content of Cynthia's complaint with impressive originality; e.g. Janan 2001, 107: 'Bringing Cynthia's ghost back from the grave to depose her lover's faithlessness and attest to her own faithfulness, against Propertius' record of the affair, is but one way that elegy 4.7 ambushes the elegy-reading audience by revealing that "everything you know is wrong".'

93. Regarding *numquam pallet ebur*, Richardson 1977, 461, explains that the high concentration of sulphur springs in the area apparently prevented the yellowing of ivory. Butler and Barber 1933, 365, give other literary references to the phenomenon: Sil. Ital. 12.229 and Martial 8.28.12.

94. On *Tiburtina*, Fedeli 1984 indicates the manuscript tradition that supports this textual emendation.

95. See Camps 1965, ad loc.: 'The piece is in the form of a monologue spoken by the dead woman. Its opening lines recall a familiar type of monumental epigram in which the dead person is represented as speaking from the tomb; but this conception is not long maintained.' See also Butler and Barber 1933 on lines 35-6: '[the wording] assumes but does not prove that the elegy was carved upon her tomb.' See also Richardson 1977 on line 35-6: '... certainly it suggests that the convention of the speaking tombstone is in Propertius' mind at this point, cf. Horace *Car*. 1.28.' See lastly Goold 1990, 383: 'the poem is also envisaged as being engraved on a funeral stone, like the *Laudatio Turiae*.'

96. I would quickly point out, however, that much of Propertius' fourth book, poems 4.1b, 2, 6, 8, 9 and 10, focuses on the aetiological and masculine narratives we expect from the stated themes in 4.1a.

97. The best example is Propertius 2.1.1-16: his poetry is inspired by the way

Cynthia looks when she sleeps, the way she speaks when she reads his works in progress, the way she walks in a silk dress (etc.)! Where is the poem that shows Cynthia helping him arrange his words for metrical ease, or giving him a line or two of her own to include in his poem? When he speaks of her writing (2.3a.19-21) he has her comparing her verses to those written by other women as if poetry-writing, like feats of strength, must be classified by gender.

98. Hallett 1982, 85-6, speculates out how this poem might have resonated with the *princeps* after the shame and exile of his daughter Julia: 'his heartbreaking experience with his own misbehaving daughter, gives additional grounds for believing that Cornelia, the morally unblemished stepdaughter he would proudly have fathered, was on his mind at the time he composed a draft of the *Res Gestae*.'

99. See Butler and Barber 1933, 378-9. Hallett 1982, passim, suggests that structural and verbal similarities between Prop. 4.11 and Augustus' later *Res Gestae* reflect that the emperor had an eye upon this poetic *laudatio* when he composed his own.

100. In fact a few lengthy inscriptions praising women are found; a few *laudationes* that celebrate the lives of women have surfaced in the epigraphic record, and more are mentioned as oral presentations in the histories; see Tylawski 2001.

101. Richardson 1977 mentions the *Somnium Scipionis* (*Re Pub*. 6.16.16) as a likely source of 4.11.101, but probably that too was influenced by Ennius' epigram, well known as it was to Cicero (*Tusc*. 5.49).

102. See also Flower 2002, 174-5, and n. 63.

103. John Keats, 1819, *Ode on a Grecian Urn*, 49-50: 'Beauty is truth, truth beauty – that is all ye know on earth, and all ye need to know.'

3. Tibullan Inscriptions: Between Self and *Persona*

1. Elder 1962, 71: 'that he had steeped himself in the Alexandrian poets is clear, despite his best efforts to conceal the fact'.

2. On the Alexandrian characteristics of the Tibullan corpus, see Bulloch 1973 for numerous correspondences between Tibullan verses and those of Callimachus and Theocritus. See also Cairns 1979, ch. 1, and passim. Foulon 1980 cites the nuanced representation of Apollo throughout the Tibullan corpus as evidence of Alexandrian and pre-Alexandrian influence, notably dramatic sources. Maltby 2002, throughout his commentary, provides very helpful references to the Hellenistic sources for the various allusions and influences – particularly Callimachean and epigrammatic sources.

3. Maltby 2002, 55-66, lays out a comprehensive summary of the evidence for dating Tibullus' works in relation to Virgil, Horace and Propertius. See also Lyne 1998, 520-4, for evidence regarding Propertian and Tibullan relative dating.

4. See Lyne 1998 for a seminal exploration of the aspects of Propertian / Tibullan response and counter-response.

5. Quintilian *Inst*. 10.1.93: *Elegia quoque Graecos provocamus, cuius mihi tersus atque elegans maxime videtur auctor Tibullus. Sunt qui Propertius malint. Ovidius utroque lascivior, sicut durior Gallus.*

6. Cf. the *Vita Tibulli* for the assertion that Tibullus was preferred by more critics: *hic multorum iudicio principem inter elegiographos optinet locum*; see Maltby 2002, 33 (text) and 39: 'on stylistic grounds this bibliography is probably derived from Suetonius' lost *De poetis*.'

7. Cf. Elder 1962, 71: 'Propertius ... was cultivating a style that was exuberant and sometimes inflated. Tibullus employs words in their usual sense and prefers the quiet way.'

8. See Elder 1962, 66-75, for a variety of characteristics that distinguish Tibullus' style and poetics from his contemporaries.

9. Propertius 4.6, the Actium poem, is another example in which the poet appears to purposely avoid rendering more than indirect praise to Rome's leadership. On social critique in 4.6 see treatments in Gurval 1995 and Janan 2001.

10. Elder 1962, 71, discusses the fact that Tibullus was the only elegist to include no references to Augustus, imperial policy or literary predecessors.

11. The third book of poems in the Tibullan corpus, referred to in most editions as [Tibullus] 3, was transmitted along with the other two in all the complete manuscripts; see Maltby 2002, 21-3. Recent scholarship has focused primarily on the poems in that third book called the 'Garland of Sulpicia' in many editions ([Tibullus] 3.8-18), of which poems 13-18 are believed to be the only extant poetic compositions by a female author from the ancient Roman world; on Sulpicia's authorship see Hinds 1987a and Tränkle 1990.

12. On the discussion regarding the completed nature of (and authorial hand in arranging) Tibullus' second book (only six poems long), see Bright 1978, 264-8; also see Dettmer 1980, 78-82, whose perceived numerical patterns offer evidence of structural integrity. On the dates of Tibullus' death see McGann 1970 and the very useful introduction in Maltby 2002.

13. On the structure of Tibullus Book 1, see Littlewood 1970, Dettmer 1980, Leach 1980, Ball 1983, and Mutschler 1985. Maltby 2002, 49-51, provides a helpful summary of the structural arguments.

14. Cairns 1979, 11: 'Like some other Hellenistic prologues [Tib. 1.1] is implicitly programmatic and achieves its ends by describing the poet's life which, by an equivalence standard in ancient poetry, symbolizes his poetic work.'

15. See Mutschler 1985, 157-9, for a summary of this process of disillusionment that evolves over the course of Tibullus Book 1.

16. Lee-Stecum 1998, 280-5, develops the notion that Tibullus' previous experiences with love draw him to an equivocation of love and war. Other evidence that Tibullus gradually adopts a viewpoint antithetical to his earlier position can be seen in view of the fact that his description of the underworld in 1.3 (early in his collection) offers argument to the Lucretian depiction of suffering Tityos as an apt representation of the sufferings of the lover, as Henderson 1969 points out.

17. Littlewood 1970, 666-7, poses briefly the purposes of these genre poems: 'Both derive their position in the book from true Tibullan artistry, maintaining unjarring transitions and harmonious contrasts with the central body of the book, the love sequence ... The two poems, 1.4 and 1.7, diversely provide appropriately contrasting moods to the love sequence, and ... balance one another in the complete scheme.'

18. On the possible identification of Titius as a historical person, see Cairns 1979, 174; Maltby 2002, 236, likes Cairns' identification. However Murgatroyd 1980, 156, points to judicial language that used the name Titius as a name for unidentifiable persons ('John Doe').

19. See Cairns 1979, 173-5, for these and other intriguingly Alexandrian traits in the poem. On the tradition of erotodidaxis, see the introduction to Ovid's *Ars Amatoria* 3 in Gibson 2003.

20. On Tibullus' participation at Aquitania see Maltby 2002 on Tibullus 1.7 and 2.3. On Roman concerns in elegy that distinguish it from purely literary elegy that originated among the Hellenistic writers, see the suggestion by Cairns 1979, 29-34;

particularly 34: 'The Hellenistic moral emphasis is much more in the private sphere; and the private interests of individuals have little connection with the public interest; ... they are almost an afterthought ... [By contrast], the Augustan poets felt themselves to be citizens, not subjects of a powerful city, and men who could, if they had wished, have had an active political career.'

21. On Callimachean praise of Ptolemy see Hutchinson 1988, 38-40.

22. Lee-Stecum 1998, 105, views this reference to women as a reflection of the Tibullan-lover as Odyssean figure: 'The mourners whom he misses are all female. This perhaps suggests the traditional role of women, especially in the heroic world of literary epic, ... fitting them into a male-viewed social scheme where they perform functions centred upon the man, in this case the poet.' But note also the important role of women in elegiac funerals as well: mentioned in Prop. 1.17.19-24 (Cynthia performs his obsequies) and in Prop. 1.21.5-10 (the dying soldier hopes his beloved will find and gather his bones); see the following chapters for more discussion on the role of women in lamentation and funerals. Murgatroyd 1980, 100, does not believe that Tibullus provides more than allusion to Odysseus: 'there are too many details in the elegy which do not fit in with an extended parallel.'

23. See Cairns 1979, 50-7, on the Hellenistic tradition that places lovers in Elysium and offenders of love in 'Hell'. I would add that Tibullus may be the first poet to relegate to Hades ('the seat of wickedness') contemporaries of his own at 1.3.81-2, an invective technique that Dante would perfect centuries later in his *Inferno*. Though these contemporary offenders are unnamed, the reference is clearly to those Romans who do not share the poet's erotic sensibilities. By contrast, when Aeneas visits the Underworld in *Aeneid* Book 6, he sees only his own fellow-legends in torment (e.g. Dido), while Romans contemporaneous with the author Virgil all appear in Elysium (e.g. Marcellus). See Henderson 1969 for further discussion on Tibullus' construction of the afterlife, particularly its responses to Lucretius.

24. Lee 1982, 114; Lee-Stecum 1998, 118.

25. See also Hanslik 1970, 145, on the ring-composition structure of 1.3 that places the inscription in the important position of centre of the poem.

26. See particularly Campbell 1973, Bright 1978, Murgatroyd 1980, 102, and a helpful summary of earlier viewpoints in Lee-Stecum 1998, 101. See also Musurillo 1967, 257-8 on the temporal contrasts laid out in poem 1.3.

27. E.g. Wilfred Owen (1917) 'Dulce et Decorum Est', and Edgar A. Guest (1918), 'The Things that Make a Soldier Great'.

28. Maltby 2002, 41: 'The *Life* and the elegies also make it clear that T.'s duties to his patron involved military as well as literary obligations .... The *Life* mentions T.'s involvement in Messalla's campaign in Aquitania, ... [and 1.7] makes the claim that T. himself took part in the action (1.7.9-12).' Lee-Stecum's conjecture (1998, 118), namely that Tibullus is blaming Messalla in some way for his predicament by placing his name in the epitaph, is unsatisfactory on the grounds that the 'protest' is entirely too subtle to register. More likely Messalla's name in the epitaph is due to Lee-Stecum's other interpretive conjecture (118): 'Roman convention'. (Ovid, who had every reason to blame Augustus for his relegation and impending death in a strange land, does not mention Augustus at all in his epitaph at *Tristia* 3.3.73-6.) Even so, I avoid going as far as Ball (1983, 56) who suggests that Tibullus is currying favour with his patron by means of these lines. If tradition and duty are to be equated with 'currying favour' then all service to homeland and all respect for tradition become unnecessarily suspect.

29. See also Kennedy 1993, 17: 'For "public" consumption, the lover who imagines himself cavorting around the Elysian fields or returning to the arms of his rapturous beloved, wishes to be seen (or fantasizes as being seen?) as the model of a loyal soldier, following his commander even to his death.'

30. I do not think it is possible to see the inclusion of inscriptions in Propertius Book 2 as anything less than responses to Tibullus' first book. The inscriptional language had been there in elegy all along, as I have shown, but the inclusion of these textual passages, quoted as if read right off the stone, is a great innovation that Tibullus pioneered.

31. Note too that Propertius also chooses not to include his name in these passages – he is (as he was in 1.1.1) *miser* at 2.1.78, and simply *qui* at 2.13.35. Notice too that the epitaph at 2.13.35-6 is not a complete distich as if something is missing, such as his name.

32. Lyne 1998, 537: 'In high and funny contrast with the sort of epitaph a conventional equestrian might construct for himself, Propertius' epitaph glances too at the epitaph Tibullus imagines for himself … . Propertius' total commitment to love and poetry exposes Tibullus' worldly collaboration.'

33. See Butler and Barber 1933 on *esseda* at Prop. 2.1.76; see also Hubbard 1974, 102, n. 1 on Ciceronian references to British chariots in a derogatory context. Even Maecenas' embossed reins (*caelatis iugis*) in the same line make reference to his love of ornament and luxury.

34. The *Oxford Classical Dictionary* lists his many offices and distinctions: victor over the forces of Sextus Pompeius, the Illyrians, the Alpine Salassi, and the Aquitani in Gaul; he held offices of co-consul with Octavian in 31, *praefectus urbi* (briefly), and *curator aquarum*; it was he who promoted the title *pater patriae* for Augustus in 2 BC. By contrast, although Maecenas did hold essential powers by the authority of Augustus, he never held a magistracy; for more on him see Syme 1960, 341-2.

35. That is until, according to Suetonius (*Aug*. 66.3; see also Syme 1960, 342), he did something to lose the confidence of the *princeps*.

36. In fact the poets refer to Maecenas as the descendant of Etruscan kings, as at Prop. 3.9.1, an association that would have offended men a generation beforehand; see Syme 1960, 341-2.

37. See also Miller 2004, 126, for a psychological interpretation of the role of Messalla in Tibullus 1.1 and 2.3, and with relevance to 1.3 as well: 'This is the realm of Messalla, the realm of the father. This realm, which Tibullus both needs and tries to escape, explains why Messalla occupies the mythic place he does in the Tibullan corpus, being both the incarnation of traditional Roman values and in 1.7 associated with Osiris and Bacchus, the founders of agriculture.' See also Johnson 1990, 95: 'Messalla is *Romanitas* incarnate'; and 103: 'the figure of Messalla blurs the dream of Arcadia, it prompts Tibullus to think of his inadequacy and irrelevance.'

38. Tibullus draws from precedents in this formulation of the ages: Maltby 2002, 199, points to Hesiod *Op*. 176-201 and Aratus *Phaen*. 108-9.

39. As I argued earlier, poems 21 and 22 in Propertius' first book demand that attention be re-directed to a campaign that brought misery to many Italian families. It was also a campaign that Augustan propaganda was most eager to overlook.

40. Maltby 2002, 322, summarizes the nature of these various inter-relationships, first clarified by Cairns 1979, 152.

41. On the dedicatory inscription as an elegiac motif, see Putnam 1973, 145, Murgatroyd 1980, 277, and Maltby 2002, 339. Actually the dates of Horace's poems are uncertain in relation to 27, the year of Tibullus' first publication; nevertheless, see Nisbet and Rudd 2004, 315-16, on Horace's lyric, inscriptional references.

42. This fragment bears the following full reference in Courtney 1993, 263: Pap. Qa°r Ibrîm inv. 78-3-11/1 (L I/2).

43. Part of this translation is suggested in Anderson, Parsons and Nisbet 1979, 143.

44. See Anderson, Parsons and Nisbet 1979, 142.

45. Anderson, Parsons and Nisbet 1979, 142: 'Gallus, in his disappointment at being left behind, ... will not even be present at the triumph, but will read about it afterwards in the history books.' Nisbet's interpretation finds further support in Mark Possanza's review of Courtney's edition: *Bryn Mawr Classical Review* 95.10.06, (http://ccat.sas.upenn.edu/bmcr/1995/95.10.06.html).

46. *Res Gestae* 19, 20 and 21 mention the temples and other civic buildings he constructs or restores, and *Res Gestae* 24 mentions his act of increasing the coffers of one temple with Asian booty.

47. Lee-Stecum 1998, 262, notices the contradiction in the poet's claim that he will be freed from love (*resolutus amore*) since merely four lines beforehand he speaks of himself fettered by a new love (*me vinctum puer*): one more manifestation, as she sees it, of the poet's pose as powerless to love.

48. Tibullus attributes to himself this *paupertas* at 1.1.5; see Cairns 1979, 20: '*paupertas* is not "poverty" in the modern sense but simple suffering without surplus ... poverty seems to have a particularly significant connection with Hellenistic manifesto poetry.'

49. Maltby 2002, 338, points also to other references to 'gold' and 'golden' in the poem, lines 17, 18 and 31.

50. See Cairns 1979, 19-20, for a summary of the pious aspects, and Hutchinson 1988, 3-5, on the 'grotesque or outmoded' nature of religious performances in Hellenistic poetry.

51. Tib. 1.2.25-6 and 99-100 and 1.6.83-4. Lines 1.2.99-100 take the form of a near-inscription, or at least a prayer (*at mihi parce, Venus*).

52. The threat comes just before his final lines, 1.6.85-6: *nos, Delia, amoris / exemplum cana simus uterque coma* (may we two, Delia, be an example of love in our old age).

53. Catullus 68b.97-8: *quem nunc tam longe non inter nota sepulcra / nec prope cognatos compositum cineres.*

4. Naso's Inscriptions

1. Harris 1989, 219: 'some special quality was thought to be inherent in a written text.'

2. *Her.* 7.195-6 (Dido's epitaph) is repeated at *Fasti* 3.549-50; the phrase *NASO MAGISTER ERAT* is repeated verbatim at *Ars* 2.744 and 3.812.

3. On other dramatic pairings of poems in Ovid (and Propertius) see Davis 1977 and McKeown 1989, 309.

4. See also Meyer 2001 on the ways that a variety of Roman poets consider *tabellae* faithful servants to their will and desire, and representations of the author who corresponds through them.

5. McKeown 1989 ad loc. informs us: 'no other work from the Augustan period bears such an introductory epigram. Ovid did, however, compose three couplets which he suggested might be used to preface the *Metamorphoses*.' These couplets are found at *Tristia* 1.7.35-40. See Van Sickle 1980 and Williams 1992 on the role of the 'book' and its representations in Latin poetry.

6. The military metaphors in the first book of the *Amores* have been the subject of much scholarship, particularly the phrases, 1.1.1: *arma gravi numero* (noticeably its irony in relation to *arma virumque cano*), and 1.2.19: *en ego, confiteor, tua sum nova praeda, Cupido* (in relation to the context of the triumphal procession in Roman society).

7. As in *Ad Fam*. 42 (16.15) and 43 (16.10).

8. McKeown 1989, ad loc.: 'One passage is clearly a reworking of the other … . It is not possible to determine priority.'

9. Sen. *Epist*. 11.

10. See Horace's *Sat*. 2.7 for a striking literary episode where a slave comes out of the woodwork to tell his master what he frankly thinks of him, his writing and his attitude. See also Fitzgerald 2000, 18-22.

11. E.g. Prop. 3.24, 25 and Ovid *Am*. 3.3.12.

12. On the absent presence of women in the elegiac text, see especially Hallett 1984 and Gold 1993; a comment by Greene 1998, 89, on *Am*. 1.7 (about an incidence of domestic abuse) applies here also: '[Corinna] becomes a pictorial object in the speaker's imaginative landscape, the "empty tablet" in which the *amator* can inscribe his poetic talents. The *amator* metaphorizes the woman right out of sentient existence and again diverts attention from his violent behaviour to his poetic virtuosity.'

13. See McKeown, 1989, ad loc., on the play on *duplex* to describe the form of the tablets and their treacherous behaviour.

14. Meyer 2001, 205: 'The medium bears with its message a certain immediacy and places pressure on the recipient to respond, for to resist such a *tabella* embodying a person is like resisting the beloved pleading with you in person.'

15. Meyer 2001, 207: 'He had marked his tablets with his hands, and as a consequence they were *fideles* (9) to him when acting as his agents, placating girls and speaking to them with *verba diserta*, all without him being there (*sine me* [9]) … so deep was his imprint that the *tabellae* always bore his mark and were always true to him.'

16. See Davis 1977, 108-17, on the pairing of Ovid 2.13 and 2.14 and the history of the scholarship discussing the pair. Note especially Davis, 116, where his conclusion focuses on the 'dramatic pause' between the paired elegies, and the 'basically comic effect' achieved by these pairings: 'the anxious solicitousness of II.13 dissolves into a rather tasteless tirade in II.14.' My interpretation will take issue with the 'tasteless' nature of the tirade.

17. The foundational works on the fiction of the elegiac mistress remain: Gold 1993; Hallett 1973 and 1984; Sharrock 1991a; and Wyke 1987b, 1989 and 1995. See also recent formulations of women in elegy, passim, in Greene 1998, James 2003, Lindheim 2003, and Wyke 2002.

18. Kennedy 1993, 69: 'The name "Corinna" does not figure before 1.5.' See Wyke 2002, 20: [as opposed to Cynthia and Delia] 'Corinna does not have a precisely recognizable character and is without authenticity, because in reality she does not exist.' See also Sullivan 1961.

19. Keith 1994, 32: 'An earlier generation of critics decried the vagueness of Ovid's portrait of Corinna, but we are now in a position to recognize and appreciate the specifically literary qualities of her *persona*.'

20. Indeed Ovid makes this promise to his (as yet) unnamed mistress in *Am*. 1.3. that if she provides herself as his inspiration, 19-20: *te mihi materiem felicem in carmina praebe: / provenient causa carmina digna sua* ('give yourself to me as the happy material for my poems, and the songs will advance as worthy of their inspiration'), they will both profit, 25-6: *nos quoque per totum pariter cantabimur orbem / iunctaque semper erunt nomina nostra tuis* ('I will be sung throughout the whole world, and my name will forever be joined with yours').

21. Severy 2003, 52-3, discusses the dates and aspects of the parts of the *Leges Iuliae*; see also her accompanying n. 90 for useful summary of scholarship on the laws.

22. See Badian 1985 on the facts of this legislation.

23. 'So I was made sole caretaker of the laws and moral customs.' See also *Res Gestae* 8: *multa exempla maiorum exolescentia iam ex nostro saeculo reduxi*, 'I ushered into the present a revival of many worthy moral practices from previous generations.'

24. *Am.* 1.2.20: *porrigimus victas ad tua iura manus*. McKeown 1989, 15, points out that the first use of *iura* in relation to a god's authority comes from Ovid (*Am.* 1.1.5: *quis tibi, saeve puer, dedit hoc in carmina iuris*). As is well known, *iura* and *leges* can be, to some extent, interchangeable – but with one important distinction: *iura* can refer to the product of juristic interpretation and thereby a law that bears an element of discourse and nuance, whereas *lex* refers more to a dominant principle, a law that bears authority in its common understanding, one without much need for nuance (see Barry Nicholas, '*ius gentium*' in *The Oxford Classical Dictionary*, 3rd edition, Oxford, 1996: 790). Therefore the word that Ovid uses to define the authority of his ruling deity is one that implies the act of interpretation. This aspect will play a role in the analysis that follows.

25. Miller 1995, 294, addresses the 'depreciation of official symbolism' in Ovid's erotic triumph; see also Cahoon 1988, 295, on Ovid's adaptation of terms of conquest and violence to the sphere of erotic activity: 'Roman love demeans and enslaves the lover'. In relation to this, see also Sharrock 1994b for an examination of the ways that Ovid situates his work politically, even when he poses as not doing so.

26. Cahoon 1988, 303, '[Ovid's *amator*] sees all relationships in terms of victory and defeat, of success and failure.' For his most excessive use of military metaphor, see in particular *Am.* 1.9 and 2.12.

27. See Hickson 1991, particularly 128: after the triumph of Cornelius Balbus in 19 BC, 'the only generals who were awarded triumphs were Augustus' potential successors'.

28. See a similar suggestion in Harvey 1983 (considered in Miller 1995, 294) that the ritual's exclusivity makes triumphal reference an automatic reference to Augustus' household, whereby the connection between Cupid in the poem and Cupid within the Julian line makes Ovid's poem a direct attack on the Augustan household.

29. See Versnel 1970, 64-93, and Beard 2003, 25.

30. See Ovid *Trist.* 4.2.27-32 for a description of barbarian leaders in a triumphal procession.

31. Beard 2003, 26, poses a relevant question: 'What mechanisms of control allowed the Romans to parade thousands of soldiers and prisoners through the streets, watched by at least as many spectators, and then disperse them safely afterwards?'

32. See Beard 2003, 32, on 'the role of writing as representation: whether as an object of display itself, inscribed on placards that proclaimed cities conquered and founded; or as a caption – a decoding device to make some required sense of the strange visual icons on parade.'

33. Suet. *Iul.* 37.

34. Holliday 1997, 147, also uses this passage in his analysis of the 'contrasts of potential responses conditioned by cultural and literate sensitivity'. In addition, Beard 2003, 36, uses this passage to illustrate 'the slipperiness of triumphal imagery'.

35. Clarke 2003, 10: 'what [Ovid] says about making up interpretations pokes fun at the elite practice of *ekphrasis*, or the explanation of paintings.'

36. Beard 2003, 336, considers the identifications a trick: 'Was it not a dumb decision to pretend to distinguish so easily the two rivers that, more than any other, are the natural twins of the world's waterways?'

37. See also Elsner 1995, 24-8, and 35.

38. See Holliday 1997, 133 and accompanying notes, for ancient sources.

39. See Holliday 1997, 133, n. 34, on early Roman dedications to Jupiter Feretrius rather than Jupiter Optimus Maximus.

40. Holliday 1997, 142 (fig. 9), includes in his analysis a figure of a late fifteenth-century painting by Andrea Mantegna representing the triumph of Julius Caesar over Gaul. The inscription in the painting reads: *IMP IVLIO CAESARI / OB GALLIAM DEVICT / MILITARI POTENCIA / TRIUMPHUS / DECRETUS INVIDIA / SPRETA SUPERATA*. According to Holliday, 146, this artistic rendition was probably inspired by reliefs from the Arch of Titus.

41. Gibson 2003, 405, adds that, by calling himself *magister*, 'he acknowledges the example of Tibullus who was the first to call himself by this title and ask for remembrance in this way, ... (1.4.75: *vos me celebrate magistrum*)'. The *sphragis* operates throughout Roman poetry without necessarily taking an inscriptional form; for example Virg. *Georg*. 4.5.69ff. and Hor. *Carm*. 4.6.41-4.

42. See Sharrock 1994b, 106-08, and Leach 1964 on the way Ovid manipulates his most significant predecessor, Virgil's *Georgics*.

43. On wooing readers, see Sharrock 1994a, ch. 2, and note also 296: 'Just as texts are magically seductive, so is interpretation, so is theory.'

44. E.g. *Ars* 3.3: *ite in bella* ***pares*** ... (go into battle as equals); 3.5: *non erat armatis* ***aequum*** *concurrere nudas* (it was not a fair fight for armed men to take on defenceless women); 3.794: *et ex* ***aequo*** *res iuvet illa duos* (and let the 'event' be pleasurable for both equally); and 3.800: *quo* ***pariter*** *debent femina virque frui* (whereby the woman and the man ought equally to derive enjoyment).

45. See also Gibson 2003, 20-1 and 35-6, on the male audience of *Ars* 3 and the precepts delivered 'at the expense of the female audience', and on the problems with Ovid's 'adoption of the position of the *lena*'. See also Myerowitz 1985, ch. 4 ('The Lover's *Materia*'), on the disadvantage that Ovid's female 'pupil' is intrinsically rendered with respect to nature and capability.

46. On transvestitism within Roman poetry, see DeBrohun 2003, 161-5, and Janan 2001, 142-3 and n. 55, on the transvestitism of Hercules. DeBrohun 2003, 162 (and elsewhere), suggests parallels between the cross-dressing hero and the position of the elegiac *amator*.

47. See Gibson 2003, 13-21, on the revolutionary nature of the *Ars* in addressing women in didactic verse, but note also his findings on the 'erotodidactic' tradition and the similarities between such works (frequently directed to or authored by women) and *Ars* 3.

48. Ovid writes in his exile poetry of the *Ars* as the poem that turned Augustus against him (e.g. *Trist*. 1.67-8 and 112-14). There are many speculations as to why the poem would have angered Augustus; see especially Gibson 2003, 25-37.

49. Cf. Tibullus 1.3.55-6: *HIC IACET IMMITI CONSUMPTUS MORTE TIBULLUS / MESSALLAM TERRA DUM SEQUITURQUE MARI*.

50. Cf. Propertius 1.7.23-4, 2.1.71-8, and 2.13.35-6.

51. Herescu 1958 points out the similarities between Ovid's simplified curriculum vitae and the epitaphs of other writers. Nevertheless, the choice Ovid makes astounds one scholar (Zielinski, cited in Herescu 1958, 420): 'Étrange! Dans le quatrain funèbre qu'il composa dans son exil, il passe sous silence ses oeuvres sérieuses.'

52. Green 1994, 238: 'Despite all his earlier disclaimers regarding his erotic *oeuvre*, Ovid now comes out with a flat statement that it is this, and this alone, for which he wishes to be remembered: perhaps the strongest evidence for accepting the historicity of his illness and fear of death, a determination to set the record straight *in extremis*, an abandonment of all his careful self-exculpatory arguments.'

5. The *Heroides* Inscriptions

1. See Hopkins 1983, 212-17, on the masculine membership of such of such *collegia*.

2. See Lefkowitz and Fant 1992, 159-60, 165, 190, 207 and 212. Out of five inscriptions that claim to be authored by women, only three (190: *ILLRP* 971; 207: *CIL* 6.38605; and 212: *CIL* 9.2029) appear truly designed by women. Mothers present the first two for their daughters, and a freedwoman prepares the third one for herself, for her family and for a procuress. The mothers indicate that they oversaw their daughters' honours, and the freedwoman makes clear that she pays for the monument entirely with her own money. Purdie 1935, 68-9, also features Latin inscriptions by women for their husbands. See Saller and Shaw 1984, 126-7, on the ante-mortem monument and its implication to the content and authority of epitaphs.

3. Some of the material in this chapter is extracted and revised from my 2005 article (Ramsby 2005), with permission of course.

4. Lindheim 2003, passim, argues throughout that Ovid's heroines are not effective narrators of their own feelings or perspectives, for they frequently marginalize themselves in their letters; even so, as stated in her ch. 2 she cannot evade the idea that Ovid has done something exciting and psychologically sensitive with the women he creates and authorizes.

5. Ovid's *Heroides* were published before the *Ars*; see Hollis 1977, xiv.

6. Cf. Kauffman 1986, 58, on the use of the epitaph in conjunction with the suicide as 'the threat of publicity. She (the heroine) will make sure the world knows who caused her death by inscribing his name on her tomb (58).'

7. See Hall 1989, 14-16, on the evolution of Thracians from admirably bellicose allies to degenerate, greedy barbarians. Greek sources to this effect include Plato, Herodotus, Aristotle, Strabo and Duris of Samos. The Roman attitude may well be reflected in the revival of the story of the Thracian king Tereus in the 104 BC play of Accius, a work admired by Cicero (*Ad Att.* 16.2.3 and 16.5.1) and probably an influence on Ovid's story of Tereus and Philomela in *Metamorphoses* 6.

8. Besides Dido and Phyllis, Ariadne, Hysipyle and, arguably, Medea all suffer similar fates and appear in the *Heroides*.

9. See Knox 1995, 30-1, on the syllepsis of *praebuit* with *causam* and *manum* to render an emotional response that simultaneously focuses on 'Demophoön's culpability in causing her suicide'.

10. On *manus* as a term to describe a type of marriage, see Treggiari 1991, 16-34. Regarding literary uses of the term to suggest appropriation, matrimonial and otherwise, the *Oxford Latin Dictionary* (Oxford, 1982) lists such near contemporaries as Cicero, Livy and Velleius Paterculus.

11. E.g. *Aen.* 4.1: *regina gravi iamdudum saucia cura*; *Am.* 2.9.34: *notaque purpureus tela resumit Amor*; and *Her.* 7.190: *ille locus saevi vulnus amoris habet.*

12. Jacobson, 131, calls this piety 'a pose'. His analysis however depends far too much on subtle shifts in tonality in various distichs: 'a twinge of regret', for example (131). The significant aspect in the epitaph is that it lies distinctly separate from the other poetic inflections of her, quoting Jacobson, 'girlish helplessness' (131). Ovid provides her claim of piety with significant dignity.

13. There is a lengthy scholarly debate as to whether or not Ovid actually authored this letter (and the same is true to a lesser extent for other letters in the contemporary collection). For a useful summary of the arguments and the bibliography, see Lindheim 2003, 136-41 and all accompanying notes. See Jacobson 1974, 277-80, for a summary of the arguments and a disposal of major concerns regarding this letter's authenticity. Knox 1995, 12-14 and 36-7, is not convinced, though he concedes (310) 'to include a dedicatory inscription is entirely in Ovid's manner'.

14. *Am.* 3.9.67-8: *ossa quieta, precor, tuta requiescite in urna, et sit humus cineri non onerosa tuo.* One might have expected Ovid to have Tibullus speak from his tomb, but perhaps the absence of the epitaph can be attributed to his self-commemoration in his own poem, 1.3.

15. See Kleiner and Matheson, eds, 2000 and Flower 2002 on the variety of ways that women were commemorated, principally among the upper classes. See also Hallett 1982 on the possible influence of Propertius' eulogy for Cornelia on Augustus' composition of the *Res Gestae*. A rather remarkable example of female accomplishments receiving commemoration is found in Pliny, *NH* 7.34, who mentions that Pompey placed effigies in his theatre representing women who had given birth to many or strange offspring.

16. See Hutchinson 1988, 30-1, on the historical sources of Callimachus' aetiological narratives.

17. Unfortunately, the part of the story in which this event occurs is lost to us, but we do have enough evidence in ancient summary accounts of Callimachus' works to make it clear that the phrase was a part of the poem; see Nisetich 2001, 141.

18. *Aitia*: Pfeiffer 1949, fr. 73; see Clausen 1994, 307 (on *Ecl.* 10.53-4), regarding the influence of Callimachus' story on Roman narrative. See also Clausen 1994, 157 (on *Ecl.* 5.13) for the inscription of a poem upon a tree and some implications. For further implications of that use of text upon a tree, see Breed 2006, ch. 3.

19. On the literary history of Oenone, see Jacobson 1974, 176-7: 'Our pre-Ovidian sources for this Romance are largely scholia and mythographic accounts, purely of a narrative nature, generally schematic and concerned with the bare exposition of the plot.'

20. See Knox 1995, 147, on the possible interpolation of these lines: *populus est, memini, fluviali consita rivo, / est in qua nostri littera scripta memor.*

21. See Jacobson 1974, 182-3, and Knox 1995, ad loc. on the authorship of the oath-inscription – most commentators attribute it to Paris. Nevertheless Jacobson, loc. cit., asks whether we should take 'this inscription as a concrete reality or perhaps as the product of Oenene's imagination'.

22. Kenney 1996, ad loc.: the oath follows the formula of pledges that state impossible conditions, *adunata*, such as also appear at Hor. *Carm.* 1.33.9: *quam turpi Pholoe peccet adultero*; and Prop. 3.19.9: *quam possit vestros quisquam reprehendere cursus*; and Prop. 2.1.65-6: *hoc si quis vitium poterit mihi demere, solus Tantalea poterit tradere poma manu.* See also Canter 1930.

23. *Ecl.* 10.53-4: *malle pati tenerisque meos incidere amores / arboribus: crescent illae, crescetis, amores*, I prefer to suffer, and to carve my loves into the sapling-trees: they will grow, and you, my loves, will grow.

24. Respectively, Jacobson 1974, 190 and 192.

25. Kenney's introduction (1996) provides a sound defence of their Ovidian characteristics. Even so, Kenney points out that the double-epistles are 'still relegated by some scholars to a pseudo-Ovidian penumbra' (ix). I am working under the assumption that Ovid is the author.

26. Ovid had another significant elegiac predecessor as well; Wheeler 1915, 171, points approvingly to Catullus 65.19-22: 'this allusive reference without even a name to the famous apple-girl elegy of the master, the *Cydippe*.'

27. *Am.* 1.11 and 12 speak of the use of the *tabella* in carrying messages of love; *Ars* 3.329-48 instructs the reader to recite poetry to infatuate the listener, and two separate passages from the *Ars* (1.437-86 and 3.467-98) encourage the pupil to read letters carefully for signs of the lover's intentions, and to write letters to achieve their aims. Of course the *Heroides* is an epistolary collection that provides literary examples of women's correspondence.

28. Lindheim 2003, 75: Ovid's heroines 'highlight the constraints placed upon what they write by their all-consuming preoccupation with their addressees'.

6. Ovid's Epic Inscriptions

1. Part of this chapter is a revised excerpt from my 2005 article (Ramsby 2005).

2. See also Knox 1986 who points throughout to many elegiac tendencies in Ovid's epic poem.

3. See my first chapter on studies that have examined the purposes of Virgil's inscriptions within the *Aeneid*. Those inscriptions render innovative approaches to the structural integrity of the hero's journey; see Barchiesi 1979 and Kyriakidis 1998. The presence of inscriptions in metres other than elegy does not damage my argument, for I have been claiming that poetic inscriptions are linked to a Roman preoccupation with commemoration and preservation. Virgil's inscriptions are also reflective of this cultural practice.

4. Cf. Feldherr 2002, 177; and Hardie 2002, 83-4.

5. See Lefkowitz and Fant 1992, 190, where the bereaved demonstrate in inscriptions that the act of leaving a memorial for their beloved substitutes for the acts of care they would have offered the living; the act provides a modicum of consolation. See Spentzou 2003, 106-11, for an interesting correlation between the notion of feminine writing and the process of mourning.

6. Translation: 'in dying you have made my entire estate a grave, [and with you have all my joys perished entirely, joys that your cherished love nourished when you lived.] Now a foreign land possesses your poor corpse buried not among familiar tombstones near the ashes of your ancestors, [but in faraway soil, in ominous Troy.]'

7. This is very much in line with the recently touted Lacanian view of thwarted feminine desire, a well-written and concise version of which appears in Lindheim 2003, 83-9.

8. Admittedly, Ovid creates a situation where Peneus' friends (and assumedly Peneus himself) aren't sure whether or not they should mourn or rejoice that Daphne has been turned into Apollo's laurel (1.578: *gratentur consolenturne parentem*).

9. See Wheeler 1997 on the ambiguous nature of the name Iphis and its wordplay on virility and the lack thereof.

10. See also Hallett 1997, 263: 'Ovid's narrative displays immense sympathy toward Iphis' plight, a sympathy contrasting with Iphis' own self-condemnation and negative view of female homoeroticism.'

11. On Ovid's play with pronouns, see Tissol 1997, 59-62.

12. Cf. Sharrock 2002, 96: 'the story shows the anxieties surrounding the acquisition of gendered identity, and especially male gender'.

13. Heyob 1975, ch. 4, believes there has been exaggeration regarding the extent to which women served as priestesses in the cult of Isis, but note especially 110: 'The fact that women did participate in the religion even to the small extent that they did is in itself significant, however, since their participation in the Greek and Roman religions was very narrowly limited.'

14. Flower 2002, 160: 'It is evident that the breakdown of the Republic and the establishment of one man rule led to a new public prominence for the women related to the first *princeps*.

15. See particularly Sharrock 1991a, Elsner 1991, Sharrock 1991b and Leach 1974.

16. E.g. Tacitus *Hist.* 1.49; see Weaver 1972, 10 on the attitudes of historians towards imperial freedmen. On the notable contribution of slave and freedmen labour in imperial administrations, see esp. 259-96.

17. See Ando 2000, 13: 'As we shall see, provincials who sought to identify themselves as Romans but who acknowledged the differential legal ranks imposed by Rome discovered a unifying tendency in the administrative rituals of Roman government.'

18. Woolf 1998, 241-6, discusses the integrity of Gallo-Roman culture as something quite different from Italian-Roman culture.

19. On the notion of non-elite Romans, I point the reader to Clarke 2003, 4-7, for a helpful summary of the distinctions.

Conclusion

1. *Sat.* 71.7: *hoc monumentum heredem non sequatur*, 'this monument may not be inherited' – a typical instructions in funerary inscriptions, abbreviated H. M. H. N. S.; and 71.12: *C. POMPEIUS TRIMALCHIO MAECENATIANUS HIC REQUIESCIT. HUIC SEVIRATUS ABSENTI DECRETUS EST. CUM POSSET IN OMNIBUS DECURIIS ROMAE ESSE, TAMEN NOLUIT. PIUS, FORTIS, FIDELIS, EX PARVO CREVIT, SESTERTIUM RELIQUIT TRECENTIES. NEC UNQUAM PHILOSOPHUM AUDIVIT. VALE: ET TU*, 'Gaius Pompeius Trimalchio, formerly a slave of Maecenas, rests here. He was decreed a member of the Augustan priesthood in his absence. He could have been made a member of all the workers' societies at Rome, but he refused. He was duty-bound, brave, true, and though he started from nothing, he died a multi-millionaire, yet he never once listened to philosophers. Good-bye Trimalchio, and to you who reads this.' See Courtney 2001, 115-16, on the likeness of this inscription to others discovered from Roman sites.

2. Trimalchio says in his inscription that he declined to join these guilds, but the fact that his membership was so widely sought after demonstrates that he was familiar with and popular among them.

3. In her paper presented at the annual conference of the Classical Association of Canada at Calgary-Banff, 11-14 May 2005, 'Stones in the Forest: Epigraphic Allusion in the *Silvae* of Statius' (now a forthcoming publication), Professor Kathleen Coleman points out the relative scarcity of inscriptions in Statius' *Silvae* and suggests that this was due to a conscious decision to break from the elegiac tendency to represent the written word. As she points out regarding Statius, 'fitting epigraphic formulae into a metrical scheme should have been just up his street.' She concludes with the following statement: 'Statius' epideictic training, and his patrons' expectation that he would render their mundane lives exotic within his verbal art, does not accommodate the nuts and bolts of that world; he replaces the functions of epigraphy with a far more oblique and sophisticated game of words. The absence of inscriptions from the *Silvae* of Statius is eloquent testimony to their fundamental role in the society whose intelligentsia and glitterati he cultivated and entertained.' I thank Professor Coleman for providing me with the text of her paper and permission to cite it.

4. See Johnson 1954 on Martial's many obituary-epigrams. Martial does not mimetically borrow from the inscriptional experience to more fully develop a fictional world; rather he is writing epitaphs for specific individuals, much like a professional epigrapher. The literary purposes of the Augustan elegiac inscriptions do not apply.

Bibliography

Ahl, Frederick. 1985. *Metaformations: Soundplay and Wordplay in Ovid and Other Classical Poets*. Ithaca.

Allen, Archibald W. 1962. '*Sunt Qui Propertius Malint*', in J.P. Sullivan, ed., *Critical Essays on Roman Literature: Elegy and Lyric*. Cambridge. 107-48.

Anderson, R.D., P.J. Parsons and R.G.M. Nisbet. 1979. 'Elegiacs by Gallus from Qa°r Ibrîm', *JRS* 69: 125-55.

Ando, Clifford. 2000. *Imperial Ideology and Provincial Loyalty in the Roman Empire*. Berkeley.

Armstrong, Henry H. 1910. *Autobiographic Elements in Latin Inscriptions*. London.

Badian, Ernst. 1985. 'A Phantom Marriage Law', *Philologus* 129: 82-98.

Ball, Robert J. 1983. *Tibullus the Elegist: A Critical Survey*. *Hypomnemata* 77. Göttingen.

Barchiesi, Alessandro. 1979. 'Palinuro e Caieta: Due "epigrammi" virgiliani (*Aen.* V.870 sg.; VII.1-4)', *Maia* 31: 3-11.

Barton, Carlin, A. 1993. *The Sorrows of the Ancient Romans*. Princeton.

———. 2001. *Roman Honor: The Fire in the Bones*. Berkeley.

Beard, Mary. 1991. 'Writing and Religion: *Ancient Literacy* and the Function of the Written Word in Roman Religion', in J.H. Humphrey, ed., *Literacy in the Roman World*. JRA Supplementary Series, No. 3. Ann Arbor. 35-58.

———. 2003. 'The Triumph of the Absurd: Roman Street Theatre', in Catharine Edwards and Greg Woolf, eds, *Rome the Cosmopolis*. Cambridge. 21-43.

Beard, Mary, John North and Simon Price, eds, 1998. *Religions of Rome*, vols 1-2. Cambridge.

Binns, J.W., ed. 1973. *Ovid*. London.

Bolter, Jay D. and Richard Grusin. 1999. *Remediation: Understanding the New Media*. Cambridge, MA.

Bömer, Franz. 1969-83. *Ovid: Metamorphoses*, 7 vols. Heidelberg.

Boucher, Jean-Paul. 1965. *Études sur Properce: Problemes d'Inspiration et d'Art*. Paris.

Boyd, Barbara Weiden. 1997. *Ovid's Literary Loves: Influence and Innovation in the* Amores. Ann Arbor.

Breed, Brian W. 2004. 'Portrait of a Lady: Propertius 1.3 and Ecphrasis', *CJ* 99.1: 35-56.

———. 2006. *Pastoral Inscriptions: Reading and Writing Virgil's Eclogues*. London.

Bright, David F. 1978. *Haec Mihi Fingebam: Tibullus in His World*. Leiden.

Brilliant, Richard. 1999. 'What is Death that I Should Fear it?: Aspects of the Roman Response', in R. Turcan, ed., *Imago Antiquitatis: Religions et Econographie du Monde Romain*. Paris. 145-8.

Bruss, Jon Steffen. 2005. *Hidden Presences: Monuments, Gravesites, and Corpses in Greek Funerary Epigram*. Leuven and Paris.

Buecheler, Franz. 1894. *Carmina Latina Epigraphica*, in F. Buecheler, A. Riese and E. Lommatzsch, eds, *Anthologia Latina, partes 2.1-2.2*. Stuttgart (1964 edition).
Bulloch, A.W. 1973. 'Tibullus and the Alexandrians', *PCPhS* 19: 71-89.
Butler, H.E. and E.A. Barber. 1933. *The Elegies of Propertius*. Oxford.
Cagnat, René 1889. 'Sur les Manuels Professionels', *Revue de Philologie* 13: 51-65.
Cahoon, Leslie. 1984. 'The Parrot and the Poet: The Function of Ovid's Funeral Elegies', *CJ* 80: 27-35.
———. 1988. 'The Bed as Battlefield: Erotic Conquest and Military Metaphors in Ovid's *Amores*', *TAPA* 118: 293-307.
———. 1996. 'Calliope's Song: Shifting Narrators in Ovid, *Metamorphoses* 5', *Helios* 23: 43-66.
Cairns, Francis. 1979. *Tibullus: A Hellenistic Poet at Rome*. Cambridge.
Campbell, C. 1973. 'Tibullus: Elegy 1.3', *YCS* 23: 147-57.
Camps, W.A. (vol. 1: 1961; vol. 2: 1967; vol. 3: 1966; vol. 4: 1965). *Propertius. Elegies. Book I-IV*. Cambridge.
Cancik, Hubert and Helmut Schneider, eds. 2002. *Brill's New Pauly: Encyclopaedia of the Ancient World*. Leiden.
Canter, H.V. 1930. 'The Figure *Adunaton* in Greek and Latin Poetry', *AJP* 51: 32-41.
Claridge, Amanda. 1998. *Rome: An Oxford Archaeological Guide*. Oxford.
Clarke, John R. 2003. *Art in the Lives of Ordinary Romans: Visual Representation and Non-Elite Viewers in Italy, 100 B.C.–A.D. 315*. Berkeley.
Clausen, Wendell. 1994. *A Commentary on Virgil: Eclogues*. Oxford.
Coarelli, Filippo. 1988. *Il sepolcro degli Scipioni a Roma*. Rome.
Cole, Thomas. 1969. 'The Saturnian Verse', *YCS* 21: 3-73.
Conte, Gian Biagio. 1992. 'Empirical and Theoretical Approaches to Literary Genre', in K. Galinsky, ed., *The Interpretation of Roman Poetry: Empiricism or Hermeneutics. Studien zur klassischen Philologie*. Frankfurt am Main.
———. 1994a. *Genres and Readers: Lucretius, Love Elegy and Pliny's Encyclopedia*. Baltimore.
———. 1994b. *Latin Literature: A History*.
Cooley, Alison, ed. 2000. *The Epigraphic Landscape of Roman Italy*. *BICS* Supplement 73. London.
Copley, Frank O. 1956. *Exclusus Amator: A Study in Latin Love Poetry*. Oxford.
Corbier, Mireille. 1974. *L'Aerarium Saturni et l'Aerarium Militare: administration et prosopographie senatoriale*. Rome.
———. 1987. 'L'écriture dans l'espace public romain', in *L'urbs : espace urbain et histoire (I s. ap. J.C.). Actes du colloque international organisé par la Centre national de la recherche scientifique et l'École française de Rome*. Paris. 27-60.
Courtney, Edward. 1993. *The Fragmentary Latin Poets*. Oxford.
———. 1995. *Musa Lapidaria: A Selection of Latin Verse Inscriptions*. Atlanta.
———. 2001. *A Companion to Petronius*. Oxford.
D'Ambra, Eve. 2002. 'Acquiring an Ancestor: The Importance of Funerary Statuary among the Non-Elite Orders of Rome', in J.M. Højte, ed. 223-46.
Davis, John T. 1977. *Dramatic Pairings in Propertius and Ovid*. *Noctes Romanae* 15. Bern.
DeBrohun, Jeri Blair. 1994. 'Redressing Elegy's *Puella*: Propertius IV and the Rhetoric of Fashion', *JRS* 84: 41-63.
———. 2003. *Roman Propertius and the Reinvention of Elegy*. Ann Arbor.
Degrassi, Attilio, ed. 1965. *Inscriptiones Latinae Liberae Rei Publicae: Imagines*. Berolini.

Degrassi, A. and J. Krummrey, eds. 1986. *Corpus Inscriptionum Latinarum*, vol. 1, altera editio, fasc. 4, partes 1-2. Berolini. [= *CIL* 1.2.4.1-2]

Dettmer, Helena. 1980. 'The Arrangement of Tibullus Books 1 and 2', *Philologus* 124: 68-82.

Dinter, Martin. 2005. 'Epic and Epigram – Minor Heroes in Virgil's *Aeneid*', *CQ* 55.1: 153-69.

Easterling, P.E. and E.J. Kenney, eds. 1989. *Cambridge History of Classical Literature,* vol. 1.4: *The Hellenistic Period and the Empire.* Cambridge.

Eck, Werner. 1984. 'Senatorial Self-Representation: Developments in the Augustan Period', in Millar and Segal, eds. 129-68.

Egbert, J.C. 1923. *Introduction to the Study of Latin Inscriptions.* New York.

Elder, J.P. 1962. 'Tibullus: *Tersus Atque Elegans*', in J.P. Sullivan, ed., *Critical Essays on Roman Literature: Elegy and Lyric.* Cambridge. 65-105.

Elsner, Jaœ. 1995. *Art and the Roman Viewer: The Transformation of Art from the Pagan World to Christianity.* New York.

———, ed. 1996. *Art and Text in Roman Culture.* Cambridge.

Elsner, John. 1991. 'Visual Mimesis and the Myth of the Real: Ovid's Pygmalion as Viewer', in J. Elsner and A. Sharrock 'Re-Viewing Pygmalion', *Ramus* 20: 154-68.

Engström, Einar. 1912. *Carmina Latina Epigraphica: post editam collectionem Buechelerianam in lucem prolatam.* Göteborg-Leipzig.

Ernout, Alfred. 1957. *Recueil de Textes Latins Archaiques.* Paris.

Fantham, Elaine. 1997. 'Images of the City: Propertius' New-Old Rome', in Habinek and Schiesaro, eds. 122-35.

Farrell, Joseph. 1998. 'Reading and Writing the *Heroides*', *HSCP* 98: 307-38.

———. 2002. 'Greek Lives and Roman Careers in the Classical *Vita* Tradition', in P. Cheney and F.A. de Armas, eds, *European Literary Careers: The Author from Antiquity to the Renaissance.* Toronto. 24-46.

———. 2003. 'Classical Genre in Theory and Practice', *New Literary History* 34: 383-408.

———. 2004. 'Ovid's Virgilian Career', in G.W. Most and S. Spence, eds, *Re-presenting Virgil: Special Issue in Honor of Michael C. J. Putnam. Materiali e discussioni per l'analisi dei testi classici* 52. Pisa. 41-55.

Fedeli, P. 1984. *Sexti Properti Elegiarum Libri IV.* Stuttgart.

Fejfer, Jane. 2002. 'Ancestral Aspects of the Roman Honorary Statue', in J.M. Højte, ed. 247-56.

Feldherr, Andrew. 2002. 'Metamorphosis in the *Metamorphoses*', in Hardie, ed. 163-79.

Fitzgerald, William. 2000. *Slavery and the Roman Literary Imagination.* Cambridge.

Flower, Harriet. 1996. *Ancestor Masks and Aristocratic Power in Roman Culture.* Oxford.

———. 2002. 'Were Women Ever "Ancestors" in Republican Rome?' in J.M. Højte, ed. 159-84.

Foulon, Albert. 1980. 'Tibulle II, 3 et L'Alexandrianisme', *REL* 58: 252-73.

Fowler, Don. 1991. 'Narrate and Describe: The Problem of Ekphrasis', *JRS* 81: 25-35.

———. 1996. 'Even Better than the Real Thing: A Tale of Two Cities', in J. Elsner, ed. Cambridge. 57-74.

Franklin Jr., James L. 1991. 'Literacy and the Parietal Inscriptions of Pompeii', in J.H. Humphrey, ed., *Literacy in the Roman World.* JRA Supplementary Series, No. 3. Ann Arbor. 77-98.

Fredrick, David. 1997. 'Reading Broken Skin: Violence in Roman Elegy', in Hallett and Skinner, eds. 172-93.

Freeman, Philip M. 1998. 'Saturnian Verse and Early Latin Poetics', *JIES* 26: 61-90.

Fuller, Joseph. 2003. 'Classical Genre in Theory and Practice', *New Literary History* 34: 383-408.

Galinsky, Karl. 1969. 'The Triumph Theme in the Augustan Elegy', *Wiener Studien* 82: 75-107.

———. 1975. *Ovid's Metamorphoses: An Introduction to the Basic Aspects*. Los Angeles.

———. 1996. *Augustan Culture: An Interpretive Introduction*. Princeton.

Gamel, Mary-Kay. 1989. '*Non Sine Caede*: Abortion Politics in Ovid's *Amores*', *Helios* 16: 183-206.

Gibson, Roy, K., ed. 2003. *Ovid:* Ars Amatoria *Book 3*. Cambridge.

Gold, Barbara K. 1993. ' "But Ariadne was never there in the first place": Finding the Female in Roman poetry', in N. Sorkin Rabinowitz and A. Richlin, eds, *Feminist Theory and the Classics*. London. 75-101.

Goldberg, Sander. 2006. 'Ennius after the Banquet', *Arethusa* 39: 427-48.

Goold, G.P. 1990. *Propertius: Elegies*. Cambridge, MA.

Gordon, Arthur E. 1983. *Illustrated Introduction to Latin Epigraphy*. Berkeley.

Gowing, Alain M. 2005. *Empire and Memory: The Representation of the Roman Republic in Imperial Culture*. Cambridge.

Green, Peter, ed. 1994. *Ovid: The Poems of Exile*. London.

Greene, E. 1998. *The Erotics of Domination: Male Desire and the Mistress in Latin Love Poetry*. Baltimore and London.

Griffin, Jasper. 1984. 'Augustus and the Poets: "Caesar Qui Cogere Posset" ', in Millar and Segal, eds. 189-218.

———. 1986. *Latin Poets and Roman Life*. Chapel Hill.

Gruen, Erich. 1992. *Culture and National Identity in Republican Rome*. Ithaca.

Gurval, Robert A. 1995. *Actium and Augustus: The Politics and Emotions of Civil War*. Ann Arbor.

Gutzwiller, Kathryn. 1985. 'The Lover and the Lena: Propertius 4.5', *Ramus* 14.2: 105-15.

———. 1998. *Poetic Garlands: Hellenistic Epigrams in Context*. Berkeley.

Habinek, Thomas. 1997. 'The Invention of Sexuality in the World-City of Rome', in Habinek and Schiesaro, eds. 23-43.

———. 1998. *The Politics of Latin Literature*. Princeton.

Habinek, T. and A. Schiesaro, eds. 1997. *The Roman Cultural Revolution*. Cambridge.

Hall, Edith. 1989. *Inventing the Barbarian: Greek Self-Definition Through Tragedy*. Oxford.

Hallett, Judith. 1973. 'The Role of Women in Roman Elegy', *Arethusa* 6: 103-24.

———.1982. 'Queens, Princeps and Women of the Augustan Elite: Propertius' Cornelia-Elegy and the *Res Gestae Divi August*', in R. Winkes, ed., *The Age of Augustus: Interdisciplinary Conference held at Brown University*. Providence. 73-88.

———. 1984. 'The Role of Women in Roman Elegy: Counter-Cultural Feminism', in J. Peradotto and J.P. Sullivan, eds, *Women in the Ancient World*. Albany, NY. 241-62.

———. 1989. 'Women as *Same* and *Other* in Classical Roman Elite', *Helios* 16.59-78.

———. 1997. 'Female Homoeroticism and the Denial of Roman Reality in Latin Literature', in Hallett and Skinner, eds. 255-73.
Hallett, Judith and Marilyn Skinner, eds. 1997. *Roman Sexualities*. Princeton.
Halliwell, Stephen. 2002. *The Aesthetics of Mimesis: Ancient Texts and Modern Problems*. Princeton.
Hanslik, Rudolf. 1970. 'Tibulls Elegie 1 3', in W. Wimmel, ed., *Forschungen zur römischen Literatur: Festschrift zum 60. Geburtstag von Karl Büchner*. Wiesbaden. 138-45.
Harder, M.A., R.F. Regnuit and G.C. Wakker. 2002. *Hellenistic Epigrams*. Leuven and Paris.
Hardie, Philip. 2002. *Ovid's Poetics of Illusion*. Cambridge.
———, ed. 2002. *Cambridge Companion to Ovid*. Cambridge.
Hardie. P., A. Barchiesi and S. Hinds, eds. 1999. Ovidian Transformations: Essays on Ovid's Metamorphoses and its Reception. CPS Supplementary Volume 23. Cambridge.
Harris, William V. 1971. *Rome in Etruria and Umbria*. Oxford.
———. 1989. *Ancient Literacy*. Cambridge, MA.
Harvey, F.D. 1983. '*Cognati Caesaris*: Ovid *Amores* 1,2,51/52', *Wiener Studien*. 17: 89-90.
Henderson, A.A.R. 1969. 'Tibullus, Elysium and Tartarus', *Latomus* 28.3: 649-53.
Herescu, N.I. 1958. 'Le sens de l'epitaphe Ovidienne', in N. Herescu, ed., *Ovidiana: Recherches sur Ovide*. Paris. 420-42.
Heyob, Sharon Kelly. 1975. *The Cult of Isis Among Women in the Graeco-Roman World*. Leiden.
Heyworth, S.J. 1992. 'Propertius 2.13', *Mnemosyne* 45.1: 45-59.
Hickson, F.V. 1991. 'Augustus *Triumphator*: Manipulation of the Triumphal Theme in the Political Program of Augustus', *Latomus* 50: 124-38.
Hinds, Stephen. 1987. *The Metamorphosis of Persephone: Ovid and the Self-Conscious Muse*. Cambridge.
———. 1987a. 'The Poetess and the Reader: Further Steps toward Sulpicia', *Hermathena* 143: 29-46.
Hodge, R.I.V. and R.A. Buttimore. 1977. *The* Monobiblos *of Propertius*. Cambridge and Ipswich.
Højte, Jakob Munk, ed. 2002. *Images of Ancestors*. Aarhus.
Holland, Tom. 2003. *Rubicon: The Last Years of the Roman Republic*. New York.
Holliday, Peter J. 1997. 'Roman Triumphal Painting: Its Function, Development, and Reception', *Art Bulletin* 79: 130-47.
Hollis, A.S. 1977. *Ovid: Ars Amatoria, Book I*. Oxford.
Hope, Valerie. 2000. 'Inscription and Sculpture: the Construction of Identity in the Military Tombstones of Roman Mainz', in Oliver, ed. 155-85.
———. 2001. *Constructing Identity. The Roman Funerary Monuments of Aquileia, Mainz and Nimes*. BAR International Series, 960. Oxford.
Hopkins, Keith. 1983. *Death and Renewal: Sociological Studies in Roman History*, vol. 2. Cambridge.
Hubbard, Margaret. 1974. *Propertius*. London.
Huskey, Samuel. 2005. 'In Memory of Tibullus: Ovid's Remembrance of Tibullus 1.3 in *Amores* 3.9 and *Tristia* 3.3', *Arethusa* 38.3: 367-86.
Hutchinson, G.O. 1988. *Hellenistic Poetry*. Oxford.
Hutton, James. 1935. *Greek Anthology in Italy to the Year 1800*. Ithaca.
Iser, Wolfgang. 1978. *The Act of Reading: A Theory of Aesthetic Response*. Baltimore and London.

J. Paul Getty Museum. 2004-. *Thesaurus Cultus et Rituum Antiquorum*. Los Angeles; and Fondation pour le lexicon iconographicum mythologiae classicae, Basel.

Jacobson, Howard. 1974. *Ovid's Heroides*. Princeton.

James, Sharon. 1997. 'Slave-Rape and Female Silence in Ovid's Love Poetry', *Helios* (24.1): 60-76.

———. 2003. *Learned Girls and Male Persuasion: Gender and Reading in Roman Love Elegy*. Berkeley.

Janan, Micaela. 2001. *The Politics of Desire: Propertius IV*. Berkeley.

Johnson, Skuli. 1954. 'The Obituary Epigrams of Martial', *CJ* 49: 265-72.

Johnson, W.R. 1990. 'Messalla's Birthday: The Politics of Pastoral', *Arethusa* 23: 95-113.

Jordan, H. 1860. *M. Catonis Praeter Librum De Re Rustica Quae Extant*. Leipzig.

Kajanto, Iiro. 1974. 'On the Idea of Eternity in Latin Epitaphs', *Arctos* 8: 59-69.

Kauffman, Linda S. 1986. *Discourses of Desire: Gender, Genre, and Epistolary Fictions*. Ithaca.

Keith, Alison. 1994. '*Corpus Eroticum*: Elegiac Poetics and Elegiac Puellae in Ovid's *Amores*', *CW* 88: 27-40.

———. 1999. 'Versions of Epic Masculinity in Ovid's *Metamorphoses*', in Hardie, Barchiesi and Hinds, eds. 214-39.

Kennedy, Duncan. 1992. ' "Augustan" and "Anti-Augustan": Reflections on Terms of Reference', in A. Powell, ed., *Roman Poetry and Propaganda in the Age of Augustus*. London. 26-58.

———. 1993. *The Arts of Love: Five Studies in the Discourse of Roman Love Elegy*. Cambridge.

Kenney, E.J. 1973. 'The Style of the *Metamorphoses*', in Binns, ed. 116-53.

———. 1995. *P. Ovidi Nasonis: Amores, Medicamina Faciei Femineae, Ars Amatoria, Remedia Amoris*. Oxford.

———. 1996. *Ovid: Heroides XVI-XXI*. Cambridge.

Keppie, Lawrence. 1991. *Understanding Roman Inscriptions*. London.

King, Margaret. 2000. 'Commemoration of Infants on Roman Funerary Inscriptions', in Oliver, ed. 117-54.

Kleiner, D.E.E. and S.B. Matheson, eds. 2000. *I, Claudia II*. Austin.

Knox, Peter, ed. 1986. *Ovid's Metamorphoses and the Traditions of Augustan Poetry*. Cambridge.

———. 1995. *Ovid: Heroides. Select Epistles*. Cambridge.

Koortbojian, Michael. 2005. 'Mimesis or Phantasia? Two Representational Modes in Roman Commemorative Art', *CA* 24.2: 285-306.

Kurke, Leslie. 1993. 'The Economy of *Kudos*', in C. Dougherty and L. Kurke, eds, *Cultural Poetics in Archaic Greece: Cult Performance, Politics*. Cambridge. 131-63.

Kyriakidis, Stratis. 1998. *Narrative Structure and Poetics in the Aeneid: The Frame of Book 6*. Bari.

Laird, Andrew. 1993. 'Sounding out Ecphrasis: Art and Text in Catullus 64', *JRS* 83: 18-30.

———. 1996. '*Ut Figura Poesis*: Writing Art and the Art of Writing in Augustan Poetry', in J. Elsner, ed. Cambridge. 75-102.

Langner, Martin. 2001. *Antike Graffitizeichnungen: Motive, Gestaltung und Bedeutung. Palilia* (Deutsches Archäologisches Institut Rom) 11. Wiesbaden.

Lattimore, Richmond. 1942 [reprinted in 1962]. *Themes in Greek and Latin Epitaphs*. Urbana-Champagne.

Leach, Eleanor W. 1964. 'Georgic Imagery in the *Ars Amatoria*', *TAPhA* 45: 142-54.
———. 1974. 'Ekphrasis and the Theme of Artistic Failure in Ovid's *Metamorphoses*', *Ramus* 3: 102-42.
———. 1980. 'Poetics and Poetic Design in Tibullus' First Elegiac Book', *Arethusa* 13: 79-96.
———. 1988. *The Rhetoric of Space: Literary and Artistic Representations of Landscape in Republican and Augustan Rome*. Princeton.
———. 1997. 'Horace and the Material Culture of Augustan Rome: A Revisionary Reading', in Habinek and Schiesaro, eds. 105-21.
Lee, Guy. 1982. *Tibullus: Elegies*. Liverpool.
———. 1990. *The Poems of Catullus*. Oxford.
Lee-Stecum, Parshia. 1998. *Powerplay in Tibullus: Reading* Elegies *Book One*. Cambridge.
Lefkowitz, Mary and Maureen Fant. 1992. *Women's Life in Greece and Rome: A Source Book in Translation*. 2nd edition. London and Baltimore.
Lier, Bruno. 1902. '*Topica Carmina Sepulacrium Latinarum*', *Philologus* 62: 445-77 and 563-603.
Lindheim, Sara. 2003. *Mail and Female: Epistolary Narrative and Desire in Ovid's* Heroides. Madison.
Lindsay, W.M. 1897. *Handbook of Latin Inscriptions, Illustrating the History of the Language*. Boston.
Lissberger, Ewald. 1934. *Das Fortleben der römischen Elegiker in den Carmina Epigraphica*. Tübingen.
Littlewood, R.J. 1970. 'The Symbolic Structure of Tibullus Book 1', *Latomus* 29: 661-9.
Lommatzsch, Ernst, ed. 1918. *Corpus Inscriptionum Latinarum*, vol. 1, altera editio. Berolini. [= *CIL* 1.2]
———. 1926. *Carmina Latina Epigraphica: supplementum*. in F. Buecheler, A. Riese and E. Lommatzsch, eds, *Anthologia Latina*, pars 2.3. Stuttgart, 1964 edition.
Luck, Georg. 1969. *The Latin Love Elegy*. London.
Lyne, R.O.A.M. 1980. *The Latin Love Poets*. Oxford.
———. 1998. 'Propertius and Tibullus: Early Exchanges', *CQ* 48.2: 519-44.
MacMullen, Ramsay. 1982. 'The Epigraphic Habit in the Roman Empire', *AJP* 103: 233-46.
Makowski, John. 1996. 'Bisexual Orpheus: Pederasty and Parody in Ovid', *CJ* 92: 25-38.
Maltby, Robert. 2002. *Tibullus: Elegies: Text, Introduction and Commentary. ARCA Classical and Medieval Texts, Papers and Monographs* 41. Cambridge.
Mann, J.C. 1985. 'Epigraphic Consciousness', *JRS* 75: 204-6.
McGann, M.J. 1970. 'The Date of Tibullus' Death', *Latomus* 29.3: 774-80.
McKeown, J. 1987, 1989 and 1998. *Ovid: Amores. Text, Prolegomena and Commentary*. Leeds.
McKinley, Kathryn L. 2001. *Reading the Ovidian Heroine:* Metamorphoses *Commentaries 1100-1618*. Leiden.
Merrill, Elmer T. 1893. *Catullus*. Boston.
Meyer, Elizabeth. 2001. 'Wooden Wit: *Tabellae* in Latin Poetry', in E. Tylawski and C. Weiss, eds, *In Honor of Gordon Williams: Twenty-Five Years at Yale*. New Haven.
Millar, Fergus and Erich Segal, eds. 1984. *Caesar Augustus: Seven Aspects*. Oxford.

Miller, John F. 1993a. 'Ennius and the Elegists', *ICS* 8: 277-95.

———. 1993b. 'Apostrophe, Aside and the Didactic Addressee: Poetic Strategies in *Ars Amatoria* III', in A. Schiesaro, P. Mitsis and J.S. Clay, eds, *Mega Nepios: Il Destinatario nell'Epos Didascalico. Materiali e Discusioni per l'Analisi dei Testi Classici*, 31. Pisa. 231-41.

———. 1995. 'Reading Cupid's Triumph', *CJ* 90.3: 287-94.

Miller, Paul Allen. 2004. *Subjecting Verses: Latin Love Elegy and the Emergence of the Real*. Princeton.

Mouritsen, Henrik. 1988. *Elections, Magistrates, and Municipal Elite: Studies in Pompeian Epigraphy. Analecti Romana Instituti Danici, Supplementum XV*. Rome.

———. 2005. 'Freedmen and Decurions: Epitaphs and Social History in Imperial Italy', *JRS* 95: 38-63.

Murgatroyd, Paul. 1980. *Tibullus I: A Commentary on the First Book of Elegies of Albius Tibullus*. Pietermaritzburg.

Musurillo, Herbert. 1967. 'The Theme of Tome as a Poetic Device in the Elegies of Tibullus', *TAPhA* 98: 253-68.

Mutschler, F.H. 1985. *Die poetische Kunst Tibulls. Studien zur klassischen Philologie* 18. Frankfurt.

Myerowitz, Molly. 1985. *Ovid's Games of Love*. Detroit.

Myers, K. Sara. 1994. *Ovid's Causes: Cosmogony and Aetiology in the Metamorphoses*. Ann Arbor.

Nadeau, Yvonne. 1984. 'Catullus' Sparrow, Martial, Juvenal and Ovid', *Latomus* 43: 861-8.

Nagle, Betty Rose. 1980. *The Poetics of Exile: Program and Polemic in the* Tristia *and* Epistulae ex Ponto *of Ovid*. Brussels.

Nagy, Gregory. 1979. *The Best of the Achaeans: Concepts of the Hero in Archaic Greek Poetry*. Baltimore.

Nicolet, Claude. 1984. 'Augustus, Government, and the Propertied Classes', in Millar and Segal, eds. 89-128.

Nielsen, H.S. 1997. 'Interpreting Epithets in Roman Epitaphs', in B. Rawson and P. Weaver, eds, *The Roman Family in Italy: Status, Sentiment and Space*. Oxford. 169-204.

Nisbet, R.G.M. and Margaret Hubbard. 1978. *A Commentary on Horace: Odes, Book II*. Oxford.

Nisbet, R.G.M. and Niall Rudd. 2004. *A Commentary on Horace: Odes, Book III*. Oxford.

Nisetich, Frank. 2001. *The Poems of Callimachus*. Oxford.

Oliensis, Ellen. 1997. 'The Erotics of *Amicitia*: Readings in Tibullus, Propertius, and Horace', in Hallett and Skinner, eds. 151-71.

Oliver, G. J. 2000. 'An Introduction to the Epigraphy of Death: Funerary Inscriptions as Evidence', in Oliver, ed. 1-23.

———, ed. 2000. *The Epigraphy of Death: Studies in the History and Society of Greece and Rome*. Liverpool.

Ong, Walter. 1977. *Interfaces of the Word: Studies in the Evolution of Consciousness and Culture*. Ithaca.

———. 1988. *Orality and Literacy: The Technologizing of the Word*. London and New York.

Owen, S.G. 1915. *P. Ovidi Nasonis: Tristium Libri Quinque Ibis Ex Ponto Libri Quattuor Haelieutica Fragmenta*. Oxford.

Parsons, Jed. 1999. 'A New Approach to the Saturnian Verse and its Relation to Latin Prosody', *TAPA* 129: 117-37.

Petersen, Lauren H. 2003. 'The Baker, His Tomb, His Wife, and Her Breadbasket: The Monument of Eurysaces in Rome', *Art Bulletin* 85.2: 230-57.

Pfeiffer, R. 1949. *Callimachus, I: Fragmenta*. Oxford.

Pintabone, Diane. 2002. 'Ovid's Iphis and Ianthe: When girls won't be girls', in N.S. Rabinowitz and L. Auanger, eds, *Among Women: From the Homosocial to the Homoerotic in the Ancient World*. Austin. 256-85.

Postgate, J.P. 1962. *Select Elegies of Propertius*. London.

Purdie, Albert B. 1935. *Latin Verse Inscriptions*. London.

Putnam, M.C.J. 1973. *Tibullus: A Commentary*. Norman.

Quinn, K. 1973. *Catullus: The Poems*. London.

Ramsby, Teresa. 2005. 'Striving for Permanence: Ovid's Funerary Inscriptions', *CJ* 100.4: 365-91.

Raval, Shilpa. 2000. 'Cross-Dressing and "Gender Trouble" in the Ovidian Corpus', *Helios* 29: 149-72.

Richardson Jr, L. 1977. *Propertius: Elegies I-IV*. Norman.

Richlin, Amy. 2001. 'Emotional Work: Lamenting the Roman Dead', in E. Tylawski and C. Weiss, eds, *Essays in Honor of Gordon Williams: Twenty-Five Years at Yale*. New Haven. 229-48.

Rodriguez Herrera, G. 1999. 'Propertius 2.1.71-78 and the Latin Epitaphs', *Mnemosyne* Ser. 4.52.2: 194-7.

Rolfe, John C. 1927. *The Attic Nights of Aulus Gellius*, 3 vols. Cambridge.

Rosenmeyer, Patricia. 1997. 'Ovid's *Heroides* and *Tristia*: Voices from Exile', *Ramus* 26.1: 29-56.

Rossi, Laura. 2001. *The Epigrams Ascribed to Theocritus: A Method of Approach*. Leuven and Paris.

Saller, Richard and Brent Shaw. 1984. 'Tombstones and Roman Family Relations in the Principate: Civilians, Soldiers and Slaves', *JRS* 74: 124-56.

Sandys, J.E. 1927. *Latin Epigraphy: An Introduction to the Study of Latin Inscriptions*. Chicago.

Scheid, John and Jesper Svenbro. 1996. *The Craft of Zeus: Myths of Weaving and Fabric*. Cambridge.

Severy, Beth. 2003. *Augustus and the Family at the Birth of the Roman Empire*. New York and London.

Sharrock, A. R. 1991a. 'Womanufacture', *JRS* 81.36-49.

———. 1991b. 'The Love of Creation', in J. Elsner and A. Sharrock 'Re-Viewing Pygmalion', *Ramus* 20: 169-82.

———. 1994a. *Seduction and Repetition in Ovid's* Ars Amatoria *II*. Oxford.

———. 1994b. 'Ovid and the Politics of Reading', *Materiali e discussioni per l'analisi dei testi classici* 33: 97-122.

———. 2002. 'Gender and Sexuality', in Hardie, ed. 95-107.

Skinner, Marilyn B. 2003. *Catullus in Verona: A Reading of the Elegiac* Libellus, *Poems 65-116*. Columbus.

Skutsch, Otto. 1985. *The Annals of Q. Ennius*. Oxford.

Smith, R.R.R. 1988. '*Simulacra Gentium*: The *Ethne* from the Sebasteion at Aphrodisias', *JRS* 78.50-77.

Solodow, J.B. 1988. *The World of Ovid's Metamorphoses*. Chapel Hill.

Sörbom, Göran. 1966. *Mimesis and Art: Studies in the Origin and Early Development of an Aesthetic Vocabulary*. Stockholm.

Sparrow, John. 1969. *Visible Words: A Study of Inscriptions in and as Books and Works of Art*. Cambridge.

Spentzou, Efrossini. 2003. *Readers and Writers in Ovid's Heroides*. Oxford.

Stahl, Hans-Peter. 1985. *Propertius: 'Love' and 'War': Individual and State Under Augustus*. Berkeley.
Stein, Arthur. 1931. *Römische Inschriften in der antiken Literatur*. Prague.
Sullivan, Francis A. 1955. 'Vergil and the Latin Epitaphs'. *CJ* 51: 17-20.
Sullivan, J.P. 1961. 'Two Problems in Roman Love Elegy', *TAPA* 92: 522-36.
———. 1976. *Propertius: A Critical Introduction*. Cambridge.
Susini, Gian Carlo. 1973. *The Roman Stonecutter: An Introduction to Latin Epigraphy*. Oxford.
———. 1988. 'Spelling Out Along the Road: Anthropology of the Ancient Reader, Or Rather, the Roman Reader', *Alma Mater Studiorum* 1:117-24.
Syme, Ronald, 1960. *The Roman Revolution*. Oxford.
Tanner, R.G. 1961. 'The Arval Hymn and Early Latin Verse', *CQ* 11: 209-38.
Tarrant, Richard. 2002. 'Ovid and Ancient Literary History', in Hardie, ed. 13-33.
———. 2004. *P. Ovidi Nasonis: Metamorphoses*. Oxford.
Thomas, Richard F. 1998. 'Melodious Tears: Sepulchral Epigram and Generic Mobility', in Harder, Regtuit and Wakker, eds. 205-23.
Tissol, Gareth. 1997. *Wit, Narrative and Cosmic Origins in Ovid's Metamorphoses*. Princeton.
Toynbee, J.M.C. 1971. *Death and Burial in the Roman World*. Ithaca.
Tränkle, H. 1990. *Appendix Tibulliana. Texte und Kommentare* 16. Berlin.
Treggiari, Susan. 1991. *Roman Marriage: Iusti Coniuges from the Time of Cicero to the Time of Ulpian*. Oxford.
Tylawski, Elizabeth. 2001. 'Supplying a Genealogy: Self-promotion by Praising Dead Women', in E. Tylawski and C. Weiss, eds, *Essays in Honor of Gordon Williams: Twenty-Five Years at Yale*. New Haven. 283-93.
Van Sickle, J. 1980. 'The Book-Roll and Some Conventions of the Poetic Book', *Arethusa* 13: 5-42.
Varner, Eric R. 2004. *Mutilation and Transformation:* Damnatio Memoriae *and Roman Imperial Portraits*. Leiden and Boston.
Versnel, H.S. 1970. *Triumphus: An Inquiry into the Origin, Development and Meaning of the Roman Triumph*. Leiden.
Veyne, Paul. 1988. *Roman Erotic Elegy: Love, Poetry and the West*. Chicago.
Weaver, P.R.C. 1972. *Familia Caesaris: A Social Study of the Emperor's Freedmen and Slaves*. Cambridge.
Welch, Tara. 2005. *The Elegiac Cityscape: Propertius and the Meaning of Roman Monuments*. Columbus.
Wheeler, Arthur L. 1915. 'Catullus as an Elegist', *AJP* 36.2: 155-84.
Wheeler, Stephen. 1997. 'Changing Names: the Miracle of Iphis in Ovid *Metamorphoses* 9', *Phoenix* 51 (2): 190-202.
———. 1999. *A Discourse of Wonders: Audience and Performance in Ovid's* Metamorphoses. Philadelphia.
Wilkinson, L.P. 1966. 'The Continuity of Propertius 2.13', *Classical Review* 14: 141-4.
Williams, Gareth. 1992. 'Representations of the Book-Roll in Latin Poetry: Ovid *Trist*. 1.1.3-14 and Related Texts', *Mnemosyne* 45: 178-89.
———. 1994. *Banished Voices: Readings in Ovid's Exile Poetry*. Cambridge.
Wolff, Étienne. 2000. *La Poesie funeraire epigraphique a Rome. Collections 'Études anciennes'*. Rennes.
Woolf, Greg. 1996. 'Monumental Writing and the Expansion of Roman Society in the Early Roman Empire', *JRS* 86: 22-39.
———. 1998. *Becoming Roman: The Origins of Provincial Civilization in Gaul*. Cambridge.

Wyke, Maria. 1987a. 'Written Women: Propertius' *Scripta Puella*', *JRS* 77: 47-61.
———. 1987b. 'The Elegiac Woman at Rome', *PCPhS* 33: 153-78.
———. 1989. 'Mistress and Metaphor in Augustan Elegy', *Helios* 16: 25-47.
———. 1995. 'Taking the Woman's Part: Engendering Roman Love Elegy', in A.J. Boyle, ed., *Roman Literature and Ideology*. Victoria. 110-28.
———. 2002. *The Roman Mistress: Ancient and Modern Representations*. Oxford.
Yardley, J.C. 1996. 'Roman Elegy and Funerary Epigram', *EMC* 40: 267-73.
Zanker, Paul. 1989. *The Power of Images in the Age of Augustus*, translated by A. Shapiro. Ann Arbor.
Zorzetti, Nevio. 1990. 'The *Carmina Convivalia*', in O. Murray, ed., *Sympotica: A Symposium on the Symposion*. Oxford.

Indices

Index inscriptionum

Index nominum

Index operum maiorum

Index rerum